A YEAR
ON THE
RUN

Written by Damian Hall

Illustrated by Daniel Seex

Aurum
Press

Quarto is the authority on a wide range of topics.
Quarto educates, entertains and enriches the lives of
our readers— enthusiasts and lovers of hands-on living.
www.QuartoKnows.com

First published in Great Britain
2016 by Aurum Press Ltd
74–77 White Lion Street
Islington
London N1 9PF
www.quartoknows.com

A catalogue record for this book is available from the British Library.

ISBN 978 1 78131 528 6
ebook: ISBN 9781781316474

1 2 3 4 5 6 7 8 9 10
2016 2017 2018 2019 2020

Interior design by: Neal Cobourne
Printed in China

For Indy and Leif

CONTENTS

JULY
166

AUGUST
192

SEPTEMBER
218

OCTOBER
240

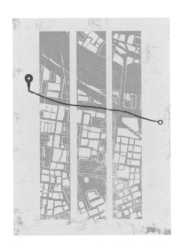

NOVEMBER
262

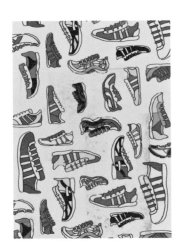

DECEMBER
290

JANUARY

1 January

The Knacker Cracker
(since 2004)

As the rest of the country sleeps off hangovers and the tail-end of Christmas overindulgence, 200 loony souls gather at the bottom of Box Hill in Surrey, southeast England, to run 10km (6.2 miles) in the mud and (usually) rain, dressed as bananas and ladybirds at the always sold-out Knacker Cracker. (Nipper Knacker and Knicker Knacker races are also available, for women and children).

After belting out the national anthem, fancy-dressed runners try to ignore the weather and bellies sloshing with mince pies, turkey sandwiches, beer and champagne to run or wobble up Box Hill, including the 'Eiger steps', five times. Amid the mild suffering, there's always banter, merriment and plenty of laughter too. Few things typify the wonderful, infectious silliness of amateur runners better.

2 January

The Hakone Ekiden
(since 1920)

On this date in Japan, people with usually no interest in running switch on the television and settle down with their New Year *mochi* (rice cakes) to watch the Hakone Ekiden. The TV audience share is similar to the Super Bowl in the US and brings the country to a standstill with spectators lining the length of the course.

It's both Japan's biggest annual sporting event and one of the toughest mass-participation endurance events in the world. The Hakone Ekiden is a 135-mile (217km) relay race shared between university teams (male only) of 10 runners. Run over two days, it starts in the centre of Tokyo, travelling to the foot of Mount Fuji and back.

Although the Hakone dates to 1920, ekidens really took off in Japan as part of the post-World War Two rebuilding process, with companies setting up sports teams in an effort to help raise worker morale. To help runners train, relay races – ekidens – were arranged, modelled on the courier system of Japan's Edo period (1603–1868) that saw runners relay messages between Kyoto and Tokyo.

Today ekidens have surpassed the marathons in popularity in Japan, with the Hakone Ekiden being the runners' – and the viewers' – favourite.

3 January

Joe Fejes runs 555 miles

(2014)

In winning 2014's Across the Years Six-Day Race in the US, Joe Fejes set an American record for most miles run on a non-track surface in six days – beating legendary ultramarathon runner Yiannis Kouros (see 13 February), albeit Kouros at fifty-eight was ten years older.

Fejes clocked 135 miles around the 400-metre loop on the first day but on day two developed severe and 'painful' tendonitis.

As hunger became more pronounced on day three he asked his support team for a bucket of fried chicken. By the day's end he had recorded 303 miles. On day four Fejes and Kouros were regularly swapping the lead but on the final day Fejes was five miles ahead. So he sat stubbornly on Kouros's tail until the win was his. Unsurprisingly, he needed wheelchair assistance at the airport for his flight home.

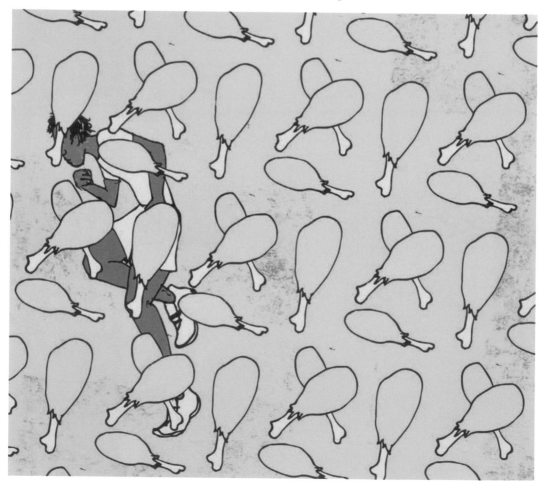

4 January

Super-coach Mihály Iglói dies
(1998)

Hungarian Mihály Iglói was an Olympic-level athlete – unusually, at both the pole vault and 1,500m – but he would have far greater success as a coach.

During his coaching career in the US and Greece, as well as his homeland, his athletes achieved an astonishing 49 world and 35 European records. The apotheosis was 1955 when his three Hungarian athletes, Sándor Iharos (see 24 January), László Tábori and István Rózsavölgyi (see 30 March), recorded nine long and middle distance world records.

Curiously his athletes had much more success against the clock than against other runners – his apparently dour approach wasn't conducive to inspiring his athletes in races.

Also a soldier and an academic, the autocratic Iglói studied physiology and concluded that interval training was better than long slow distance runs.

5 January

Reluctant feminist Kathy Switzer is born
(1947)

Born in Germany to US parents, Kathrine Switzer would be the first woman to run the Boston Marathon as a numbered entry, in 1967 – five years before women were officially allowed. The perceived wisdom of the time was that women simply couldn't cover that distance.

The 20-year-old journalism student wrote 'K.V. Switzer' on the registration form. 'I wasn't running Boston to prove anything,' she said. 'I was just a kid who wanted to run her first marathon.' But she was a serious runner, clocking a 31-mile run in training beforehand.

Switzer started the race in make-up and gold earrings on a snowy day and most runners and spectators gave her a positive reaction. But when enraged official John 'Jock' Semple attempted to remove her number mid-race he was forcibly dissuaded by Switzer's boyfriend Tom Miller, running alongside her.

Switzer finished in around 4:20, nearly an hour behind the first female Bobbi Gibb (see 2 November), who had entered as a 'bandit' (without a number). But pictures of the number removal incident were seen around the world and it became one of the all-time classic running images.

Switzer would place second at Boston in 1975 and win the New York City Marathon in 1974. Despite claiming she didn't initially run Boston as any kind of statement, Switzer was instrumental in getting the IOC to allow a women's marathon.

6 January

The American Deer runs 11 miles in an hour
(1845)

William Howitt, also known as William Jackson and more commonly referred to as 'The American Deer', became the first man to run 11 miles in an hour – and live to tell the tale. A runner named Bettridge had previously achieved the feat – but died very shortly after, from 'over-exertion'. This American Deer was actually born in Norwich, England, but the Brit adopted his moniker after a short trip to the US.

The 11-mile race took place on the Hatfield turnpike road near Barnet, England, with William Sheppard, 'the Birmingham Pet', also running. Marshals were placed a mile apart, holding a handkerchief which the runners touched before turning around, and spectators lined the course. Sheppard was ahead for most of it, but stopped at 10 miles, having clocked a new world record of 53:35. It's unclear whether he stopped due to exhaustion or because he'd miscounted the miles and thought the race was over.

7 January

Arthur Newton runs 100 miles (again)
(1928)

Legendary British ultramarathon runner Arthur Newton ran 100 miles from Bath's Bear Inn to London's Hyde Park Corner in a world record time of 14:22:10. Despite suffering 'physical problems' and encountering adverse weather along the route, a crowd of around 10,000 greeted him at the finish.

Newton had already set a 100-mile record (14:43) while living in Rhodesia (now Zimbabwe) and made two more attempts at bettering his new record in 1933, but injuries hampered him.

In 1934, aged fifty-one, and despite troublesome heart and stomach problems at 70 miles, he reached Hyde Park Corner in 14:06:00 – 16 minutes faster than his 1928 time.

Newton didn't start road running until he was thirty-eight, but still managed to win South Africa's legendary Comrades Marathon five times. He was a pioneer of long slow distance training and often logged 20 miles a day (see 20 May for more).

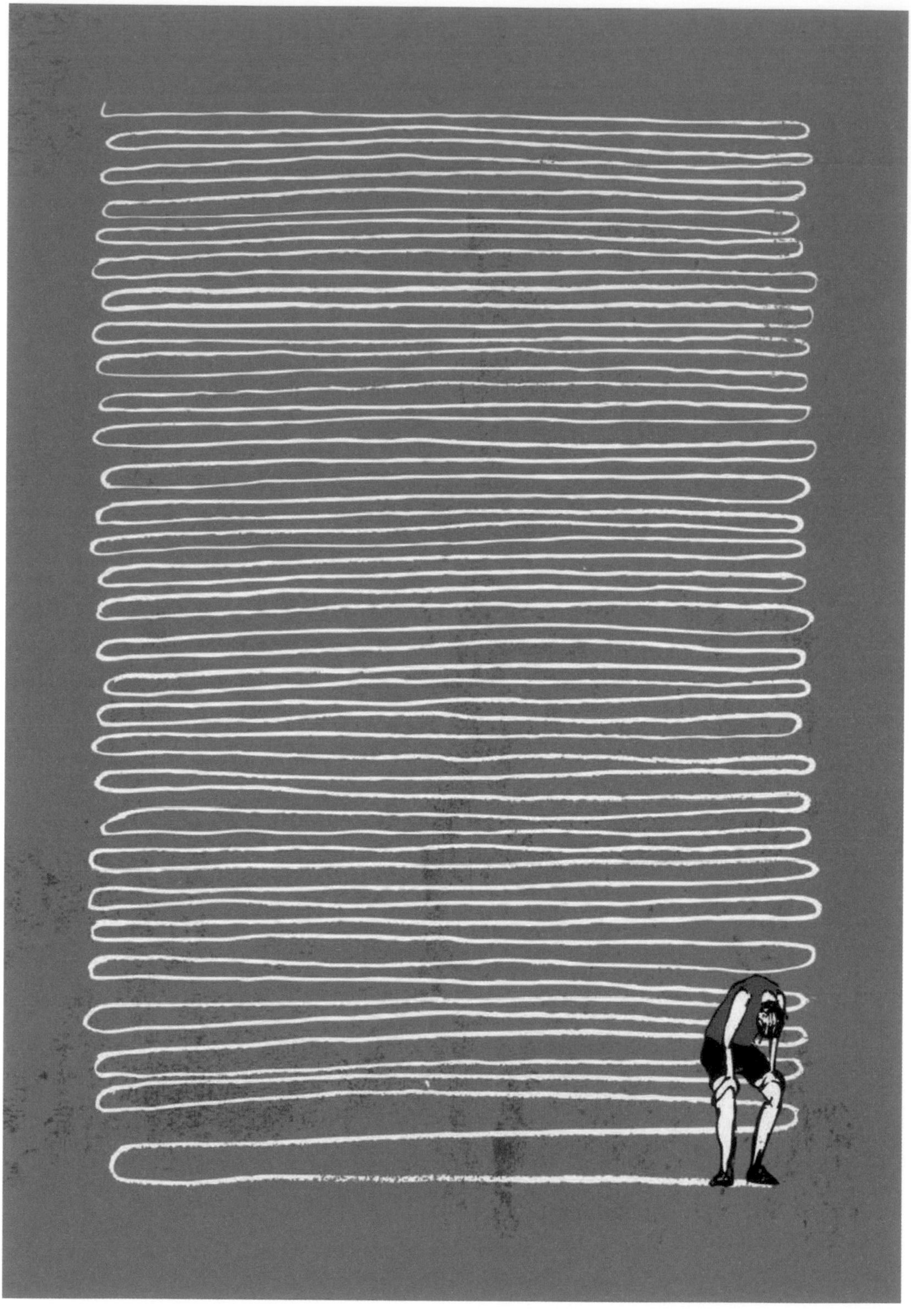

8 January

Ricardo Abad, the Spanish Forest Gump
(1971)

Born on this date, Spain's Ricardo Abad claims the world record for most marathons run on consecutive days – a not to be sniffed at 607. His project started in October 2010 as '500 marathons in 500 days' and he ran at least one marathon in each of the 50 Spanish provinces, breaking the previous record 366 set by the Belgian Stefaan Engels (before that it was Abad's record, with 150). He ran his 500th on 12 February 2012, but then decided to carry on, aiming to reach 1,000. He had to abandon his quest on 607, however, after failing to secure sufficient funding for the project.

He fitted his running around eight-hour shifts in a factory, which could be morning, afternoon or evening, so he sometimes ended up running two marathons in under 12 hours.

9 January

The day when great runners are born
(1953 & 1976)

Not one, or two, or even three, but at least four great runners were born on this date – all of them twins.

On 9 January 1953 Japanese twins Shigeru and Takeshi So arrived in the world. Shigeru would win the 1985 Tokyo Marathon and break the world record, clocking 2:09:05 at the Beppu-Oita Marathon in 1978. Meanwhile his twin brother Takeshi finished fourth, ahead of Shigeru, at the 1984 Olympic Games.

Twenty-three years later, identical Russian twins Olesya and Elena Nurgalieva were born. They went on to dominate both South Africa's prestigious Comrades Marathon and the 56km Two Oceans race. Between them they've claimed 21 podium placings – including 10 wins – at Comrades.

10 January

Controversial coach Percy Cerutty is born
(1895)

In 1938, doctors told 43-year-old Australian Percy Cerutty he only had two years to live. The news turned him on to health and fitness with zeal and he started running 100 miles a week and weightlifting. Either the doctors were wrong or his extreme exercise regime worked.

The eccentric Aussie lived to become a running coach, pioneering a system of 'Stotan' training, a blend of Stoic and Spartan principles. In practice it meant a strict diet of natural foods, swimming, weightlifting and running up and down sand dunes. He also believed in mental progress and taught poetry and philosophy to his athletes.

Though controversial for the time, Cerutty became one of the world's leading coaches in the 1950s and 1960s. His biggest success was with compatriot Herb Elliott (see 25 February), who broke world records and won Olympic gold under Cerutty's tutelage.

11 January

The Spine Race
(2014)

The Spine Race is a foot race along England's 268-mile (431km) Pennine Way National Trail, which traces the Pennines, the country's 'backbone'. It claims to be 'Britain's most brutal race', and competitors are allowed up to seven days to complete it. Northern England may not be Arctic wilderness, but the event is continuous (meaning the clock is always ticking) and the race is known for extreme weather, the real threat of hypothermia (from the country's often underestimated wet cold) and the wild hallucinations of sleep-deprived runners. Exhausted competitors have been found by Mountain Rescue on remote hilltops in their sleeping bags, while others have run into the back end of cows. The 2014 race was won by sleep-allergic Czech adventure racer Pavel Paloncý in 110 hours and 45 minutes, and he successfully defended his title the following year.

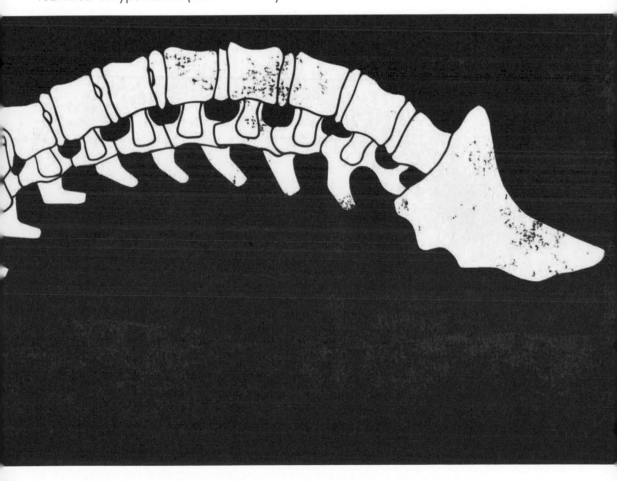

12 January

The Polar Night Half Marathon
(since 2005)

The Polar Night Half Marathon takes place in the northern Norwegian town of Tromsø, above the Arctic Circle. Along with the standard build-up of lactic acid and blisters, runners battle the fierce cold of the long Arctic night, with the average January temperature in Tromsø being –5.6° Celsius. There's only a few hours of daylight at that time of year and though the race starts at 3 p.m. it's run entirely in the dark. The track is usually covered with snow or ice and organisers recommend the wearing of spikes. Despite all this, up to 1,200 runners from more than 35 different countries usually turn up.

Some may find the summer option more attractive though. The Midnight Sun Marathon is the most northerly registered 26.2-mile race in the world. You run in the middle of the night, with the sun sitting forever above the horizon.

13 January

The fastest solo, unsupported journey to the South Pole
(2011)

According to the Guinness World Records, the fastest solo, unsupported and unassisted journey to the South Pole was recorded by 35-year-old Norwegian Christian Eide in 2011. He set off on the 715-mile (1,150km) adventure from Hercules Inlet on 20 December 2010 and covered an average of 29 miles per day to arrive in a record time of 24 days, 1 hour and 13 minutes.

Eide obliterated the previous record of 39 days, 7 hours and 49 minutes, held by the USA's Todd Carmichael. He was originally only aiming for 30 days and was so excited about reaching the pole that he said he couldn't sleep on his final night – recording 56 miles on his last leg.

Neatly, the Norwegian's record marked the 100th anniversary of the first trip to the South Pole by his compatriot Roald Amundsen. In 1911, with the aid of dogs, it took Amundsen and his team 58 days.

14 January

The Hong Kong Marathon
(since 1997)

Traditionally held close to this date, given its unpromising beginnings it's perhaps surprising to learn the Hong Kong Marathon is the world's eighth-best-attended running event, with 73,070 officially running the 2015 race (including subsidiary events).

Traced to 1981, the early years saw cancellations, changing names and rerouted courses. Yet nowadays the marathon is incredibly popular – despite high levels of humidity, which keep supporting medical staff busy. In 2007 for example, 35 participants needed hospital treatment, while 2009's injury count was a stunning 394, of which 16 were sent to the hospital. Around 30 hospitalisations per year is about average for the race.

In 2008 two runners were found both wearing the number 4. It transpired invited runner Lau Kwong Man's coach Ng Fai Yeung had taken his client's rear race number in order to run alongside him. Both were disqualified.

15 January

Ian Stewart is born
(1949)

Scottish middle-distance runner Ian Stewart is best remembered for his part in a classic 5,000m race that *Track & Field News* branded the 'hottest finish in the history of the event'.

The best middle-distance runners at the time were assembled for the 1970 Commonwealth Games 5,000m final in Glasgow, Scotland. Commonwealth and Olympic champion Kenya's Kip Keino, who had already won the 1,500m, was favourite, while most neutrals were behind popular Australian serial world-record breaker Ron Clarke in one of his final outings.

Englishman Dick Taylor led at first, but Scot Ian McCafferty hit the front with 800m left, while Keino loitered with intent. McCafferty led until 550m to go, when Stewart moved ahead. Stewart passed the bell with McCafferty just behind and Keino close on McCafferty's shoulder. Keino moved up to Stewart's shoulder, but the Scot kept increasing the pace. The speed did for ageing legend Clarke, who dropped back.

Down the back straight the lead three kept their positions, and at 200m Keino made his move. But Stewart resisted, forcing Keino to tuck in behind him around the bend. Just past the crown of the bend McCafferty made a break and was past Keino by the time they hit the final straight.

Keino sensed he was beaten, but McCafferty's incredible sprint pushed him closer to Stewart, who was still surging. With 50m to go, gold was still possible for outsider McCafferty. But he finally ran out of steam and Stewart heroically held his composure to the tape and a famous victory.

Stewart and McCafferty had become the second and third fastest 5,000m runners of all time. Keino had also run a PB – despite easing up in the final straight.

16 January

Charlotte Teske runs a world record time
(1982)

On this date, Germany's Charlotte Teske ran a world record (according to the Association of Road Racing Statisticians) of 2:29:01 to win the Miami Marathon. The joint biggest moment of her career happened the same year at the Boston Marathon when, finishing the race in what she assumed was second place, behind hot favourite Grete Waitz (see 15 May and 21 October), Teske was surprised when officials placed a laurel wreath over her head and ushered her to the winner's stage. Waitz had dropped out ahead of Teske, leaving the spoils to the German. 'I feel very sorry,' she said afterwards. 'I didn't beat her really.'

Paediatric nurse Teske represented West Germany at the 1984 Olympics as well as European and World Championships, but would never repeat the success she achieved at road running on the track. She would win city marathons in Frankfurt, Hamburg (twice each), Berlin and Munich. Her preparation included running over 220km a week, plus strength training and aerobics. After her running career she retrained as a physiotherapist.

17 January

Super Swede Dan Waern
(1933)

Born on this date, Swedish middle-distance runner Dan Waern became the first Swede to run a sub-four-minute mile, recording 3:58.5 in 1957 – albeit three years after Briton Roger Bannister broke the famous barrier. For his efforts, Waern was awarded the Svenska Dagbladet Gold Medal – an annual award 'for the most significant Swedish sports achievement of the year'.

The former amateur boxer also ran the 1,500m at both the 1956 and 1960 Olympics, placing fourth in the latter. In 1958 he won 1,500m silver at the European Championships and broke a three-year-old world record in the 1,000m with 2:18.1. He would do better the following year with 2:17.8 – another world record.

His appearances guaranteed crowds in Sweden and he accepted payment to run at a one-off gala. This was against the strict International Association of Athletics Federation amateur rules however and he was disqualified in 1961, retiring to work on a farm and do fitness coaching for a local football team.

18 January

The legendary Deerfoot dies
(1897)

Native American Indians were great runners, doing so to hunt, fight and carry messages. But much of their greatness isn't known to us because it wasn't done on circular tracks or recorded in notebooks. That is except for Louis Bennett, also known as Deerfoot and, according to Edward Sears's book *Running Through the Ages*, 'The greatest American distance runner of the nineteenth century'.

Deerfoot's most noted achievements took place in England on a 20-month tour in 1861 and 1862. His English manager George Martin pitted him against the best long-distance runners of the time, in what became the Deerfoot Running Circus. He defeated nearly all of them. Though many races were fixed in his favour to grow his aura and market the events, the American was no imposter. He set world records for 10 miles (51:26), 12 miles (1:02:02) and one hour (11 miles, 970 yards) – the latter record lasting 34 years.

Deerfoot and his manager knew a thing or two about putting on a show. The Native American would appear in a wolf-skin cloak, eagle-feather headdress, bell-festooned red apron, necklace and earrings, and parade around a venue. He ran in moccasins rather than the spikes popular at the time and would release signature 'war-whoops'.

Deerfoot's diet consisted of meat, vegetables, beer and sherry and he sometimes covered 40 miles a day in training, cajoled by a whip-toting coach. He was known for his 'spurting' tactic during races – essentially dashing ahead, then waiting for others to catch up, then spurting off again. This technique was unheard of and threw many a top runner off their game.

The American was a sure-fire crowd-puller and his fame attracted high society to the sport of pedestrianism, with the future King Edward VII inviting him for dinner.

Another Deerfoot legend has it that he once raced a horse until it died from exhaustion. The extraordinary American eventually died, aged sixty-nine, on this date.

19 January

Christopher Chataway, star of 1954, dies

(2014)

The British runner, who later became a TV broadcast journalist, businessman and politician, only had a brief career, but one full of significant moments. He was one of Roger Bannister's two pacers when the four-minute mile was broken (see 23 March), won gold over 3 miles at the Commonwealth Games and set a 5,000m world record of 13:51.6, in so doing beating the legendary Vladimir Kuts by 0.1 seconds (see 13 October) – all in 1954. And all apparently on four training sessions a week and despite being a smoker. He had such an impact in this year that he became the first winner of the BBC's Sports Personality of the Year award.

In 2006, at the age of seventy-five, he ran the Great North Run half marathon in 1:38:50 – still faster than most people decades his junior. Chataway passed away in 2014.

20 January

The Mumbai Marathon
(2013)

Held on the third Sunday of January each year, the Mumbai Marathon is the largest mass-participation sporting event on the Subcontinent and Bollywood celebrities are often found amid the sweaty, panting throng. Inspired by the London equivalent, the event debuted in 2004, with the route passing many of the city's famous landmarks such as Flora Fountain, Marine Drive, Chowpatty, Haji Ali and Mahim Church.

The race may be relatively young but there's plenty of experience in its organisation.

The race director is the first British man to win the London Marathon, Hugh Jones, also secretary of the Association of International Marathons and Distance Races.

A prize pool of US$350,000 attracts elite runners and the course records set in 2013 were the fastest times ever run for a marathon in India – by Uganda's Jackson Kiprop (2:09:32) and women's winner, Kenyan Valentine Kipketer (2:24:33).

21 January

Nicholas Bourne runs the length of Africa
(1998)

Former male model Nicholas Bourne started running from Cape Town, South Africa, today in 1998, aiming to reach Cairo, Egypt, and become the first person to run the length of Africa. It took the Briton over 10 months (officially 318 days – arriving 5 December) and he wore out 30 pairs of shoes over 7,500 miles (12,069km). Bourne passed through Botswana, Zambia, Tanzania, Kenya, Ethiopia, and Sudan, to claim one of the harder-earned Guinness World Records.

The Briton braved deserts, floods, war zones and wild animals, but his biggest obstacle was border crossings. His original plan was to run the continent north–south, but Egyptian soldiers stopped his progress at the Sudanese border. Bourne simply caught a plane to South Africa and started again in the other direction. Egyptian attitudes had softened when he arrived back and at an official reception at the Pyramids he was presented with a bouquet of flowers.

22 January

The biggest ever race
(2012)

The snappily named Kahit Isang Araw Lang Unity Run, in the SM Mall of Asia, Pasay, Philippines, is thought to be the largest mass-participation running event ever, with 209,000 runners (by way of comparison the London Marathon has around 35,000) – and a claimed total of 300,000 participating worldwide, in South America, New York, Los Angeles, USA, Papua New Guinea and Singapore.

The mass-participation event that makes its rivals look like cult gatherings in comparison was the idea of Daniel Razon, also known as 'Mr Public Service' and CEO of a Philippines TV station, whose aim was to raise money to provide educational aids such as computer facilities for school children.

23 January

Horace Ashenfelter, the steeplechase spy, is born
(1923)

American Horace Ashenfelter's 1952 Olympic win in the 3,000m steeplechase is widely regarded as one of the biggest upsets in Olympic track history.

In elite terms he was a novice, with only around seven steeplechase races to his name, previously preferring hurdles. Not only did the upstart pip the much-fancied Vladimir Kazantsev, but the American broke the Russian's world record too, posting 8:45.4.

So great was Kazantsev's perceived superiority beforehand that Ashenfelter's team-mates had teased: 'Horace, how is it going to feel to be out there running on the track when Kazantsev is in taking a shower and on his way home?'

As Ashenfelter worked for the Federal Bureau of Investigation there was more humour to be had on the theme of him being the first American spy who allowed himself to be chased by a Russian.

24 January

Hungarian great Sándor Iharos dies
(1996)

Along with László Tabori and István Rózsavölgyi, Sándor Iharos was part of the trio of star Hungarian athletes who burst on to the international scene in the 1950s. Thanks partly to injury and the Soviet Union's occupation of Hungary, he did little at major tournaments. But Iharos set over 11 long distance world records, including a stunning seven in 14 months in 1955 and 1956. In fact he's one of only two athletes (the other being nine-time Olympic champion Paavo Nurmi) to have held outdoor world records over 1,500m, 5,000m and 10,000m. He was one of the star pupils of the famous coach Mihály Iglói (see 4 January).

25 January

The Commonwealth Games 10,000m final
(1974)

New Zealand's Dick Tayler may have been coached by legendary coach Arthur Lydiard (see 6 July), but he suffered from arthritis and apparently wasn't even highly rated by his team-mates for the 10,000m final in Christchurch. He faced Commonwealth 5,000m champion Ian Stewart (see 15 January), favourite David Bedford and David Black (both from England) and three Kenyans, including Richard Juma.

As the Kenyans and Bedford jostled early on, Tayler stayed some 50 metres behind, keeping his powder dry. When he eventually made his move, the crowd noise grew with him. As he burst through to lead with half a lap to go the excitement proved too much for one spectator, who collapsed and died. The unfancied Tayler's moment of euphoria as he crossed the line in first place was voted New Zealand's favourite sporting moment in 1999.

26 January

Non-flying Finn Paavo Kotila dies
(2014)

A Finnish runner not nicknamed a 'Flying Finn' makes a refreshing change, but Paavo Kotila was from a different era. Paavo Nurmi and his pals set the athletics world alight in the 1920s, while their compatriot Kotila was at his peak in the 1950s. Kotila's predecessors were middle-distance runners who collected gold medals and set world records, while Kotila's most notable championship appearance was 13th in the marathon at the 1956 Olympics. But when he tried road marathons he found his forte.

Kotila broke the marathon world record in 1956, with 2:18:04, in Pieksamaki, Finland. He also won the Boston Marathon in 1960, the highlight of his career.

27 January

A mile world record and a classic race
(1962)

The mile has produced more than its fair share of classic races. Though when New Zealander and 800m Olympic champion Peter Snell, Australian sub-four-minute-miler Albie Thomas and British barefoot-three-mile specialist Bruce Tulloh lined up at Cooks Gardens in New Zealand's Wanganui in 1962, few were predicting a world record.

The runners certainly had pedigree – Snell's legendary coach Arthur Lydiard (see 6 July) had unhelpfully announced his runner was capable of a 3:55 mile – the current record was 3:54.5. But wet weather was forecast and the track was grass, though a crowd of 16,000 gathered to watch anyway.

Snell started in last place, but was second by the end of the first lap. At halfway he was third, but local runner Barry Cossar was pulling away, so Snell moved ahead of him, with Tulloh close behind. Crowd noise grew as they sensed a fast time. The bell for the final lap rang at 2:58. It looked good for Snell, but surprisingly Tulloh dashed past him into the lead.

Snell waited until the back straight. 'I was holding nothing back,' he later said. 'I don't think I've ever felt such a glorious feeling of strength and speed without strain.' Snell broke the tape at 3:54.4. Tulloh also finished under four minutes with 3:59.3 (and was seen dancing up and down the field in delight).

Snell, who later said the race changed his life, had surprised everyone – except his coach.

28 January

The oldest person to trek to the South Pole unsupported
(2004)

Briton Simon Murray, aged 63 years and 309 days, completed his unsupported overland trek to the South Pole on this date, earning himself a Guinness World Record. The former French Foreign Legionnaire started from the coast near Hercules Inlet on 2 December 2003 and arrived at the bottom of the world, with his trekking partner Pen Hadow, having covered around 1,100km (684 miles). The pair pulled all their own equipment and supplies. Murray had prepared for the trip by dragging tyres around Dartmoor and sleeping in a bin bag. 'The worst thing was the wind – 100mph winds that took your face off,' he said. 'But it was amazing.'

They have a taste for adventure records in his household. Simon's wife Jennifer was the first woman to fly around the world in a helicopter.

29 January

Shackleton arrives on Antarctica
(1908)

Along with Norwegian Roald Amundsen and British naval captain Robert Scott, Irishman Ernest Shackleton was one of the main protagonists of the Heroic Age of Antarctic Exploration, and he arrived at the world's only unpeopled continent in the Nimrod today in 1908.

After one trip with Scott – and before his mentor's second, ill-fated expedition (see 19 March) – Shackleton snuck in there with an effort to be the first to reach the South Pole. With three companions, he travelled 180km (112 miles) across uncharted snow and ice to establish a new 'Farthest South' record (at latitude 88°S, 156km from the Pole).

Shackleton was knighted by King Edward VII on his return home. He would be part of four attempts at reaching the Pole and would die trying in 1922. This was his most successful effort.

30 January

The London to Brighton Race
(1837)

The 55-mile (89km) London to Brighton Race claims the longest history of any ultramarathon in the world.

A popular route for pedestrians and cycle races, the first recorded running race on the Brighton Road was in 1837 when professional runners John Townsend and Jack Berry set off from the Elephant and Castle in London. The next known foot race wasn't until 1897, and was repeated in 1899 (for amateurs) and in 1903 (for professionals) – won by Len Hurst (see 19 July) in 6:32:34.

In 1924 legendary ultra runner Arthur Newton (see 7 January) set a London–Brighton record of 5:53:43. When the race finally became an annual fixture in 1951 the winner traditionally collected the Arthur Newton Cup. Runners came from all over the world to race here and from the 1960s to the 1980s the London–Brighton Race was the de facto Ultra Distance World Championships. However, from 2005 the legendary road race stopped taking place, partly due to increased traffic. A trail race now goes from London to Brighton on a similar route.

31 January

Unlucky John Zander is born
(1890)

Thanks in part to his trademark long sprint finish to races, Sweden's John Zander was one of the world's best middle- and long-distance runners before World War One.

He competed at two Olympics either side of the Great War (1912 and 1920), at both 1,500m and 3,000m. At Stockholm in the 1912 Olympics he placed seventh in the 1,500m and tenth in the 3,000m, to help his country to a team silver, though he didn't get a medal as – harshly – only the top three scorers received them.

It may have been some consolation then for Zander to set two world records, 3:54.7 for 1,500m and 8:33.2 for 3,000m. Both were eventually broken by Flying Finn Paavo Nurmi (see 22 June), but not for five and seven years respectively.

FEBRUARY

1 February

The Great Trans-Canada Race
(1921)

A crowd of 2,000 turned out in Halifax, on Canada's East Coast, to cheer off husband and wife Jenny and Frank Dill, the final entrants of the Great Trans-Canada Race. They were two of only five contestants – the other three already well ahead – in the 3,645-mile (5,866km) pan-Canadian race to Vancouver.

A welcome distraction from post-war hurt and high unemployment, the extraordinary event caught the public imagination with regular newspaper coverage and large crowds turning out en route, offering sustenance, new shoes and even lifts – though apparently none were taken – to the contestants, comprising a postman and his son, Jack and Clifford Behan, and athlete Charles Burkman.

Jack and Clifford thought they'd won, 138 days of hiking later, when they arrived on the West Coast. Three days later, however, the Dills arrived, in four days less overall.

2 February

Jez Bragg runs the length of New Zealand
(2013)

At around 4 p.m. on Saturday, 2 February, British ultra runner Jez Bragg reached Bluff, the southern end of the South Island, recording a Fastest Known Time for the 3,054-kilometre (1,900-mile) Te Araroa Trail that runs from the top to the bottom of the country.

Taking 53 days and 9 hours, the former winner of the Ultra-Trail du Mont-Blanc completed the journey despite suffering from giardiasis, which rendered him too weak to leave his bed for three days.

The trail also involved a perilous 44km, nine-hour kayak trip across Cook Straight between New Zealand's two main islands. Aside from the three days lost to illness, the athlete averaged 12–18 hours per day on his feet.

3 February

Don Ritchie starts running 100 miles
(1990)

Today Scottish runner Don Ritchie began what would, on 4 February, become a world record for 100 miles (indoor) of 12:56:13, which stood for 25 years. It was one of 14 world records set by the extraordinary Ritchie, ranging from 'tiddlers', as he called 50-milers, to 24-hour races – his best being a world record 166 miles, when aged forty-six, which stood for decades. His (absolute) 100km world record of 6:10:20 still stands over three decades later, too.

In 1989 he set the Land's End to John o'Groats (the length of Britain) solo record, completing it in 10 days, 15 hours and 25 minutes. He lost 14lb (6.4kg). 'It took me five months and seven courses of antibiotics to recover,' he told the *Independent*.

'I think you need to be a calm, determined and patient person [to run long distances], with a high tolerance for prolonged discomfort.'

4 February

Thirty-two false starts
(1851)

Bellevue, Manchester, hosted a memorable 150-yard contest between sprinter William Hayes, known as 'the Ruddington Hero', and Charles Westhall, the first man to break 4:30 for the mile on a track.

It was a cold day and the track was covered in snow, which may have accounted for many if not all of the 32 false starts. After an hour of surreal non-running, the runners finally left the line in a manner satisfying to the officials. Only for Westhall to promptly slip over. Hayes had a lead of three yards at the 80-yard mark.

In a moment you imagine Hayes rather regrets, he turned to his pursuer and put his hand on his nose in a mocking gesture. Westhall wasn't in a mood to be ridiculed and, fired up, responded by catching and passing his rival.

After winning Westhall was said to press his hand on his 'nether end' in a gesture of retaliation. He had also recorded the fastest time for 150 yards, in 15 seconds flat.

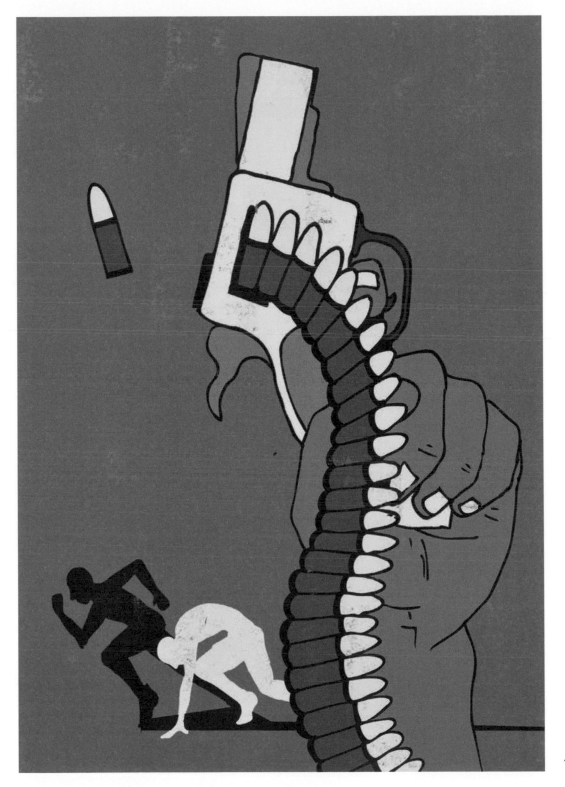

5 February

'Blower' Brown breaks six-day record
(1880)

Among his many achievements, pedestrian colossus American Edward Weston (see 22 February and 17 March), also enviously known as 'the Wily Wobbler', set a world record for six-day racing, recording 550 miles (885km), at June 1879's prestigious fourth Astley Belt.

The British Champion Henry 'Blower' Brown, so monikered because he puffed out his cheeks as he strolled, came second in that contest. Brown's fitness came partly from his brickmaking work, where he repeatedly transported wheelbarrow loads of bricks to and from the kiln.

His career wasn't as distinguished as Weston's, but he performed well in several Astley Belts. In February 1880 Brown even bettered Edward's world record for distance covered in a six-say race, clocking a whopping 553 miles and 176 yards.

According to *Running Through the Ages*, Brown was fond of a beer and his trainer would keep him motivated by shouting, 'Go it, Blower! You have 'em all beat, my beauty! Yes! Blower shall have a barrel of bear all to himself if he wins, go it Blower!' In the November 1880 Astley Belt, however, he had to retire with severe chafing in the groin region.

6 February

The longest human-powered polar journey
(2014)

On this day Britons Ben Saunders and Tarka L'Herpiniere were on the brink of completing the first return journey to the South Pole from Ross Island, along the same route attempted by both Sir Ernest Shackleton and Captain Robert Scott around a century beforehand.

At 1,795 miles (2,888km) Saunders and L'Herpiniere's 'Scott Expedition' was the longest human-powered polar journey in history. The adventurers set out from Ross Island on 26 October 2013, reached the South Pole on 26 December and finished their expedition back at Ross Island on 7 February 2014.

They hauled sleds with a starting weight of almost 200kg each and covered 17 miles per day on average, in wind-chill temperatures as low as -46°C.

7 February

The Flying Scotsman
(1880)

As befitted the sport, pedestrian George Cameron needed a nickname. Feeling uninspired, he simply chose his own surname backwards and the legend of Noremac was born. Perhaps to his relief, he also became known as the Flying Scotsman.

With several short-distance wins to his backwards name, in early February 1880 Noremac stepped up the miles with a seven-day pedestrian contest in Nottingham. The outcome is unclear, but he went on to win three 72-hour (six days, 12 hours per day) races in Scotland between late February and early April – ending at Show Hall, Edinburgh, with a new 72-hour world record of 384 miles (618km).

After similar wins in England he sailed for the US with manager George Beattie. Noremac wasn't always as successful across the Atlantic, but he bought a bar and both families lived on the premises.

However, Noremac liked a drink and everyone fell out, resulting in Beattie shooting Mrs Cameron, before turning the gun on himself.

8 February

The American Wonder and the American Deer
(1846)

American runners George Seward, 'The American Wonder', and William Jackson, 'The American Deer', toured the UK in 1846, appearing in specially staged running contests. Jackson surprisingly lost his race on this date, a rare event. Despite his nickname, Jackson was born in England (originally named William Howitt) and spent most of his life in the UK, winning 138 races in the country.

Starting off by betting he could jump over a horse with a small run-up, Seward also spent much of his pedestrian career in Britain. He was a phenomenal sprinter, sometimes called 'American's first great runner' (though that rather ignores indigenous runners).

He initially crossed the Atlantic because no one in the US would race him any longer, possibly because he liked to race in flesh-coloured silk attire.

It wasn't long before he'd beaten every respectable sprinter in England too. Initially though, he intentionally won races by small margins, to instigate a lucrative re-match.

After beating William Robinson in 1844 Seward was crowned Champion of England, and the Wonder and the Deer went back to tour the US together. Seward took on the shorter races, Jackson four miles and upwards. Soon no one would race them there again, despite the offer of head-start handicaps.

9 February

New Zealand pedestrian Joe Scott dies
(1908)

Joe Scott started work as a bootmaker in Dunedin aged thirteen. But his lunchbreaks were spent racing other boys on the streets, where he was spotted and trained as a competitive walker. At his first event in 1874, however, he was disqualified for running.

When Australian champion William Edwards came to town and walked 100 miles (161km) in 24 hours soon after, Scott promptly walked the distance in 23 hours 53 minutes. Edwards challenged him to a seven-mile race; Scott beat him again.

In 1886 Scott travelled across the Tasman Sea and was declared champion of Australia after walking 424 miles in a six-day contest, again against Edwards. Then in the Agricultural Hall, London, in May 1888, he covered 363 miles 1,510 yards in a 72-hour contest, winning him the 'world championship' belt. He arrived home to a hero's welcome in 1889, paraded around as a band played 'See the Conquering Hero Comes'.

Scott made very little money though and died leaving his wife and seven children in near-poverty. Fellow sportsmen donated over £45 for a memorial headstone.

10 February

'Iron' Joss Naylor is born
(1936)

'The hardest man in the hardest sport' is how many see Joss Naylor and the British sport of fell running. Naylor, who would earn the nicknames 'King of the Fells', 'Iron Man' and 'Iron Joss', grew up under the shadow of England's highest fell (i.e. mountain), Scafell Pike.

Yet his youth never hinted he would be a sporting legend. He was hindered by a serious back condition and rarely took part in school sports, leaving at fifteen to work on a farm. He was deemed unfit for national service and at eighteen had an operation to remove the cartilage from his right knee. That didn't go well: it prevented him fully extending his knee and gave him an unusual running gait. And yet he knew – and ran – the fells like no one else.

Aside from the Bob Graham Round (see 13 June), the most coveted fell-running record is the number of Lake District peaks scaled inside 24 hours. In July 1975, Naylor ran through a heatwave to raise his own record by nine to 72 peaks, an achievement that earned him an MBE.

Among his other records are reaching all 214 of the summits listed in Alfred Wainwright's Lake District guides in seven days, one hour and 25 minutes – in 1986 at the age of fifty. And he didn't stop there. At the age of sixty he ran 60 Lakeland fell tops in 36 hours. In 2006, aged seventy, he ran 70 Lakeland fell tops, covering more than 50 miles and ascending more than 25,000 feet, in under 21 hours.

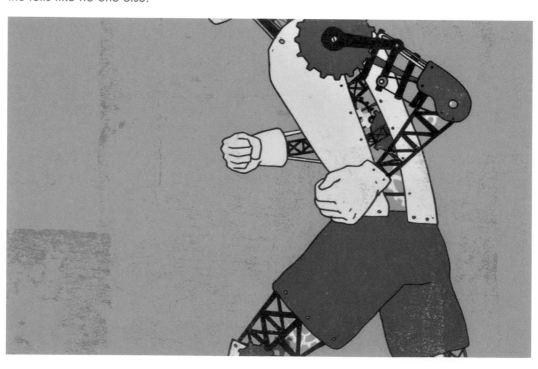

11 February

Ryoichi Sekiya sets a new 12-hour world record

(2007)

However much they deserve it and however gruelling they are, both 24-hour races and 12-hour races are not events to attract a high number of spectators. Put simply, they require runners to see how far they can run (around a track) in the time period.

Japan's Ryoichi Sekiya is rather good at both. In 2007 he set a new 12-hour world record (indoor), in Lohja Citymarket, Finland, of 146.296km (nearly 91 miles).

He is also the Asian record holder for 24 hours, with a distance of 274.884km, also recorded in 2007, and a four-time IAU 24 Hour World Championship winner – more wins than anyone else.

He also won Greece's notorious 153-mile Spartathlon in 2002 and again in 2009 when aged forty-two and has also completed Badwater (see 31 July).

12 February

James Clark sets new marathon world record

(1909)

The day of New York's 1909 Brooklyn Marathon coincided with celebrations for the centenary of former president Abraham Lincoln's birth. Crowds were estimated at around a quarter of a million and 40 troops were on hand to aid the police in trying to keep the course clear.

A little before 2 p.m., 164 runners started out from the Thirteenth Regiment Armory on Sumner Avenue (now Marcus Garvey Boulevard). They puffed and panted along various New York streets to Seagate, turning back half a mile beyond it and returning to the Armory for eight laps around the track to finish.

The 39km race was won by American James Clark in a new world record time of 2:46:52. Little is known of Clark, though *The New York Times* reported he also set an American record of 1:57:27 in a 20-mile race on 14 November the same year.

13 February

Yiannis 'Running God' Kouros is born
(1956)

If running has ever had a Superman, it is Yiannis Kouros. Creator of 160 world records, Kouros is the greatest ultramarathon runner of all time, if not simply the greatest runner.

Greek-born, he immigrated to Australia and rose to prominence when he won the first Spartathlon (153 miles) in 1984 and the 544-mile Sydney to Melbourne Ultramarathon a year later. He's won Spartathlon four times and the four fastest recorded times for the race are all his.

Kouros has set world records from 100 to 1,000 miles (10 days, 10:30:36, if you were wondering) and every road and track record from 12 hours to six days – he still holds the vast majority of them.

He takes three months off running each year, sometimes five, and aside from events rarely runs more than seven or eight miles at a time. Impressively, he also has a talent for the arts, with a master's degree in literature and has had many poems published. Fittingly the Greek played the role of Pheidippides in the 1995 film *A Hero's Journey*, about the history of the marathon.

14 February

Ice-cream-eating record-breaker is born
(1933)

New Zealander 'Millie' Sampson only ever ran two marathons. Her preference was cross country and she was national champion in 1966, 1968 and 1972.

The intensity of off-road running prepared her well and her 3:13:58 marathon time in Auckland in 1970 was the sixth fastest in the world that year. But in 1964 at her first attempt she had done relatively better.

On 21 July 1964, with a time of 3:19:33, also in Auckland, she set a world best at the women's marathon. She was very much a pioneer as very few marathons allowed female participants until well into the 1970s. She was encouraged to enter the event by fellow runners at the Owairaka Athletic Club – made famous by legendary coach Arthur Lydiard (see 6 July) – thinking her participation would attract attention to the race and club.

Sampson had been out dancing into the small hours the night before. That, and no breakfast, certainly added to the fatigue she felt towards the end of the race. But the ice cream she ate during the last few miles seemingly did her more good than harm.

15 February

Lon Myers is born
(1858)

Being a sickly child who would endure a lifelong battle with malaria, American Laurence Myers took up running simply to improve his health. He was said to have legs so long they were out of proportion to his body. Nevertheless, he got a coach and in 1879 ran 440 yards in a claimed record of 49.5 seconds, despite his shoe coming off with 120 yards to go.

In 1880 he collected national records like they were gold coins, from 100 yards to the mile. But there was suspicion from across the Atlantic, as it was thought US courses were rarely measured accurately. So Myers got on a boat to Britain and irrefutably broke several more short- and middle-distance world records. Overall he set records at 11 distances.

His greatest performance came in 1881, back in the US, an attempt at the 1,000-yard amateur record held by Englishman Walter George. Twenty expert time-keepers were there to defy any British cynicism. He recorded 2:13, five seconds quicker than George and four seconds inside the professional record.

Myers and George became great friends and raced in America and Australia over the mile, quarter-mile and 1,000 yards, in front of huge crowds. Myers' aggregate win was 6–3.

16 February

Cathy Freeman is born
(1973)

At the 2000 Olympics in Sydney Cathy Freeman created not just one of the great Olympic moments, but a great moment for post-colonialism. Most of Freeman's relatives were Aborigines, her grandmother part of the 'stolen generation', forcibly removed from their families as children and raised by white parents.

As in most post-colonial countries, relations between Indigenous and non-Indigenous Australians haven't always been harmonious, but they were able to come together in 2000 to celebrate the brilliance of Freeman.

The 400m runner was the first Indigenous Australian to become a Commonwealth gold medallist, in 1990, aged just sixteen, and she competed in the 1992 and 1996 Olympics, taking silver at the latter. She was World Champion in 1997 and 1999, and prior to the 2000 Games had won 37 of her previous 38 finals. The expectation was huge.

There were 112,000 people inside the stadium and half of Australia watching on television. Wearing a curious hooded bodysuit, Freeman started cautiously. She seemed to tire slightly in the final 200m and was level with two others entering the home straight. But her strides grew in length as she powered away, the will of the host nation pushing her along, to win by nearly half a second.

The lack of smile at the finish line perhaps gave away the release of pressure, rather than pure elation, she must have felt. Overwhelmed, Freeman sank to the track and sat for two full minutes as the crowd cheered. She carried both the Australian and Aboriginal flags on a lap of honour – despite the fact 'unofficial' flags are banned at the Games. On her upper right arm, the side closest to spectators on an athletics track, she has 'Cos I'm Free' tattooed.

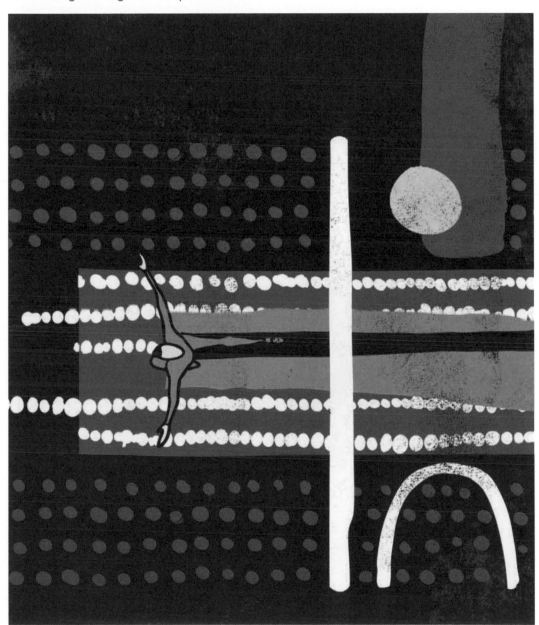

17 February

Toru Terasawa breaks marathon world record
(1963)

Japan's Toru Terasawa broke the marathon world record at the Beppu-Oita Marathon on Japan's island of Kyushu. He took off at a ferocious speed, holding his record-setting pace for most of the race. Predictably he began to tire near the end and his pace slowed. But he hung on heroically and managed to narrowly break Abebe Bikila's world record by under half a second with 2:15:15.8.

He would run a faster 26.2 miles though. Two years later, at London's Polytechnic Marathon, Terasawa recorded 2:13:41.

Compatriot Morio Shigematsu, however, was just ahead of him, to set a world record with 2:12:00. Terasawa's PB was the third fastest ever at the time.

He won Beppu-Oita Marathon for four consecutive years (1963–66), as well as two wins at Fukuoka Marathon and one at the Nagano Marathon.

A year after his world record, however, he could only manage 15th at the Olympics. But in 1965 he set his second world record, running 30km in 1:31:51.6 in Kumanichi.

18 February

The first Tokyo Marathon
(2007)

The Tokyo Marathon is one of the official six World Majors – the others being Berlin, Boston, Chicago, New York and London. Though it officially dates only to 2007, there were two marathons in the Japanese capital beforehand: the Tokyo International Marathon, which took place on even years, and the overexcitedly named Tokyo-New York Friendship International Marathon, which took place on odd years. Both date to 1981, when the two took place only a month apart, a situation wisely deemed unsustainable. So they simply took it in turns, until 2007.

The 2011 Tokyo Marathon was the first one without rain.

19 February

Buddy Edelen dies
(1997)

Like George Seward (see 16 October), Ellison 'Deerfoot' Brown (see 18 January) and Lon Myers (see 15 February), Leonard 'Buddy' Edelen was an American who spent his prime running years in England.

Edelen ran the world's first sub-2:15 marathon at London's 1963 Polytechnic Marathon with 2:14:28 (see 15 June). He was consequently labelled 'America's great hope' for gold at the 1964 Olympics in Tokyo.

Edelen was a poorly paid private-school teacher in England and had to wash cars and appeal for donations to afford to travel to the US for Olympic Trials. His efforts were rewarded, as he made the US team. A sciatic nerve condition caused him severe back trouble at the Olympics, but he still finished sixth.

Edelen ran 13 more marathons, winning seven, but he stopped competing at the age of twenty-eight. Although he ran 130 miles (209km) a week at his peak, he drank a beer a day and smoked.

20 February

4,000-mile run across the Sahara
(2006)

Charlie Engle (US), Ray Zahab (Canada) and Kevin Lin (Taiwan) reached the Red Sea and the end of an incredible 4,300-mile (nearly 7,000km) run across the Sahara. Their journey, starting from the coast of Senegal, had lasted 111 days – the equivalent of two marathons a day for 100 days – and had taken them through six countries (also Mauritania, Mali, Niger, Libya and Egypt). They were the first contemporary runners known to have crossed the famous desert, and a Matt Damon-narrated documentary, *Running the Sahara* (2007), tracked their progress.

Lin and Zahab were competitive ultramarathon runners (even if the latter used to smoke a pack of cigarettes a day), but Engle had a more unlikely past. The American is an ex-drug addict, alcoholic and convict, who enjoyed running marathons but entered his first ultramarathon by accident, thinking he was entering a 10K event. And won it.

21 February

Ron Clarke is born
(1937)

Australia's Ron Clarke set 17 middle- and long-distance world records – 12 of them in 1965, including nine in a stunning 21 days. Yet oddly Clarke is more commonly remembered for misfortune and near misses. He won four Commonwealth Games silvers and one Olympic bronze, but never the gold his performances elsewhere merited.

At 1968's Mexico City Olympics, Clarke – unprepared for the altitude – nearly blacked out late in the 10,000m final. Virtually unconscious, he went from challenging for the lead to staggering to sixth place. (He damaged his heart as a result, requiring open-heart surgery years later and daily medication.)

He did get an Olympic gold, however, donated to him by Czech legend Emil Zátopek, recognising how much the Australian deserved one.

Off the track, Clarke was a successful businessman, author and politician, becoming the mayor of the Gold Coast, Queensland. He died in June 2015.

22 February

Wily Wobbler Edward Weston loses a bet
(1861)

When Edward Weston made an ill-judged bet with a friend, he wouldn't have known subsequent events would define his life. They wagered on the outcome of the 1860 US election: whoever's candidate lost would walk to see the new president's inauguration. Abraham Lincoln won and Weston, later known as 'the Wily Wobbler', had to dust off his walking boots.

With a showman's awareness, he started his 478-mile (769km) trek from Boston to Washington on 22 February, followed by a carriage full of supporters and a band of drummers. He faced snow and rain, rarely slept and fell several times. But after 10 days and 10 hours on his feet he arrived on 4 March, just hours late for Lincoln's inauguration.

But word had spread and Weston was invited to the inauguration ball at the White House. He even received a congratulatory handshake from the new president and the offer of his train fare home. But Weston declined, insisting he would walk back. Newspaper coverage had given him ideas...

Weston would go on to be one of the most famous people in the English-speaking world (see 17 March and 29 June).

23 February

Paula Radcliffe sets 10,000m women's world record
(2003)

Britain's Paula Radcliffe is better than good at marathon running. Her world record of 2:15:25, set at London in 2003, is unsurpassed since. She's a three-time winner of London (also 2002 and 2005), and New York (2004, 2007, 2008), with another win at Chicago (2002). She's so good at 26.2 miles that her achievements at 10,000m often get overlooked.

Radcliffe is a former European Champion at 10K (as well as cross country) and a World Championship silver medallist. In the same year as her marathon world record she set a new 10,000m women's world record – which, like her London record, still stands well over a decade later. She ran 30:21 at the 'World's Best 10K', a road race in San Juan, Puerto Rico.

Not bad for an asthma sufferer.

24 February

Arun Bhardwaj, India's top ultra runner, is born
(1969)

Arun Bhardwaj is an ultra runner from a place where few have heard of ultra running. On his website he claims to be the 'only ultra runner in India' and he's certainly the first to gain international recognition. He says he enjoys the 'spiritual ecstasy' of running long distances.

He's completed New York's famous Self-Transcendence 3,100 Mile Race, the notorious Badwater Ultramarathon (see 31 July) in the US, and in 2010 he won South Africa's 564km (350 miles) George Archer Six Day Circuit Race (by being the only finisher).

He works as a planning commissioner for the government in New Delhi, where he often runs the 40km round trip to work.

25 February

Herb Elliott is born
(1938)

Australia's Herb Elliott first got the running bug watching legendary Russian Vladimir Kuts (see 23 November) at the 1956 Olympics. The same year, Elliott hooked up with unorthodox coach Percy Cerutty, who initiated a training regime that included swimming in surf, sprinting up sand dunes and eating raw vegetables.

In 1957 he ran his first sub-four-minute mile, three years after Roger Bannister broke the barrier. In August 1958 he set a world record for the mile, clocking 3:54.5, 2.7 seconds under Derek Ibbotson's record. Later that month he set a 1,500m world record, running 3:36.0.

Between 1957 and 1961 he ran 45-mile and 1,500m races and didn't lose once. He won gold, and bettered his own 1,500m world record (with 3:35.6) at the 1960 Olympics, despite not understanding the lap times, called out in Italian. He dominated middle-distance running as few, if any, have before or since.

However, he retired aged just twenty-two, to study at Cambridge University, England, and went on to become chairman of an iron ore mining company.

26 February

Sanya Richards-Ross is born
(1985)

This 400m runner ranked number one in the world from 2005–09 and again in 2012. Born in Jamaica, Richards-Ross became a US citizen in 2002 and represents them internationally. She's the type of runner who doesn't like too much colour variety in her medal collection. She has five World Championship golds (seven medals in total) and four Olympic golds (five medals in total), albeit three for the 4×400m relay.

It'll be no surprise that the 2002 National High School Female Athlete of the Year and 2006 IAAF Female World Athlete of the Year started running at the age of seven. It may or may not be a surprise that she also has her own reality TV series, *Sanya's Glam and Gold*. She's also married to American Football star, Aaron Ross.

27 February

Pam Reed, Badwater winner, is born
(1961)

In 2002 America's Pam Reed became the first woman to win the notoriously hot, 135-mile Badwater Ultramarathon outright – aged forty-one and by a margin of five hours, setting a women's course record by nearly two hours. She then went on to win it overall again the next year, beating Dean Karnazes (see 17 September) into second place.

In 2005, Reed ran 300 miles without sleep and is the female American record holder in six-day marathons, after completing 490 miles at 2009's Self-Transcendence Six-Day Race in New York.

With five sons and her own race to direct, Reed sneaks in short training runs between school drop-offs and collections, several times a day.

28 February

James Kwambai is born
(1983)

Kenya's James Kwambai is one of those incredible athletes you sense was simply born at the wrong time. The marathon specialist has the unenviable knack of coming second, being beaten by a world record or world record holder.

In 2006 Kwambai won the Brescia Marathon and Beijing Marathon, his first two 26.2-mile races. He's also won the JoongAng Seoul Marathon three times consecutively (2011–13).

But he's better known for finishing second (with 2:05:36) at the 2008 Berlin Marathon, where Haile Gebrselassie set a new marathon world record of 2:03:59.

At the 2009 Rotterdam Marathon the nearly man again finished second, this time behind Duncan Kibet. Extraordinarily both runners were credited with 2:04:27, the third-fastest performance of all time.

MARCH

1 March

Pheidippides runs many marathons
(490 BC)

The Ancient Greek story behind the marathon is a mythology classic, told in schools around the world. But it's become a bit muddled.

The common version is that a Greek runner – a full-time and valued job back then, primarily to carry messages – Pheidippides (spellings vary), ran around 25 miles from Marathon to Athens, to deliver news of a military victory against the Persians in the Battle of Marathon before dropping dead.

In the excellent *Running Through the Ages*, however, author Edward S. Sears uses several historical sources to argue the tale is confused with a story of another Greek messenger – running around 140 miles from Athens to Sparta and possibly back again. And not dropping dead.

In both Greek and Roman histories there are also references to a Pheidippides running from Athens to Sparta, dating to 490 BC. The first reference to a Marathon-to-Athens run, of around 26 miles, isn't until around AD 46–120.

In 1879 American poet Robert Browning published the poem, 'Pheidippides', which combines various versions of the legend. The poem's climax is a run from Athens to Marathon – the likely influence for the founders of the modern Olympics. The 153-mile Spartathlon ultramarathon from Athens to Sparta is based on the original account of Pheidippides.

'Pheidippides' run from Athens to Sparta and back is historically sound,' argues Sears. After all, a professional runner dropping dead after 26 miles isn't very, well, professional.

2 March

Patrick Makau is born
(1985)

Kenya's Patrick Makau broke the marathon world record in 2011, with 2:03:38 at Berlin (see 25 September). Oddly, however, 26.2 miles isn't his best distance. His record as a half-marathon runner is even better.

Makau has two individual silvers and two team golds for the IAAF World Half Marathon Championships 2007 and 2008.

He has 11 half-marathon wins to his name, mostly in Europe and usually finishing in under an hour.

In 2007 he finished second at the Ras Al Khaimah Half Marathon in 59:13 minutes, beaten only by Samuel Wanjiru, who set a world record of 58:53. Makau returned to win the race in 2009.

3 March

Charles Rowell runs 150 miles in 24 hours
(1882)

In a six-day race in New York, British pedestrian and six-day racer Charles Rowell continued with his experimental tactic of building a huge early lead and simply trying to hold on to it as the hours and days waned.

In the first 24 hours of the race starting, he clocked up a staggering 150 miles. However, on the third day he mistakenly gulped down a cup of vinegar; the liquid condiment succeeded where poison and violence hadn't in previous races (see 11 March) and forced him to retire, leaving George Hazael to win – and become the first man to cover 600 miles in six days.

Rowell didn't try his fast-start strategy again, or presumably a mid-race vinegar. But his 24-hour record stood until 1953.

4 March

The start of the Bunion Derby
(1928)

Billed as 'the greatest test of human endurance in history', 1928's Great Transcontinental Footrace measured 3,423 miles (5,508km) from Los Angeles to New York City in 84 daily stages of between 30 and 75 miles. A $25,000 prize lured 199 runners to the start line of the 'Bunion Derby' and an unprecedented 15 million Americans would turn out to see the race.

British-born Arthur Newton (see 7 January and 20 May) was the star attraction, along with Willie Kolehmainen, older brother of Olympic hero Hannes (see 7 July). Kolehmainen was out by day three, however, thanks to an absurdly fast start. Newton, too, crashed out injured with a nine-hour-lead, though the star continued as 'technical advisor'.

As the event started losing money, race director Charles C. Pyles began lengthening the stages, up to 75 miles at a time, to try to complete it sooner. After 84 days, 55 runners finished, many in rags and some shoeless. The victor, Andy Payne, paid off the mortgage on his father's farm with the winnings, then retired from running after a doctor judged the race had taken 10 years off his life.

5 March

Rudi Harbig dies
(1944)

In 1936, a 22-year-old Rudolf 'Rudi' Harbig helped the German 4x400m team to a bronze medal at the Berlin Olympics. He then went unbeaten in 1937 and 1938. The following year he set world records for both 400m and 800m, with 46.0 and 1:46.6 respectively. Not bad for someone who trained lightly by contemporary standards, according to Fred Wilt's *How They Train* (though he abstained from alcohol, tea and coffee).

When World War Two intervened, Harbig was deemed useful to the Nazi propaganda machine and allowed to continue training and racing (in Germany, Italy and Sweden) until 1942. Eventually, the double world record holder was sent to the Eastern Front, where he died in 1944 at the age of thirty.

6 March

George Littlewood starts his six-day world record attempt
(1882)

England's George Littlewood, or the 'Sheffield Flyer', was one of the best pedestrians around. He competed in most of the Astley Belts and other six-day races, regularly winning.

Between 6 and 11 March 1882, on a track in the Norfolk Drill Hall, Sheffield, England, he beat the then 142-hour heel-and-toe world walking record of 530 miles, albeit by just one mile. His 531 miles is still the six-day walking world record today. The following year he raced against a horse called Charlie in a 17-mile race and lost by only three-quarters of a mile.

He really showed his grit at Madison Square Garden, New York, between 26 November and 1 December 1888 in another six-day race, recording 623 miles and 1,320 yards. That was despite a match being deliberately dropped into his alcohol bath during a break, probably by a disgruntled backer of a rival. Littlewood's feet and legs were badly burned, but he carried on, hobbling at times, walking on raw bone, to complete 85 miles on the final day and earn the nickname 'Littlewood the Lionheart'.

7 March

John Muir nearly blinds himself
(1867)

While working in an Indianapolis wheel factory, 28-year-old John Muir's tool slipped and struck him in the eye, confining him to a darkened room for six weeks. There he had an epiphany: he resolved to follow his dual passions of exploration and nature.

The following September, Muir walked some 1,000 miles (1,600km) from Indiana to Florida, recounted in his book, *A Thousand-Mile Walk to the Gulf*. Not long after, he found himself living in a hut in Yosemite, California, where his work really began.

Muir was a wanderer, a mountaineer, a naturalist, a writer, an amateur botanist and geologist, an engineer and an activist who would help turn Yosemite into the world's first national park. He's seen as the father of the modern conservation movement and his Ralph Waldo Emerson-inspired writing is worshipped by similar-minded folk the world over.

8 March

Otto Peltzer is born
(1900)

Germany's Otto Peltzer was a sickly child, with heart and hip problems and poor immunity. His parents thought him lazy. But at university he tried running and quickly progressed; he was soon greedily clocking up national titles at 400m, 800m and 1,500m.

In 1926 he set a world record for 800m in London (see 3 July). He was told before the start that his shorts were too short and, after failing to locate any alternatives, simply turned them round and pulled them down a bit, which fooled the over-officious officials.

In 1927 he ran a 1,000m world record of 2:25.8 and faced multiple world record holder Paavo Nurmi in a 1,500m race; the Finn was considered unbeatable over this distance. Peltzer caused two false starts, but won in a dramatic three-way struggle down the finishing straight, setting a new world record of 3:52.6.

Peltzer was later persecuted by the Nazi Party for homosexuality, and continued to be discriminated against after the war.

9 March ⫸

9 March

Edit Bérces runs on a treadmill for 24 hours
(2004)

In 2000, Hungarian Edit Bérces won the World and European 100K Championships. In 2001 she won the IAU 24 Hour World Championship. In 2002, she won the European 24-Hour Championship and (just two weeks later) set a 24-hour world record on the track and a 100-mile world record en route. Having seemingly run out of road and track races to win, in 2004 Bérces turned to the treadmill.

The Hungarian set a 24-hour world treadmill record of 247.2km (153.6 miles), which at the time was better than the men's record. She again set a 100-mile world record in the process. 'I felt like a caged bird,' she said at the time, 'who will be freed only after 24 hours.'

Although she had four breaks 'for hygienic reasons', she never once stepped off the treadmill.

10 March

Glenn Cunningham dies
(1988)

In 1917, aged eight, American Glenn Cunningham's legs were so badly burned in an accident with a kerosene can, in which his older brother died, that his limbs were only saved from amputation at the last minute, because of his distress. He had lost all the flesh on his knees and shins, and all the toes on his left foot. It was two years before he could attempt to walk again. Yet this astonishing man would one day be nicknamed the 'Kansas Flyer', the 'Elkhart Express' and the 'Iron Horse of Kansas'.

The middle-distance runner earned a 1,500m silver at the 1936 Olympics and set world records for the mile (4:06.8 in 1934, 4:04.4 in 1938) and 800m (1:49.7 in 1936).

After serving in the US Navy during World War Two, Cunningham and his wife cared for thousands of troubled and underprivileged children, as well as having 12 children of their own. A Kansas park is named after him.

11 March

Day two of the third Astley Belt
(1879)

Sir John Astley cajoled and mentored unknown Englishman Charles Rowell into the Astley Belt six-day race series, to try and get the belt back across the Atlantic from Irish-American Dan O'Leary. While most of the great pedestrians were predominately walkers, five-foot six-inch Rowell was known for his 'dogtrot' technique, more of a slow run.

The third Astley Belt garnered huge interest, with thousands turned away from Madison Square Garden, New York, and updates posted in nearby shops and bars.

Holder O'Leary was the favourite, but he quit on 215 miles. Near the end of the race, a drunken spectator attempted to assault Rowell, who was winning. The interloper was led away by police, cursing the English as he went. According to the book *Running Through the Ages*, Irish competitor John Ennis addressed the crowd: 'If this man (Rowell) is injured, I will leave the track . . . He is an Englishman. I am an Irishman. But if he wins it is because he is the best man.'

The two men grasped hands and continued on together, Rowell winning the race with 500 miles, and Ennis second on 475.

12 March

Yohann Diniz sets a world record
(2011)

French racewalker Yohann Diniz has three European golds and one World Championship silver to his name, all over the 50km distance.

He's had setbacks though. He failed to finish in the 2008 Olympics on an extremely hot day. He was disqualified at the 2011 World Championships for collecting three red warning cards, and again at the 2012 Olympics, after finishing eighth, for taking a bottle of water outside the official zone.

He probably feels he had the last laugh, as he currently holds the world records for 50km on both track (3:35:27 in 2011) and road (3:32:33 in 2014) – the latter despite stopping to ask for a Portuguese flag, in homage to his late grandmother.

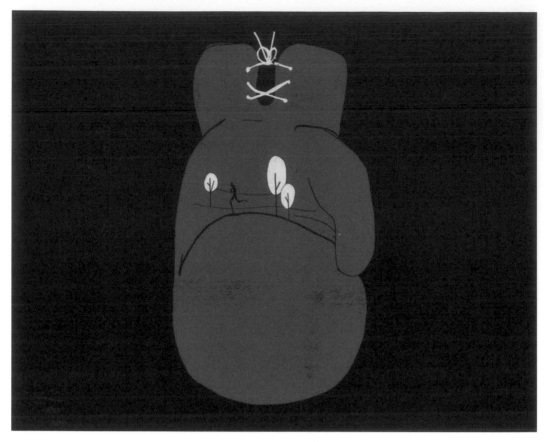

13 March

Jack Holden is born
(1907)

Britain's John 'Jack' Holden discovered running while training as a boxer. Indeed he was built like a pugilist and was said to run on pure grit. He won his first race, a three-mile handicap, but had to decline the first prize of a live pig as it would have forced him to turn professional, barring him from amateur races. Holden represented England in the International Cross-Country Race for 10 consecutive years (1929–39), winning three times, and he was the favourite for the 1948 Olympic marathon. However, he abandoned the race due to blisters. He'd bathed his feet in permanganate of potash to toughen them up, but admitted, 'I over-pickled them'.

At forty-one he sensed it was a good time to retire, but his wife talked him out of it.

He went on to win marathon gold at the 1950 Empire Games in Auckland, running the last nine miles barefoot after his shoes fell apart, and being chased by a Great Dane three miles from the finish.

Aged forty-three he won the European Championships marathon in Brussels and he is still the oldest athlete to win a European running title. Introduced to Prince Baudouin of Belgium, he said, 'Glad to meet you, sir. Met your father and grandfather before you.'

14 March

The Jerusalem Marathon
(2011)

The historically turbulent city of Jerusalem has been destroyed at least twice, besieged 23 times, attacked 52 times, as well as captured and recaptured 44 times. The marathon, which since 2011 has taken place in mid-March, runs through the centre of the ancient city and to several historical sites.

Competitors start the race in modern times, in the shadow of the Knesset (Israel's parliament), and puff and pant their way through the Valley of the Cross (a site consecrated in the fourth century by the Roman Emperor Constantine the Great), and past Mount Scopus, before entering the Old City through the Jaffa Gate, passing the Tower of David, the cobbled streets of the Armenian Quarter, leaving Old Jerusalem through the Zion Gate.

As well as history buffs, the hilly route appeals to 'destination' marathon runners, more than PB chasers. Which is a good job, because in 2011 the three leading runners veered off course and arrived at the wrong finish line. Despite that, 2015 saw 25,000 runners from 60 nations participate in the marathon.

15 March

Wilson Kipsang is born
(1982)

As this book was published, Kenyan Wilson Kipsang was the second fastest ever human over the marathon distance. At the 2013 Berlin Marathon he recorded 2:03:23, chopping 15 seconds off the previous world record, set two years previously on the same course by compatriot Patrick Makau (see 25 September).

Kipsang trained specifically to break the record for two years, after missing it by an agonising four seconds at 2011's Frankfurt Marathon.

As the 2013 race unfolded, Kipsang hung patiently near the rear of the lead pack, which included his pacesetters. They reached halfway in 1:01:32. At about 21.7 miles, with the pace 20 seconds slower than Makau's record time, Kipsang surged to the front, eventually outpacing the field. 'I was really inspired by [fellow Kenyan] Paul Tergat (see 22 August) when he broke the world record here 10 years ago,' Kipsang said.

The marathon specialist has run under 2:05 six times, won seven major city marathons and earned a bronze medal at the 2013 Olympics. He eventually had his world record taken off him by training partner and friend Dennis Kimetto (see 30 September), who clocked 2:02:57 at Berlin in 2014.

16 March

Willie Day's greatest race
(1890)

Cross-country races gained popularity in the UK and US towards the end of the nineteenth century and American Willie Day was an early character. The five-foot five-inch (1.65m) runner appeared to live on pies, doughnuts, sarsaparilla (a soft drink) and cigarettes, according to Edward Sears's *Running Through the Ages*, which labels him a 'strange young man'.

On 16 March 1890 he raced his greatest race, an eight-miler with a handicap, meaning his main rival, Sidney Thomas, had a 30-second head-start, the rest of the field some seven and a half minutes. The lapped course included 10 fences, and it was raining and windy. Nevertheless, Day caught Thomas before three miles and worked his way through the entire field of 200 to take victory. Two months later he won the National Cross Country Championships with apparent ease.

In 1894 Day was in the newspapers for very different reasons. He'd been arrested as a suspect when $12 went missing from the laundry where he worked. Shortly afterwards, this shy man, uncomfortable with the publicity, was found hanged in local woods. Tragically, the laundry accountant later confessed to an admin error. But there were other rumours – of women, debts, even an ambush, and that his arms were tied behind his back when found.

17 March

Septuagenarian walks from San Francisco to New York
(1910)

This was the third day of the great but ageing American pedestrian Edward Weston's walk from San Francisco to New York. His route covered some 3,600 miles (5,800km) and he'd pledged to arrive within 100 days.

Perhaps the Victorian and Edwardian eras' greatest sportsman, Edward Weston (see 22 February and 29 June) had almost run out of pedestrian challenges. As well as various US journeys, he'd spent eight years touring Europe, where he'd walked more than 5,000 miles around Britain and attempted to walk 2,000 miles around the shires of England within 1,000 hours – missing out by just a few miles. In 1879 he won the fourth prestigious Astley Belt for six-day racing.

Weston was outspoken in his opposition to the 'lazy culture' encouraged by cars and saw walking as the perfect antidote. He was also openly enthusiastic about recreational drug use to aid sporting performance, including cocoa leaves and cocaine. Despite his age, Weston completed his trek from California to New York in just 77 days.

Ironically, a week after his 88th birthday, Weston was knocked down by a New York taxi and never walked again, dying two years later.

18 March

The first six-day race
(1878)

As the clock struck 1 a.m., 17 Englishmen and one Irish-American started walking, shuffling, jogging and using other undefinable but purposefully forward methods around a tanbark track in the Agricultural Hall, Islington, London. It was the first of seven international versions of the Astley Belt, a six-day 'go-as-you-please' event. The aim was simple – to get around the track as many times as possible over the next six days. A military band played while bookmakers shouted the odds and adjacent bars and restaurants teemed with customers.

It was the first of five 'world championship' Astley Belts in the UK and US, with a prize of £500 at stake. Thousands attended and updates dominated newspaper front pages. Eventual winner Irish-American Dan O'Leary accumulated 520 miles.

Sir John Astley, the man behind the series, was a Conservative MP and great-great-grandfather of Samantha Cameron, wife of UK Prime Minister David.

19 March

Three men put a tent up in Antarctica
(1912)

Britons Henry Bowers, Edward Wilson and Robert Scott made camp to sit out an Antarctic blizzard, just 18km (11 miles) from the next food and fuel depot, assuming they'd reach it in a day or two – after travelling 2,842km (1,766 miles) through the white wilderness.

Their goals were to be the first to the South Pole and conduct scientific research. They were beaten to the Pole by Norwegian Roald Amundsen, but they were lugging 14kg of rock specimens.

With their morale deflated, their return journey was increasingly gruelling. Edwardian nutritional ignorance, fuel leakages, the physical strain of man-hauling sleds and, above all, unseasonably cold temperatures even for Antarctica, were taking their toll. Two members of the party had already died. But they were so close to the next depot. They had enough food for four days and if they could just wait out this blizzard . . . But the storm lasted nine days.

They are thought to have died on 29 March. Without the blizzard they would have made it home. If a dog team had gone looking for them, as instructed, they probably would have made it. And if the depot had been placed where it was originally planned, they probably would have made it.

It's still perhaps the greatest polar journey. 'I do not believe men have ever shown such endurance at any time,' said Helmer Hanssen, one of Amundsen's men, 'nor do I believe there ever will be men to equal it.'

'Their deaths are more triumphant than most of our lives,' acknowledged Amundsen.

20 March

Uta Pippig breaks women's half marathon record
(1994)

For many, breaking a world record, as Germany's wonderfully named Uta Pippig did today in 1994, clocking 1:07:59 for the half marathon at Kyoto, would be their greatest sporting moment, but not Pippig. Almost a year to the day later, at the same race, she knocked one second off her time, for another world record.

The former East German medical student, now a US citizen, also won the Berlin and Boston Marathons three times each, New York once and ran the marathon in the Olympics in 1992 (placing seventh) and 1996 (DNF).

Her 1996 Boston win came despite not being well, and she showed amazing courage to overcome a 220-metre deficit to Kenya's Tegla Loroupe at Heartbreak Hill (a notorious climb on 20 miles).

21 March

The first (second, third and fourth) sub-2:30 marathon(s)
(1937)

There's a popular phrase in Britain that goes, 'You wait ages for a bus to come along, then three turn up at once.' So too, it seems, with running world records.

According to the Association of Road Running Statisticians, Japan's Son Kitei (see 9 August) ran the marathon in 2:26:14 in Tokyo, hacking over four minutes off Harry Payne's world record, which had stood for six years. Kitei's compatriot Fusashige Suzuki also broke the old barrier, with 2:27:49.

Admittedly there's some confusion over the exact dates – though they were both recorded in March 1935 in Tokyo – and whether the times occurred in the same race. But what is clear is that just a few days later, on 3 April, compatriot Yasuo Ikenaka also broke the 2:30 barrier, with 2:26:44, also in Tokyo.

Kitei would better his record in November, running 2:26:42, a time that wouldn't be beaten for 12 years.

Kitei, however, was actually Korean, not Japanese, but Korea was then part of the Japanese Empire. In 1988, under his real name of Sohn Kee-chung, he carried the Olympic torch into the stadium at the opening of the Seoul Games.

22 March

António Pinto is born
(1966)

Portugal's António Pinto won the London Marathon in 1992, 1997 and 2000 – in six London races up to 2000 he was always on the podium. The former cyclist also won Berlin in 1994 and was the 10,000m European Champion in 1998. Pinto also competed in four consecutive Olympics (1988–2000), firstly for 10,000m, then three times in the marathon. His best placing was 11th in Sydney 2000.

Much more interestingly, however, he is an advocate of drinking red wine, owning a vineyard near Porto in Portugal; he swore by a glass (or more) of red the night before races. 'I enjoy a few glasses of wine and there's nothing wrong with it the night before a race as long as it's in moderation,' he said. 'It helps settle you, makes you sleep well and is very nice to drink, too.'

23 March

Roger Bannister is born
(1929)

British medical student Roger Bannister was the country's top middle-distance runner in the 1950s, but disappointed with only fourth place in the 1,500m at the 1952 Olympics. His new focus was to break the four-minute mile, four laps of a standard athletics track at an average pace of 15mph (24kph).

The record had been stuck at 4:01 for nearly a decade. The *Daily Telegraph* called it 'sport's greatest goal'. Both Bannister and Australian rival John Landy had run close to the time, but breaking the barrier was proving elusive. Landy had branded it 'a brick wall'.

The weather in Oxford was far from ideal on 6 May 1954. It had been raining and was very windy. Bannister nearly called the attempt off. Some 3,000 spectators and two pacemakers, fellow middle-distance athletes Chris Brasher and Chris Chataway (see 19 January), were there in support.

Brasher took the lead for the first two laps, which were on target pace. But as Chataway took over, the pace slowed. After three laps, the time was 3:07.

'I felt like the moment of a lifetime was upon me,' Bannister has since said. He overtook Chataway and went for it crossing over the line in 3:59.4.

Landy bettered the record the following month, with 3:57.9. It was a faster time, but he hadn't been the first. Later that year, the two would race each other (see 7 August).

24 March

The emergence of William Cummings
(1877)

Long before the Roger Bannister and John Landy rivalry over the mile, William Cummings and Walter George competed with each other over the same distance (and others), leading to the fastest mile of the nineteenth century. The 1,500m has superseded the mile today, but in late-1800s England it was all the rage, attracting huge crowds and wagers.

William Cummings burst on to the scene on 24 March 1877, winning a one-mile handicap. The next year he became Professional Mile Champion of England and brought the pro record down over several years, to just over 4:16 in 1881. In training he ran an easy mile every day, mixed with 10-mile walks and faster runs.

In turn Walter George, whose training diet was bread, cheese and beer, emerged to challenge Cummings. A crowd of 10,000 watched their first race in 1884, with many thousands angrily turned away. Despite Cummings unsportingly tapping his rival's heels from behind, George won. Cummings won their next two meets, albeit over longer distances, and one with George ill from a suspected poisoning.

A disillusioned George left for America to race Lon Myers (see 15 February), but returned in 1886 to race Cummings again. Their epic 'Mile of the Century' duel saw George win in a world record time of 4:12¾, a time not surpassed by an amateur or professional athlete for another 29 years.

25 March

Derartu Tulu arrives just in time
(1995)

Ethiopia's Derartu Tulu is the first black African woman to win an Olympic medal. She claimed gold in 1992 before joining second-placed athlete Elana Meyer for a hand-in-hand lap of honour. Tulu has another Olympic gold and a bronze to her name, and has won the London, Tokyo and New York Marathons. Her crowning moment was perhaps her remarkable 60.3-second final lap in the 2000 Olympic 10,000m final to win gold.

But another moment shows her prowess equally. She almost didn't get to the 1995 IAAF World Cross Country Championships in England. And when she did, she was in a far-from-ideal state. The athlete had been stuck in Athens airport without sleep for 24 hours and only arrived an hour before the start. Tulu still won though.

She comes from the same Ethiopian village as Kenenisa Bekele (6 April).

26 March

The first women's six-day race
(1879)

The pedestrian movement wasn't just for men. The first major women's six-day race was held on 26 March 1879 at New York's Madison Square Garden. The winner, Bertha Von Berg, received $1,000 for covering a distance of 372 miles.

Only five of the 18 participants would finish, and the women were described as: 'A queer lot, tall and short, heavy and slim, young and middle-aged, some pretty and a few almost ugly'. The misogyny didn't stop there, with *The New York Times* calling the event 'cruel' and the women 'unfortunate',

plus the mostly male crowd heckling unkindly at times.

Some female peds were certainly ill-prepared, racing in dancing slippers that quickly filled with sawdust. But they were also required to wear heavy velvet dresses, which undoubtedly hindered them.

The second major female six-day race became a duel between 17-year-old Amy Howard from Brooklyn and a Madame Tobias. The former was crowned Champion Pedestrian of the World in 1880 and her record of 409 miles stood for 102 years.

27 March

Garside finally gets his Guinness World Record
(2007)

Leaving London in 1996 with £20 in his pocket, Britain's Robert Garside aimed to become the first person to run around the world. The trainee clinical psychologist would dodge Russian Gypsy bullets, be jailed in China on suspicion of espionage, become entangled in Afghanistan's civil war, get attacked with stones and axes, and twice mugged at gunpoint.

Worse than all that, when he got home, some people didn't believe him. A few of his claims didn't quite seem to add up – especially when he seemed to have set a

world speed record of 10 days from Mexico City to the US border.

When quizzed by journalists Garside finally admitted he'd made parts of the story up. He'd had to fly home for a family medical emergency and said he wanted to throw competitors off the scent.

Guinness World Records spent four years evaluating the evidence before, to the surprise of many, awarding Garside with the title of the first person to run around the world.

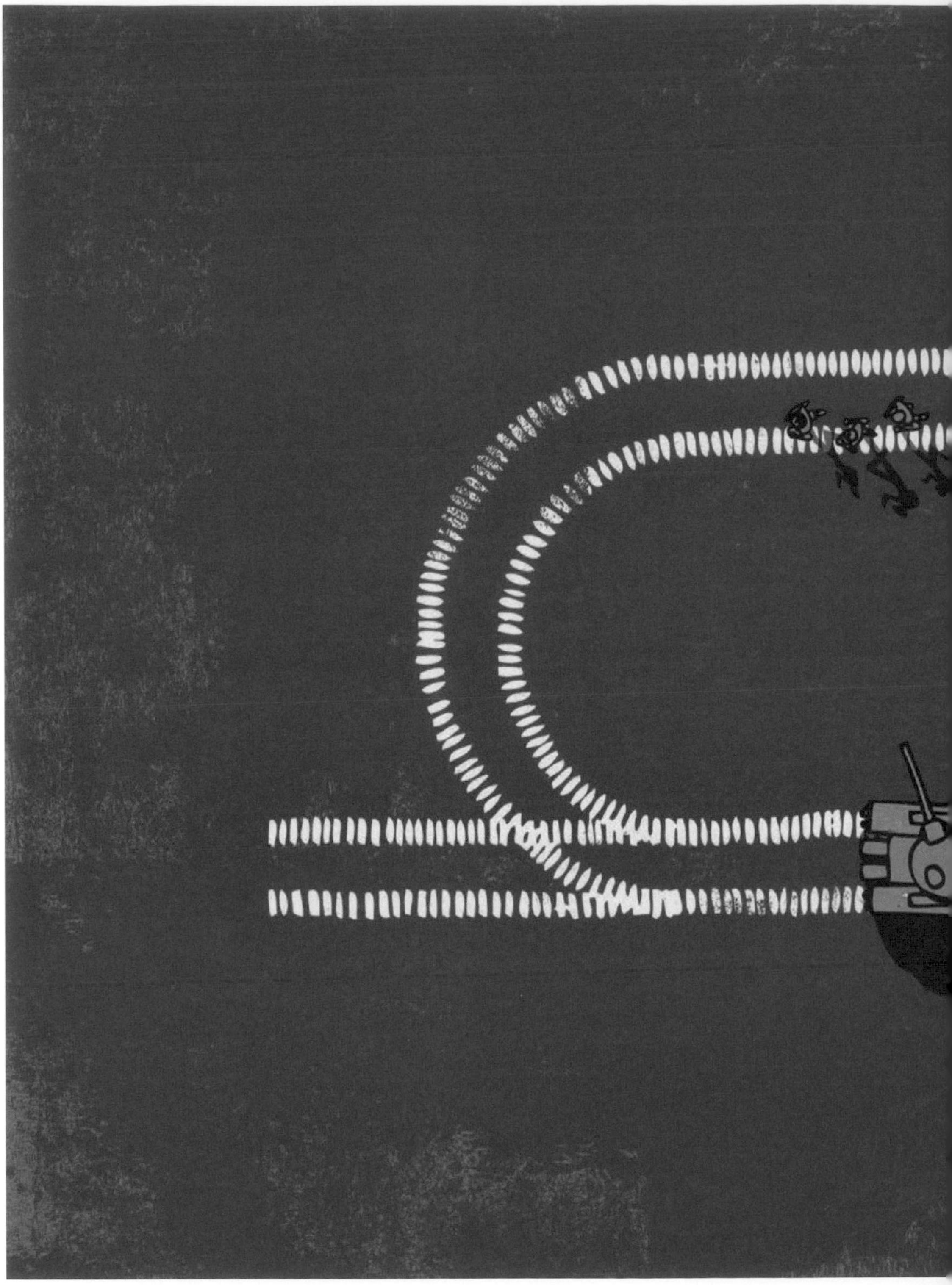

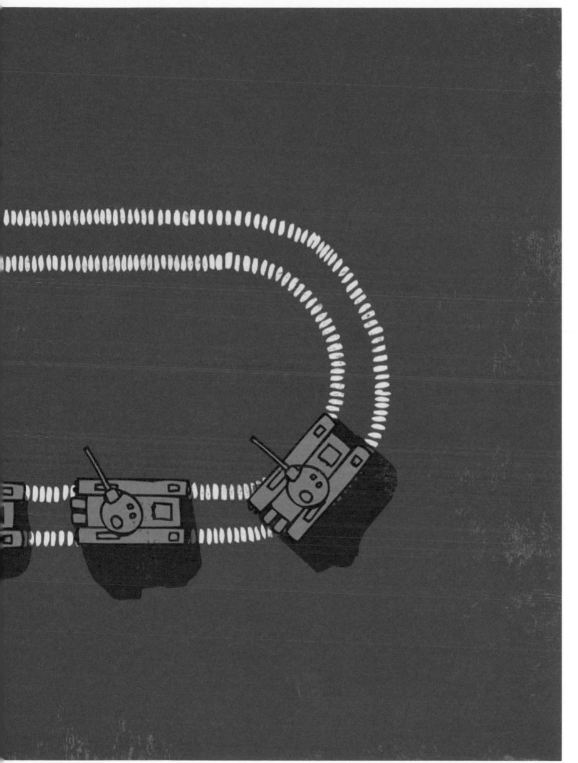

30 March ⫸

28 March

Wally Herbert closes in on the North Pole
(1969)

Today in 1969 British polar explorer Wally Herbert found himself just nine days away from becoming the first man to indisputably walk to the North Pole, dubbed 'the last great journey on Earth'.

Herbert, who Sir Ranulph Fiennes called 'the greatest polar explorer of our time', led a 3,800-mile, 15-month expedition, which was also the first surface crossing of the Arctic Ocean. At one point his team was forced to camp for two months, drifting around the Pole on the trans-Arctic ice-stream, until sunlight returned. They finally reached the North Pole via the Pole of Inaccessibility on 6 April 1969. Despite his vast experience as a navigator, Herbert was said to sometimes choose a day's route relying on dreams. Air-dropped supplies included 27kg of tobacco.

Herbert took his first steps towards polar regions when a newspaper fell from a luggage rack on to his lap on a bus, opening on an advert for people to join an Antarctic expedition. He was also a prize-winning author and an artist, and later took his family to live with Greenland's Inuit for two years.

29 March

The first London Marathon sees joint winners
(1981)

In a fitting image for the debut of what's now one of the world's six prestigious Marathon Majors, Norwegian Inge Simonsen and American Dick Beardsley (who would soon be famous for another very close marathon finish – see 19 April) were joint winners of the first London Marathon.

Co-founders athlete John Disley and journalist and Olympian Chris Brasher were inspired by stories of the New York Marathon, and after trying it out they were suitably inspired to stage one in London in 1981.

England had marathons already, not least London's Poly, but they were enthusiast events, not mass participation.

From 7,055 runners at the first London Marathon, more than 90,000 applications were received for the second. The event had certainly captured the public imagination, not least with the fairy-tale finish. 'What does it matter who won?' said Beardsley. 'As far as I'm concerned, everyone who finished this thing is a winner.'

30 March

István Rózsavölgyi is born
(1929)

A former footballer, István Rózsavölgyi was one of the trio of Hungarian middle-distance runners – the others being Sandor Iharos (see 24 January) and László Tábori – who broke world records in the 1950s, all coached by pioneering Mihály Iglói (see 4 January).

Rózsavölgyi's greatest year was 1955, when he bagged world records for 1,000m (2:19.0) and 2,000m (with 5:02.2). A year later he broke the 1,500m world record, with 3:40.5 in Tata, as well as surpassing the 3,000m world record (but being narrowly beaten to the tape).

The following year was something of a disappointment. The speedy Hungarian went to the 1956 Olympics in Melbourne as a favourite for 1,500m gold. At home, however, the Hungarian Revolution had just been quashed by the Soviet Union, which must have been a major distraction, and Rózsavölgyi failed to make the final.

Past his peak at the 1960 Olympics, he did however snare a bronze medal.

31 March

The second Bunion Derby starts
(1929)

Harry Abrams, who'd placed 11th in 1928's Great Transcontinental Footrace (see 4 March), was back for more in 1929, as was two-time Comrades Marathon winner and 100-mile world record holder Arthur Newton, who hadn't finished the first race.

They joined another 75 men to begin the 3,554-mile (5,720km), second 'Bunion Derby', this time going from New York City to Los Angeles – 43 of them were veterans from the previous race.

Newton's misfortune continued when he was hit by a car and retired with a broken shoulder blade. The remaining runners often covered more than 60 miles a day over 78 days. Just three minutes separated American winner Johnny Salo from England's Pete Gavuzzi in Los Angeles, while Harry Abrams became the first person to twice run across the continental US.

1 April

Arne Andersson: half of a record-smashing double act
(2009)

Sweden's Arne Andersson, who passed away on this date, was a world-record breaking middle-distance runner who had an intense rivalry with compatriot Gunder Hägg (see 18 July and 27 November).

On his 1939 international debut, aged twenty-one, Andersson was meant to be a pacer for Åke Jansson in a 1,500m race in Finland. But he announced his arrival in athletics by winning it, in the year's fastest time (3:48.8, only a second outside the world record).

The next year Andersson's rivalry with front-runner Hägg began, with a 1,500m defeat. In 1941 he got revenge by beating his nemesis to become national cross country champion, but of 27 races in the ensuing track season he lost only five, four of them to the pesky Hägg. And that, loosely, was the pattern of his career.

Over numerous mile and 1,500m races, Hägg just about got the better of Andersson. But they both owe wins and world records in part to each other, as the presence, real or theoretical, of their nemeses spurred their athletic prowess on ever further. Most of Andersson's world records – and he set three for the mile – were superseded by times recorded by Hägg (who also set three) – and vice versa.

2 April

Ffyona Campbell leaves Cape Town
(1991)

At just sixteen, Briton Ffyona Campbell walked from John o'Groats to Land's End – she was the youngest person to ever walk the length of Britain. Continuing that pedestrianism spirit, two years later she claimed she'd walked across the US. At twenty-one she walked across Australia, covering 50 miles a day from Sydney to Perth – a total of 3,200 miles (5,150km) in 95 days.

On 2 April 1991, she set off from Cape Town to walk the length of Africa, arriving in Tangiers, Morocco, over two years later on 1 September 1993. She'd covered over 9,900 miles, joined for part of it by British survival expert, TV presenter and ex-boyfriend Ray Mears. They had to be evacuated from Zaire due to an uprising and walked an extra 2,500 miles around another war zone.

In 1994 Campbell walked across Europe. Then she caused outrage by confessing she hadn't really walked across the US. She had accepted occasional rides from her companion and driver, as she fell behind schedule and sponsors threatened to pull out . . . and she discovered she was pregnant.

'When things got too hard, I just got in the van,' she admitted, 'till I was walking very little at all. Nobody knew, nobody was hurt, I rationalised.'

But as far as we know, her other claims are true.

3 April

The Alexander the Great Marathon

(since 2006)

Every year around this date the Alexander the Great Marathon takes place between Pella, the birthplace of the legendary Greek king, and the capital of ancient Macedonia, Thessaloniki. Alexander biographer Guy MacLean Rogers believes he was an impressive runner. 'He was a naturally gifted athlete. He was a fine runner, and was tough as nails. He had superhuman powers of endurance.'

Indeed, running was greatly valued in Greek mythology and society: Apollo famously beat Hermes in a race. Achilles (despite that famous heel problem) and Atalanta (a female, refreshingly) were also great runners. The latter was said to be only willing to marry someone who could beat her in a race. In Greek society, the poet Homer and the philosopher Xenophanes both lauded running as the greatest physical attribute of a man.

The Greek public too loved athletics and the best runners were feted like celebrities, earning fortunes, being exempt from taxes and granted pensions – and free olive oil – for the rest of their lives. Leonidas of Rhodes was perhaps the first great runner. The Ancient Greek won three Olympic running events – they were run naked apart from the 'Race in Armour' – in four consecutive Olympiads from 164–152 BC. An unmatched 12-medal haul.

4 April

The North Pole Marathon

(since 2006)

'Have you got the nerve to travel to the [Geographical] North Pole and run on Arctic ice floes, with 6 to 12 feet separating you from 12,000 feet of Arctic Ocean?' reads the website for the North Pole Marathon. 'This marathon is not run on land – it is run "on" frozen water, in the high Arctic Ocean.' Not forgetting the sub-zero temperatures and polar bears (though the website doesn't mention the latter).

Operating since 2006 and recognised by Guinness World Records as the world's northernmost marathon (although not registered with the Association of International Marathons unlike the slightly more southerly Midnight Sun Marathon, see 12 January), the race usually attracts around 50 entrants, who've paid a cool (pun intended) £11,900 (including flights – planes and helicopters – from Norway) to do so.

The race record is 3:36:10 and the event is part of the Marathon Grand Slam Club – runners who've completed a marathon distance or longer on each of the seven continents.

5 April

Nicky Spinks tackles Bob Graham again
(2015)

At the stroke of midnight and the start of 5 April, Nicky Spinks set off on a Bob Graham Round (see 13 June), a 106km (66 miles) circuit of 42 summits in Britain's Lake District with 8,200m (27,000ft) of ascent. She was attempting to beat her own record and therefore record the fastest cumulative time for all three major British fell running Rounds, the other two being the Paddy Buckley in Wales and the Charlie Ramsay in Scotland.

Yorkshire farmer Spinks is known as the woman who beat cancer twice, beats men in running races and beats mountain running records.

She completed this Bob Graham Round in 18:06, outside the 17:21 she needed to record the fastest cumulative time for all three rounds – but she suffered a large cut to the hand early on and still managed a new women's record time by six minutes. Spinks is the only person to have completed each challenge in under 20 hours and holds the women's record for the fastest combined time over the three challenges.

6 April

Kenenisa Bekele wins the Paris Marathon
(2014)

Ethiopian Kenenisa Bekele won the 2014 Paris Marathon with a new course record of 2:05:04. His performance was the sixth fastest marathon debut ever (on a record-eligible course), which might make it sound as if he shot to fame unnoticed, but far from it. Bekele already had three Olympic golds and one silver for 10,000m and 5,000m – and currently holds the world records for both – plus five World Championship and 11 World Cross Country Championships golds.

Until Paris, the marathon was the distance Bekele wasn't yet reigning supreme at. He had considered making his marathon debut at London the same year but couldn't reach financial agreement with the organisers.

The decisive break at Paris came after 15 miles, with Bekele quickly opening up a large gap on the rest of the field, though the 31-year-old admitted that his victory was far from straightforward after enduring an attack of cramp in his hamstring that left him grimacing in pain in the final stages. 'I had no marathon experience before today and it was very tough,' said Bekele. 'But I ran the time that I expected.'

7 April

Paris Marathon
(1976)

The first marathon in Paris, the 40km Tour de Paris Marathon, took place in 1896, when Englishman Len Hurst (see 19 July) was the fastest of 191 runners, winning in 2:31:30. The world's first recorded female marathon run is disputed (see 29 September), but may also have happened at the race, in 1918.

The modern incarnation of the event dates to 1976 and, despite its history, Paris isn't one of the six World Major Marathons. Other characteristics include a more muted crowd than other big-city races, some cobbled sections and the Bois de Vincennes at 23 miles, where a surprising amount of runners take a shortcut across the grass.

Paris is known as one of the more scenic city marathons, with a route including many famous Parisian landmarks, such as the Eiffel Tower, Notre Dame Cathedral, the Avenue des Champs-Élysées and the Louvre. It's more economical than taking a tourist bus tour of the French capital, although a little more demanding on the legs.

8 April

Mami Kudo starts running

(2011)

On this date Japanese ultra runner Mami Kudo began her attempt at the women's 48-hour road record. She clocked a staggering 368.687km (229 miles) to claim a new world record.

Such feats weren't new to Kudo though. The same year, she set a new world record in the 24-hour track distance at the Soochow International 24 Hour race in Taipei, Taiwan – beating her own record, set in 2009, by one kilometre, with 255.303km. She led the women's race from the start, finishing second overall.

9 April

The fastest run around the world
(2015)

Today Kevin Carr became the fastest man to run around the world. The 34-year-old British runner set off from Haytor, Devon, in July 2013, running approximately a marathon a day for 621 days to complete his world record – and beating the previous record by just 24 hours.

Carr wore through 16 pairs of shoes, pushing all his kit along in a stroller, as he ran through 26 countries and covered 16,299 miles (26,231km). 'I have encountered some pretty scary things,' he said, 'from packs of wild dogs in Romania to the most extreme weather conditions imaginable. Most frightening of all, however, was coming face to face with bears. One of the bears stalked and then actively came for me. I had severe heatstroke in India and have twice been hit by cars.'

10 April

Spiridon Louis wins the first Olympic marathon
(1896)

Held on 6–10 April 1896 in Athens, the first modern Olympics saw Spiridon Louis of Greece win the first (40km) marathon, in a time of 2:58:50.

Before the 11 a.m. start, each runner was given milk and two pints of beer. As the race progressed, many of the 17 competitors dropped out. At around 34km Louis, a 24-year-old Greek farmer, caught race leader Edwin Flack of Australia. Louis gradually pulled away from Flack, who also dropped out.

When Louis entered the stadium alone, Greece's Prince George and Crown Prince Constantine ran alongside him, escorting him to the finish line in front of 100,000 cheering spectators. No track or field event at the Games had yet been won by a Greek and the water carrier became a national hero.

Two more Greek runners entered the stadium to finish in second and third place, adding to the party atmosphere, though third-place finisher Spiridon Belokas was later found to have covered part of the course by carriage and was disqualified.

The King offered Louis any gift he desired, and Louis requested a donkey-drawn carriage to help him in his water-carrying business.

11 April

Stamata Revithi runs a marathon
(1896)

Women were barred from competing in the 1896 Olympics, but Greece's Stamata Revithi was determined to run the marathon. She was turned away on the day, the official reason being that the date for participation had expired. So at 8 a.m. the next morning Revithi set off to run the course alone. Before starting, she asked a teacher, mayor and a city magistrate to sign a statement confirming the time she departed.

She ran at a steady pace and finished the 40km in approximately five and a half hours (though she wasn't allowed to enter the Panathinaiko Stadium at the end).

Some sources claim a second woman, Melpomene, also ran the Olympic marathon. There's debate among Olympic historians, however, as to whether or not Revithi and Melpomene are the same person.

12 April

The third Sydney-to-Melbourne Ultramarathon starts
(1985)

Five days later, and in a record time of five days, five hours and seven minutes, Yiannis Kouros (see 13 February) was welcomed as the first finisher by Melbourne's huge Greek population, who lined the streets, many in national costume, for the final stretch of the 960km (586-mile) race. After collecting a cheque for $20,000 and taking a bath Kouros told reporters he 'felt terrific' and as if he had 'just started the race'. Of 27 starters only 13 made the finish.

The Sydney-to-Melbourne Ultramarathon was held annually between 1983 and 1991 and the inaugural race was won by Cliff Young, an unknown 61-year-old potato farmer from Victoria. The extraordinary Kouros would win the race four more times, from 1987 to 1990.

13 April

Paula Radcliffe breaks the marathon world record

(2003)

Britain's Paula Radcliffe won the London Marathon in two hours, 15 minutes and 25 seconds, beating her own previous world record of 2:17:18, set the previous October in Chicago. Race director Dave Bedford called it 'the greatest distance-running performance I have seen in my lifetime'. Over ten years on and no other woman has finished a marathon within three minutes of her world record.

One contentious aspect of her record performance is that she ran the marathon paced by two men – as most elite male runners do – a practice that has since been banned for female athletes.

Radcliffe, who always uses the same lucky safety pins for her race number, is asthmatic and anaemic, but her father had been a keen amateur marathoner as a young man. He took up the hobby again in an attempt to lose weight after giving up smoking and took his daughter on training runs from the age of seven. At ten she watched her dad in the London Marathon and saw Ingrid Kristiansen set the women's world record. 'I remember thinking: "I'd love to do that",' she has said.

14 April

Marathon des Sables

(since 1986)

The Marathon des Sables, set in southern Morocco, is the brainchild of French concert promoter Patrick Bauer, who travelled across the Sahara Desert solo on foot in 1984. Two years later, 23 runners participated in a race that would grow in popularity and start calling itself 'The toughest foot race on Earth'. At a relatively modest 156 miles over six days and with a finish rate well above 90 per cent, it clearly isn't. But the boast and the striking desert imagery makes it popular with magazines.

The race has traditionally been dominated by Moroccan brothers Lahcen and Mohamad Ahansal, who've won 10 and six editions respectively. But the most memorable story comes from 1994. After an eight-hour sandstorm, Italian former Olympic pentathlete Mauro Prosperi became lost in the desert.

To stay alive over the ensuing days he cooked food in his own urine, drank bat blood and ate raw snakes and lizards. After a few days, when both a helicopter and aeroplane failed to spot him, he decided to commit suicide. But after cutting his wrists, his blood was so thick it wouldn't drain.

Finally, after 10 days of wandering lost in the Sahara he chanced upon a shepherd girl and was saved. Prosperi was 291km (181 miles) off course, in Algeria, and weighed just 45kg (99lb), having lost 16kg.

He has since returned to complete MDS and run several more desert marathons.

15 April

Plennie Wingo starts walking backwards
(1931)

Plennie Wingo, thirty-one, began to walk backwards from Fort Worth, Texas, on this day and didn't stop for over a year. 'With the whole world going backwards,' he wrote in his book, *Around the World Backwards*, 'maybe the only way to see it was to turn around.'

Wingo said the hardships of the Great Depression motivated him to take on the quirky adventure. Using glasses with rear-view mirrors to see traffic, his goal was to walk the world backwards. But Turkish police prevented him from continuing on 24 October 1932.

Wingo had covered an average of 25km each day, supporting himself by selling postcards. He totalled 517 days and 8,000 miles (12,875km). When he returned the Great Depression had worsened and his wife, having pleaded with him to quit the project and return home, had divorced him.

It may or may not have been a consolation to enter the *Guinness Book of World Records* as the greatest exponent of reverse pedestrianism.

16 April

The fastest marathon in orbit
(2007)

The Guinness World Record for the fastest marathon in orbit was run by 41-year-old American astronaut Sunita Williams on this day. Williams ran her 26.2 miles in 4:24, while orbiting on board the International Space Station. She's from Boston and has previously run the city's famous race – and was competing as an official entrant in the 2007 version. While the race is famed for its atmosphere, she had none at all – the weightless runner was strapped to a treadmill with a bungee cord to hold her down. She circled the Earth at least twice in the process, running as fast as 12.8km/h (8mph), but flying more than 8km (5 miles) each second.

17 April

Women are finally allowed to run Boston
(1972)

Against race rules, women such as Kathrine Switzer (see 5 January) and Bobbi Gibb (see 2 November) had been running the Boston Marathon for several years, albeit usually as 'bandits' (without numbers). But the 1972 event was the first to officially allow female entrants. Nina Kuscsik emerged from an eight-member field to win the race in 3:10:26.

However, it wasn't until 1984 that the women's marathon would become an Olympic event – at the 1980 Olympics there was no women's race longer than 1,500m. Despite the fact Norway's Grete Waitz had run a sub-2:30 at the New York Marathon in 1979, showing once and for all that women could be more than half-decent at distance running, there were unfounded concerns that women's health would be damaged. Also, the Olympic Charter stated a women's sport must be widely practised in at least 25 countries on at least two continents before inclusion in the Games.

18 April

Joan Benoit breaks marathon world record
(1983)

After winning the Boston Marathon in 1979 as a relative unknown (in 2:35:15, both a new course and American womens record), wearing a Boston Red Sox cap, American Joan Benoit Samuelson won again in 1983. This time she ran a world-best time of 2:22:43, which wouldn't be bettered for 11 years.

She started at a pace not seen in a women's marathon before or since. Her first 10K was 31:45 and she reached 10 miles at 51:38. She couldn't keep that up, but still finished strongly. The women's course record has only improved by two minutes in the 30-plus years since, while the men's best has improved by nearly six minutes.

In 1984 Samuelson became the first women's marathon Olympic champion (see 28 July). In her fifties she continued to run impressive marathon times, recording sub-2:50 four times from 2008–11.

19 April

The Duel in the Sun
(1982)

At Boston in 1982, Alberto Salazar and Dick Beardsley played out what's often cited as the greatest finish to a marathon. John Brant's 2006 book, *Duel in the Sun*, is devoted to their captivating contest.

Cuban-born Salazar, the best marathoner in the world at the time, was pre-race favourite, at his first Boston. But with nine miles to go he found himself on the shoulder of Beardsley – who had prepared by running numerous reps of the infamous Heartbreak Hill a week beforehand, in a blizzard. The pace was on the world record. Salazar clung on.

With the clock at 2:06 and just over half a mile to go Salazar snuck past Beardsley and made about three yards on him. But Beardsley responded, pushing back and almost catching him . . . only for a police motorbike to cut him off on a corner, which knocked him off his stride. In a desperate sprint finish, Salazar broke the tape two seconds before Beardsley, with 2:08:52 – the first time two people had run under 2:09 in the same marathon.

Neither runner was able to reach that competitive peak again. The two are friends, but Beardsley (who had previously won London and whose website says he was 'foiled by a motorcycle') suffered a series of near-fatal accidents and an addiction to prescription drugs. He is the only man known to have run 13 consecutive marathon personal bests.

Salazar, who also won the New York City Marathon three times, is currently British runner Mo Farah's coach and head coach of the Nike Oregon Project.

20 April

Bruce Tulloh runs across America
(1969)

Not long after British middle-distance runner Bruce Tulloh retired he was flicking through his son's *Guinness Book of Records* and he noticed the record for running across America was 73 days for around 3,000 miles. 'I thought, "That should be easy",' he's said. 'But of course it wasn't.'

The 1962 5,000m European gold medallist (see 15 September) and barefoot runner (though he wore shoes for this) set off from Los Angeles. Despite intensive training he developed 'the most violent cramps' in his thighs after just 24 miles and injury bedevilled much of his attempt.

Despite a four-day spell when he was not only reduced to walking, but even resorted to using a walking stick, Tulloh completed the 2,876 miles in just under 65 days, beating the record by eight and a half days. 'It was a very exciting time. Sometimes very tough. Sometimes quite boring. Forrest Gump got the credit for it. I only did it once. He did it two and a half times.'

The record has been broken six times since (see 30 April).

21 April

Lizzy Hawker runs from Everest to Kathmandu, again
(2013)

Diminutive British ultramarathon runner Lizzy Hawker has won Ultra-Trail du Mont-Blanc (see 25 August), Europe's most competitive 100-mile race, five times. The environmental scientist also won Spartathlon, the 2006 100K World Championships and previously held the women's 24-hour world record (153.5 miles in 2011).

But perhaps her most audacious feat was setting a Fastest Known Time between Everest Base Camp and Kathmandu, in Nepal, a 319km (198m) journey she completed on this day in 63 hours and 8 minutes. The brutally hilly route, with more than 10,000m ascent and nearly 14,000m descent, is known as the 'Everest Mailrun', the traditional route taken for carrying letters to and from expeditions at Everest Base Camp before the Lukla airstrip was opened in 1964.

Hawker's new best surpassed her own record of 71:25, set in 2011. Which in turn trumped her previous record of 77:36, set in 2007. During the journey she slept for just four minutes. Asked if she would run the route again, she said, 'I wouldn't say I wouldn't.'

22 April

The fastest marathon by a vegetable
(2012)

The Guinness World Record for the fastest marathon run dressed as a jester is 3:01:56, by Switzerland's Alexander Scherz at the 2012 London Marathon, run on this day.

It was a particularly fine year for costume-related world records at the famous UK race. It was also the location for fastest marathon on stilts (6:50:02), wearing an operational gas mask, in a wedding dress, the obligatory man dressed as a fairy, and in a nurse's uniform, dressed as a Roman soldier, a vegetable (male and female records – both carrots), a baby, a nun, a monk, in a two-person pantomime costume, a book character (Dracula), as an insect (bee), hula-hooping, dribbling a football, and the fastest marathon run by a dairy product (ice cream).

23 April

Alfie Shrubb passes away
(1964)

Early in the twentieth century, before the Flying Finns took over, British runner Alfred 'Alfie' Shrubb dominated all distances between two and 15 miles.

He discovered his gift for speed by accident, racing four miles through the night to locate a fire, beating both a respected local runner and the horse-drawn fire engine to the scene. Shrubb loved cross country and was almost unbeatable at it, winning the national championships four years consecutively and the international championships twice in a row. He broke world records for two miles, three miles, 10 miles and the one-hour record – with 11 miles and 1,137 yards (18.7km).

However, like many of the best sportsmen at the time, he was banned from amateur sport for receiving travel expenses (for a tour of Australia). Turning pro didn't dent his record breaking though, and altogether he set 28 world records – all without pacemakers.

Shrubb practised an economical, shorter stride, saw shouted-out lap times as artificial aids and would toy with competitors in races, sometimes slowing to let others catch him before shooting off again. He raced 10 times against the Canadian legend Tom Longboat (see 4 June), winning all races shorter than 20 miles, but losing all the longer races.

24 April

Luxembourg's star athlete is born
(1927)

The running abilities of Luxembourg's Joseph 'Josy' Barthel, born today in 1927, were discovered when he was in the army, winning the Military World Championships at 800m (twice) and 1,500m.

He finished ninth in the 1948 Olympic 1,500m final, which wouldn't have unduly worried any of the stacked field for the 1952 final, including future sub-four-minute-mile record breaker Roger Bannister.

Germany's Rolf Lamers led for the first two laps and into the final curve, with the field tightly bunched behind, and Barthel a full five yards adrift of him. In one of the all-time classic race finishes, both America's Bob McMillen and Barthel broke past the German. At the tape, the Luxembourger just outreached the American for a surprise win.

It was his zenith as a runner and the only time a Luxembourg athlete had won an Olympic gold. Barthel went on to be president of the Luxembourg's Olympic and Sporting Committee, and had success in both chemistry and politics. Luxembourg's national stadium is named Stade Josy Barthel.

25 April

Two Oceans Marathon
(since 1970)

The 56km (35-mile) Two Oceans 'Marathon' has taken place on Easter Saturday since 1970. It's famed for being a sister race of the Comrades Marathon (also an ultramarathon rather than a marathon, but the word was traditionally more commonly used to mean any long run) anitsd for its spectacular coastal scenery, as it takes 11,000 runners alongside both the Atlantic and Indian Oceans.

The race began with just 26 runners, saw its first female runner in 1974, its first black runner in 1975 and its first black winner a year later, when Gabashane Vincent Rakabaele won in 3:18:05, after a close duel with Alan Robb (see 2 June).

Perhaps the greatest Two Oceans story comes from 1988, when winner Thompson Magawana improved his previous year's winning time by 1:47, with 3:03:44. This run included world records for the 30-mile and 50km distances and his time has never been beaten. This achievement is all the more remarkable as he may have been carrying a virus that would eventually lead to his death in 1995.

26 April

Gerard Nijboer breaks marathon world record (probably)
(1980)

The weather was perfect for the 1980 Amsterdam Marathon and on 23km Dutchman Gerard Nijboer broke away from the field with such impressive pace that no one followed him. He broke the tape at 2:09:01.

It was the second fastest time ever recorded, after Australian Derek Clayton's 2:08:34 in Antwerp in 1969 – however, the Association of Road Racing Statisticians believe Clayton's run was on a course short by 500m. Whether Nijboer's win was the fastest (the IAAF don't officially recognise it as such) or second fastest ever marathon time, Nijboer is the most successful Dutch marathon runner.

Amsterdam was his breakthrough and would remain his personal best. Later that year Nijboer earned a silver medal in the Olympics, the first Dutch runner to win an international marathon medal. He went on to win the European Championships in 1982 and the Amsterdam Marathon four times (1980, 1984, 1988 and 1989).

27 April

The second fastest ever marathon runner is born
(1978)

When Kenyan Duncan Kibet was in a car accident at the age of sixteen, almost losing the ability to walk, not many would have predicted he would one day become the world's second fastest marathon runner.

During his early career he was apparently still afraid to train hard. However, after following his brother to France he turned a corner. Kibet won 2006's inaugural Rock 'n' Roll Half Marathon in San Jose, USA. Then he was a pacemaker for Gebrselassie at the 2008 Dubai Marathon, where Gebrselassie ran the then second fastest ever marathon time of 2:04:53.

Kibet then won the Rotterdam Marathon on 5 April 2009, posting for himself the second fastest marathon time ever: 2:04:27.

28 April

Sammy Korir runs a slow 2:11:29 marathon
(2012)

On this day Kenya's Sammy Korir ran 2:11:29 at the Gunsan Saemangeum International Marathon. Extremely fast for almost anyone, but not for Korir. In March 2008, he won the Seoul International Marathon in 2:07:31, becoming the first man to run 11 marathons under 2:09. He was already the first to do that 10 times, which took him 11 years, but why stop there?

His tenth had been when finishing third in the 2008 Dubai Marathon in 2:08:34. The race was won by Haile Gebrselassie, who narrowly failed to break his own world record.

Despite consistently superb performances, Korir has developed an unfortunate reputation as the fastest marathon runner in history yet to win a Major City Marathon.

29 April

The greatest runner no one's heard of
(1977)

Scotland's Don Ritchie ran 50km in a world record 2:51:38 on this date. It was the first of 14 world records, ranging from what he called 'tiddlers' (50 miles) to much, much longer ones.

In 1989, he set the Land's End to John o'Groats (the length of the UK) solo record, completing it in just 10 days, 15 hours and 25 minutes. He lost 14lb (6.3kg) and it took him five months and seven courses of antibiotics to recover.

'It helps if you are a little crazy,' he told the *Independent* newspaper. 'I think you also need to be a calm, determined and patient person, with a high tolerance for prolonged discomfort. I actually find it therapeutic because the physical stress of running neutralises the mental stress caused by work. After a run I feel calm and content.'

Perhaps his finest record was running 166 miles, nonstop, in 24 hours – aged forty-six. On the track at Crystal Palace, London, in 1977, Ritchie ran 100 miles in 11:30:51, a mind-boggling 6:54-min/mile pace. He's also a sub 2:20 marathoner.

30 April

Frank Giannino runs across America
(1979)

Bruce Tulloh's record for crossing America (see 20 April) had been surpassed five times by 1979 when Frank Giannino set out from Santa Monica, California, on 1 March, attempting to break Tom McGrath's 1977 record of 53 days.

Averaging 50 miles a day, it took him 60 days and six hours to reach New York. But he had already planned to try again, with a bigger support crew. Sixteen months later, with Stan Cottrell's new record of 48 days, one hour and 48 minutes to beat, he was accompanied by his brother on a bicycle and his parents in a campervan.

Giannino needed to cover more than 64 miles a day for a new record. He averaged 60 miles per day over the first four days. It wasn't enough. So they changed tactics. Days began at 3 a.m. and Giannino did 25 miles before breakfast. Another 25, then lunch. He began covering 70 miles a day.

Frank Snr came down with dysentery in Nevada; John's bike was run over; Frank lost three toenails. But the team reached New York in a new record – which still stands – of 46 days and eight hours.

MAY

1 May

Chantal Langlacé sets new marathon world record
(1977)

Sometimes world records ping back and forth like a tennis ball. France's Chantal Langlacé set a world best for the marathon of 2:46:24 on 27 October 1974 at Neuf-Brisach, France. But it lasted only just over a month, before America's Jacqueline Hansen ran 2:43:55 in California on 1 December.

It then changed hands three times in 1975 before Langlacé, who won the Neuf-Brisach Marathon three times as well as the Paris and Lille Marathons in the 1970s and 1980s, recaptured the world marathon record on 1 May 1977, running 2:35:16 in Oiartzun, Spain.

She wouldn't get long to enjoy her world-record-holder status this time either. West Germany's Christa Vahlensieck meanly ran 2:34:47 on 10 September 1977.

2 May

Khalid Khannouchi becomes an American
(2000)

After falling out with the Moroccan athletics federation over training expenses Khalid Khannouchi moved to New York in 1992. He later married American Sandra Inoa, who doubled as his coach and agent, and became a naturalised US citizen in 2000 – controversially just in time to compete in the US Olympic Marathon Trials. Though he had to withdraw due to injury, by then he had already recorded the fastest debut marathon in history and the fourth fastest marathon of all time, winning the 1997 Chicago Marathon in 2:07:10.

Two years after that Khannouchi set his first marathon world record with 2:05:42 to win Chicago again, becoming the first man to go under 2:06. He broke his own record three years later when he won the 2002 London Marathon in 2:05:38, beating Haile Gebrselassie and Paul Tergat in what some call the best marathon ever run.

Khannouchi is one of only five men to break the marathon world record more than once, and one of only four to break their own record (the others being Jim Peters, Derek Clayton and Gebrselassie).

3 May

The longest continuous run
(2000)

One week into his run around Australia, fifty-year-old Gary Parsons had became fully aware of the daunting task ahead.

He was not meant to be doing this. The Australian had been warned by an orthopaedic surgeon that if he ran more than 5km he would end up in a wheelchair. Indeed he took a walking frame with him and would sometimes use it for 30 minutes at the end of the day, when his back felt sore.

On his 274-day adventure Parsons also dealt with unexpected crew departures, vehicle breakdowns, plagues of flies, huge dust clouds and hundreds of kilometres of isolation. Going anticlockwise, from Perth he ran with a stress fracture in his leg.

But when Parsons limped into Brisbane with a badly injured ankle after averaging 72.4km a day for more than nine months he had set a world record for the longest continuous run. He'd clocked up 19,030km (11,825 miles), breaking the previous world record of 17,071km set by American Robert Sweetgall in 1983.

'It was my goal to run further than anyone in the history of running,' Parsons told Reuters. 'I guess it is just a bit of Aussie spirit, like the old explorers who went into the beyond and went that bit further.'

He wore out 12 pairs of running shoes during his self-powered quest.

4 May

Patrick Fitzgerald uses a 'sacrificator'
(1884)

Six-day racing could make a pedestrian very sleepy. Popular stay-awake remedies included hot baths, plunging one's head into a bucket of ice water, loud music and even electric shocks. At a six-day race at New York's Madison Square in 1884 in front of 12,000 spectators race leader Patrick Fitzgerald took things a stage further.

His effort to get past the famous Charles Rowell had come back to bite him and lethargy was kicking in, threatening to undo his hard work. His lead of 20 miles slipped

to 10 on the final day. In desperation a doctor was called for and Dr Naylor arrived with a 'sacrificator', a 'rectangular bronze instrument' with '16 retractable razor-sharp blades', reports *Running Through the Ages*. It was placed on Fitzgerald's thighs and a trigger pulled, slashing the fatigued pedestrian 16 times on each quad muscle.

With leg pressure eased, a revived Fitzgerald went on to set a world record of 610 miles (982km). Yet oddly the sacrificator never really caught on.

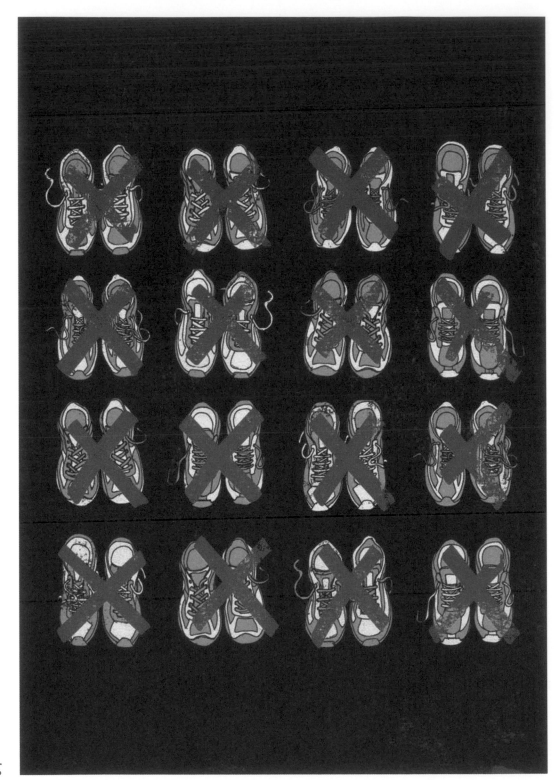

5 May

Born to Run is published
(2009)

Born to Run: A Hidden Tribe, Superathletes, and the Greatest Race the World Has Never Seen, written by the American author and journalist Christopher McDougall, has sold three million copies and is the world's most popular running book.

The narrative follows McDougall's attempts to track down members of the reclusive ultramarathon-running tribe, Mexico's Tarahumara, along with the elusive and enigmatic Caballo Blanco.

As well as introducing the wider world to US ultra running legends Scott Jurek, Ann Trason and Jenn Shelton, *Born to Run* was highly critical of the running shoe industry. McDougall argued that modern cushioned running shoes are a major cause of running injury – a claim which led to the contemporary barefoot running movement.

Rumours persist that the book is being made into a Hollywood film.

6 May

Marathon world record set by 13-year-old
(1967)

When Maureen Wilton set a new women's world record for the marathon in Toronto, finishing in 3:15:23 at a time when it was generally thought running such distances would be harmful to women, it was all the more remarkable as she was just thirteen.

Wilton's mum was waiting near the finish to give the four-foot ten-inch runner a time update, but thought her watch was playing up and told her daughter she was behind world record time. So Wilton ran the last mile in six minutes; crossing the finish line, she thought she'd fallen short. But moments later friends told her she'd set the record. 'It kind of took away from that cross-the-finish-line excitement,' she said. Much of the response from the media and officials was negative however, and she retired from running at seventeen.

Kathrine Switzer ran that day too, 16 days after her historic Boston run (see 17 April). Wilton came out of retirement to run Toronto again, with Switzer, in 2010.

7 May

Poet Robert Browning is born
(1812)

British poet Robert Browning was born on this date in London to a pianist mother and bank clerk father. Browning's father was also a scholar and book collector and his son learned Latin, Greek and French by the time he was fourteen. Robert's poetry took a while to gain popularity, but he married more illustrious poet Elizabeth Barrett and would eventually became one of the most famous wordsmiths of the Victorian era.

In 1879 he published 'Pheidippides', a poem about the famous story of a Greek runner running a long way before collapsing and dying, a combination of several historical stories (see 1 March). Inadvertently it was a key moment in the history of distance running. A few years later Frenchman Baron Pierre de Coubertin, founder of the Olympic Committee, ensured there would be a (25-mile) marathon race at the first modern Olympics in 1896. He was most likely influenced by Browning's poem.

8 May

Harry Vaughan breaks 100-mile world record
(1876)

Henry 'Harry' Vaughan made history in a 24-hour 'walking match' at the Agricultural Hall, Islington, London, on this date. He pocketed £100 for winning the 'heel-and-toe' race in front of thousands of spectators, covering a total of 120 miles (193km) and beating the previous 24-hour record by 11 miles. On his way to his total the 'ped' had also notched up a fastest ever 100-mile time of 18:51:35.

He would die of 'consumption' (tuberculosis), but was known for his long graceful strides that could carry him along at six miles an hour, seemingly effortlessly.

9 May

Tegla Loroupe is born
(1973)

One of 24 siblings (her father had four wives), Kenya's Tegla Loroupe was born on this date – a dark day for most other female runners out there. At the age of seven she started school, which involved a barefoot run of 10 kilometres each morning.

Still barefoot, she won the Goodwill Games 10,000m in 1994 (retaining the title in 1998) and the same year won the New York Marathon against a strong field. It was the first major marathon win by an African woman.

Loroupe went on to dominate at the half marathon distance with three world titles, and the marathon with wins in Berlin, Rotterdam (three times), London, Rome, Hong Kong, Cologne and elsewhere. She has twice held the marathon world record, with 2:20:47 in 1998 and 2:20:43 in 1999, plus world records for 20km, 25km and 30km.

She now devotes most of her time to humanitarian and peace work.

10 May

An epic female pedestrian race
(1880)

Held in San Francisco's Mechanics' Pavilion, the third in a series of women's six-day races (see 26 March) was the most dramatic yet. Amy Howard led the 20-woman field from the off, in her trademark 'dog trot' technique – 'I can cover seven miles an hour without distressing myself,' she had said.

By the end of the first day, Howard had recorded 95 miles, with second-placed Madame Tobias on 92. Tobias's tactic was to rest less and she overtook Howard on day two, surging seven miles ahead. The third day, as fatigue set in, was conservative and evenly matched, but by its end Howard was back in front by just four miles. As the contest remained tight, every time Tobias caught Howard, she would surge off ahead. There was usually only four miles in it. Crowds grew, as did tempers. Howard turned and accused her nemesis of interference and the two had to be separated by officials.

On the final day Howard had built a lead of seven miles and she left the track with an hour remaining, knowing a new record of 409 miles (658km) would be enough to win – a record that lasted 102 years. Tobias pushed on to reach 400 miles.

Howard would win every women's six-day race she entered.

11 May

The Gateshead Clipper beats Deerfoot
(1863)

A crowd of 8,000 gathered to see Deerfoot's (see 18 January) last race in Britain, though unfortunately he was upstaged. His opponents were William 'Crowcatcher' Lang and Jack 'The Gateshead Clipper' White, who believed he was susceptible to a fierce early pace.

Though Deerfoot covered the first three miles in 15 minutes, the other two were quicker and once lapped, Deerfoot did the customary thing at the time and stepped off the track.

White and Lang maintained their relentless pace right up to 10 miles, in 52:14. They had set world records for three, four, five, six and seven miles, but as White was the race winner all records were attributed to him.

Despite the momentous occasion, according to Edward Sears's *Running Through the Ages*, the crowd 'expressed great indignation'. They had come to see Deerfoot.

12 May

Australia's Great Train Race
(since 1981)

Australia's Great Train Race takes place in early May on the Puffing Billy railway. The narrow-gauge line dates to 1900 and was constructed through Victoria's Dandenong Ranges to open up remote areas. The 13.5km (8½-mile) race route winds through hills and fern gullies from Belgrave to Emerald Lake Park and, simply put, the 3,000-plus runners race the chuffing train to the finish line/station.

To give those not powered by steam a chance, there are two trains to race, one taking between 50 and 60 minutes and the second between 65 and 75 minutes. Around 50 runners tend to out-speed the first locomotive, while over a thousand usually beat the second one.

13 May

Ingrid Kristiansen breaks marathon world record
(1984)

Ingrid Kristiansen dominated women's long-distance running in the 1980s and first broke the world record for the marathon in London in 1984. The Norwegian won the Stockholm (three times), Houston (twice), Boston (twice), London (four times), Chicago and New York City marathons, but finished fourth at the first Olympic marathon in 1984. She wasn't bad at shorter long-distance races either. She's the only athlete, male or female, to hold the world record for 5,000m, 10,000m and the marathon at the same time – recording 2:21:06 at the London Marathon in 1985, a time that wasn't surpassed for 13 years. Kristiansen was also the first runner to hold world titles on track, roads and cross country.

Her almost tedious levels of brilliance don't stop there. She was also an elite cross-country skier, winning several Norwegian titles and a European junior championship.

14 May

A race to pick up stones
(1837)

The first half of the 1800s brought some enterprising variations on pedestrian racing, and races to collect stones were de rigueur for a time in the UK – in the US potatoes were sometimes used. Objects would be placed every yard on a straight line for the runner to collect and return to the start to place in a bucket.

On this date, a race to pick up 300 stones – meaning a total race distance of 51.3 miles (82.5km) – saw John Phipps Townsend, who had won the first London to Brighton Race (see 30 January) and humbly called himself 'The Champion of Living Pedestrians', competing against the less distinguished Edward 'Temperance' Drinkwater. By way of a handicap, reports Edward Sears's *Running Through the Ages*, Townsend had agreed to collect stones using his mouth – and he had specially sought out larger ones from Brighton Beach – while his opponent could use his hands.

Drinkwater went for the nearer stones first, while his more experienced opponent went for varied distances. He lagged behind Drinkwater for most of the race, but after eight hours Drinkwater gave up, citing exhaustion, and had to be carried to his room. Townsend picked up his last stone, and the win, after 8 hours and 19 minutes.

His party trick was to stand for long periods on one leg, which he once managed for over seven hours. He was forced to retire from pedestrianism when he lost the use of a leg, which may not be entirely coincidental.

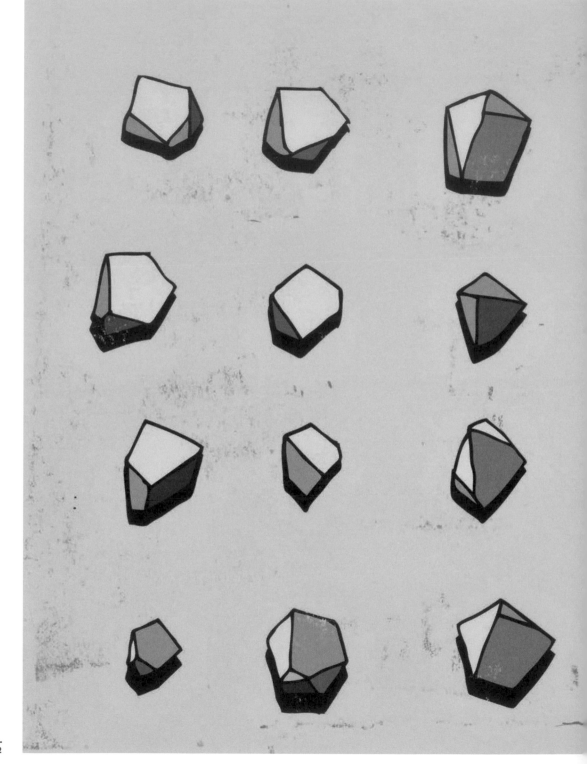

15 May

Grete Waitz sets half marathon record
(1982)

Grete Waitz ran the Gothenberg half marathon in a world-record time of 1:09:57 on this date. But it was the Norwegian's marathon running that left such a huge mark on athletics history. An unprecedented nine New York City Marathon wins (between 1978 and 1988) included setting world records three years in a row. Overall she lowered the women's world record by nine minutes, taking it from 2:34:47 to 2:25:29, and set various other world records at shorter distances.

Her first marathon, the 1978 New York win, was run after the encouragement of her husband and coach, who told her a trip to New York would be like a second honeymoon for them. The furthest she'd run in training was 13 miles and she has said the last 10 miles of the race were agony. Waitz was so angry at her husband at the finish line that she tore off her shoes and flung them at him, yelling, 'I'll never do this stupid thing again!'

In Norway there are statues created in Waitz's honour and she's been depicted on stamps and aeroplanes. Her success has clear parallels with the increased popularity of women running marathons.

16 May

The Running Doctor is born
(1910)

Many an amateur and pro runner has had cause to unknowingly curse Ernst van Aaken and his ideas, but then be grateful of them come marathon day.

The German, who was nicknamed the 'Running Doctor', is generally recognised as the founder of the long slow distance method of endurance training, initially called *Waldnieler Dauerlauf*, German for 'Waldniel endurance run'.

Until van Aaken's ideas gained traction in the 1960s interval training, championed by compatriot Woldemar Gerschler, was the common way to prepare for endurance running. But the Running Doctor, a coach and sports physician, thought the polar opposite method, running slowly for a long time, was of more benefit. (Nowadays most athletes do both.) He famously advised, 'Run long, run daily, drink little and don't eat like a pig.'

He coached Harald Norpoth to a 1964 Olympic 5,000m silver medal, but was hit by a car in 1972 while running and lost both his legs, becoming a champion of wheelchair sports. He was also a big proponent of women's running, arguing they could be better than men.

17 May

The first sub-eight-minute two miles
(1997)

Growing up in the famous Rift Valley, where the majority of Kenya's best runners come from, Daniel Komen would run six miles to school and six miles back home. In the mid-1990s Haile Gebrselassie was Komen's only equal.

In 1996 and 1997 the Kenyan produced perhaps the two most astonishing years of distance running the world has seen, winning dozens of races against top competition and setting numerous world records (for 1,5000m, 3,000m indoor and outdoor, 2 miles and 5,000m), some of which are still on the books.

His two-mile record is the most impressive, and no one has ever matched it. In a two-mile race in Hechtel, Belgium, on this day in 1997, the first mile was faster than Roger Bannister's first-ever sub-four, while his second equalled it, clocking 7:58.61 overall. To prove it wasn't a fluke, seven months later he ran 7:58.91. No other runner has ever gone under eight minutes.

Komen raced continuously in 1996 and 1997 and his body never really recovered.

18 May

Elana Meyer breaks another world record
(1991)

At eighteen months old, South Africa's Elana Meyer survived a freak accident where a vehicle drove over her head. She's said knowing she is lucky to be alive has influenced how she lives: 'Every day has to be lived to the fullest.'

She won her first half marathon aged thirteen. On 18 May 1991 she set a new women's half marathon world record of 1:07:59 – 33 seconds quicker than Norway's Ingrid Kristiansen's 1987 effort. She broke it again (with 1:07:36) almost six years later, and again 365 days after that (1:07:29). Then she did it a final time

in January 1999, with 1:06:44 – still the sixth fastest ever run (as of 2016).

But Meyer is best remembered for a moment at the 1992 Olympics in Barcelona. Having finished second in the 10,000m to Ethiopia's Derartu Tulu, the two jogged around the track, draped in flags, their hands locked together, triumphant but also defiant. It had been an epic race, but it was also a powerful symbol of post-apartheid South Africa. It was the first gold for a black African woman, while Meyer's silver marked the end of 30 years of Olympic exclusion for her country.

19 May

The world's fastest human is born
(1908)

Canada's Percy Williams had a bad knee from playing football, and a bad heart from a rheumatic fever as a child, and was advised against physical activity. He also openly confessed to not enjoying running. It's a wonder then that 'Human Flash' became his nickname, as well as the additional moniker of 'World's Fastest Human'. But bad luck followed him.

Early in his career, Williams lost out on the Canadian Championships on the toss of a coin. There were six runners and only five lanes, so he didn't get to run in the 100m final.

He did eventually qualify for the 1928 Olympics in Amsterdam, where the night before the 100m final his coach made him practise race starts in his hotel, with a mattress up against the wall to prevent injury. It worked. A perfect start led Williams to a surprise 100m gold – and then 200m gold. In 1930 he broke the 21-year-old 100m world record, clocking 10.3 seconds.

Bad luck returned however and a muscle tear ended his career at just twenty-two. He has twice been voted Canada's Greatest Athlete in polls.

20 May

Legendary ultramarathon runner Arthur Newton is born
(1883)

Born in Weston-super-Mare, England, Arthur Newton became a long-distance running legend by accident. Aged thirty-eight and living in South Africa, he was embroiled in a land dispute with the government. To attract attention to his cause, he ran the Comrades Marathon, a new 54-mile footrace. And won. So the pipe-smoking Englishman took up distance running full-time.

He won Comrades another four times, usually with a new course record (by two hours in 1923), and set numerous world-best times elsewhere. In 1924 he returned to England and ran the London to Brighton course in 5:53:43, beating the previous record by over an hour. In 1925, with the government dispute not panning out the way he wanted, he moved to Rhodesia (modern-day Zimbabwe), making the 770-mile journey on foot.

He ran in and usually won ultramarathons in the US (see 4 and 31 March), Canada and Britain (see 7 January), setting a 100-mile record at the age of fifty-one.

21 May

Sumie Inagaki runs for 48 hours non-stop
(2010)

Sumie Inagaki had already won Greece's 246km Spartathlon ultramarathon and set a women's 24-hour (indoor) world record, when she attempted a new women's 48-hour (track) record in Surgères, France. So to the casual observer it wasn't a huge surprise when the Japanese distance runner clocked a world best 397km (247 miles) two days later.

Inagaki is also two-time winner of the IAU 24-Hour World Championships. Indeed, the yoga teacher clearly likes to do things twice, as she also won America's notorious Badwater Ultramarathon in 2011 and 2012. She continues to race – and almost always wins – 24- and 48-hour races.

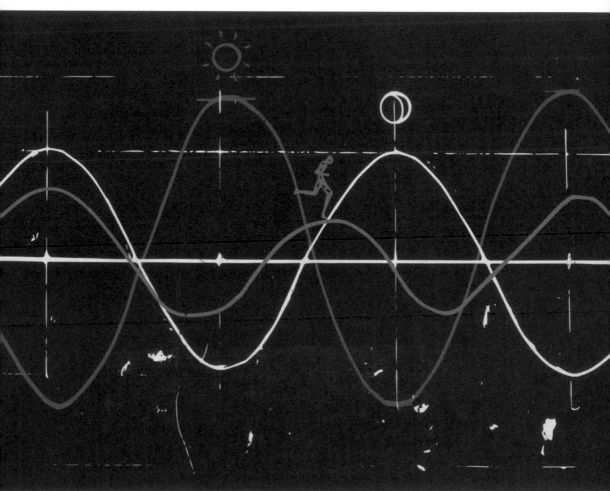

22 May

Yiannis Kouros runs 1,000 miles
(1988)

As records go, this isn't one of the more hotly contested, But in 1988 ultramarathon legend Yiannis Kouros added yet another record to his absurd pantheon of distance running achievements, with a new 1,000-mile (1,609km) world record.

It took the Australian-based Greek 10 days and 10:30.36 to reach the distance at the 1,000 Mile IAU World Championship, knocking one and a half days off Stu Mittleman's 1986 record.

He prepared himself in part by winning the previous year's 700-mile race. The races were part of the Sri Chinmoy-founded trio of 'Self-Transcendence' multi-day ultramarathons held in New York each year. The third distance is 3,100 miles (see 16 June).

23 May

The first sub-3:30 women's marathon
(1964)

Dale Greig set a new women's world record for the marathon in 1964 when she ran 3:27:45 at the Isle of Wight Marathon in the UK. She was followed around the course by an ambulance due to doubts about women's ability to cover the distance safely. Indeed, Greig started four minutes ahead of the field, and so wasn't 'officially' a part of it. It was her first marathon, though she would run up to 50 miles a day in training. Instead of celebrating her triumph, the Women's Amateur Athletic Association reprimanded the organisers for allowing her to compete.

Greig was also the first woman to run the 55-mile London–Brighton race in 1972 – seven years before female competitors were officially allowed – setting off an hour ahead of everyone else. In 1974, aged thirty-seven, she won the first international championship marathon for women, at the world veterans' championships in Paris.

24 May

First Comrades 'Marathon' run
(1921)

While serving with the South African infantry in what is now Tanzania, British-born Vic Clapham and his fellow soldiers marched over 2,700km (1,678 miles). In the aftermath of the war he looked for ways to commemorate the soldiers' suffering and their camaraderie. Inspired by both what he had been through and England's 55-mile London–Brighton ultramarathon (see 30 January), his idea was a 56-mile race between Pietermaritzburg and Durban.

Most organisations he approached with the idea thought it was mad. But he persisted and, thanks in part to a £1 loan, the first Comrades Marathon was born on this date, to 'celebrate mankind's spirit over adversity'.

It's now one of the most popular ultramarathons on the planet, with around 20,000 runners – and, as the London–Brighton wasn't yet a regular fixture, it claims to be the world's oldest.

Uniquely the race changes direction each year, one being the 'up', the other the 'down', reflecting the change in elevation; copper medals – known as the Vic Clapham medal – go to those athletes who finish the race between 11 and 12 hours.

Renowned for its infectious atmosphere, the likes of Arthur Newton (see 20 May), Wally Hayward, Hardy Ballington, Jackie Mekler, Alan Robb (2 June), nine-time winner Bruce Fordyce (3 December) and Russian twins Olesya and Elena Nurgalieva (9 January) have all become part of Comrades folklore. So too have the near-identical Motsoeneng brothers, by repeatedly swapping places during the 1999 race. Their cheating was proven by TV footage showing they were wearing watches on different wrists.

25 May

Ville Ritola breaks Paavo Nurmi's record
(1924)

If Finland-born US resident Ville Ritola hadn't been running around tracks at absurd speeds at the same time as compatriot Paavo Nurmi, his place in history would have been written in larger letters (see 13 July).

The 'Flying Finn' won five Olympic golds and three silvers in the 1920s and on this date Ritola broke Nurmi's three-year-old 10,000m world record, clocking 30:35.4 in Helsinki. He lowered his own record in July. But, of course, that pesky Nurmi broke it again just a month later.

Ritola moved back to Finland late in life and while both a sports hall and a statue pay tribute to him, his legacy reaches further. The Finnish phrase to 'pull a Ritola' means to make a quick exit.

26 May

Chasing a cheese
(2014)

The idea is simple, if totally crackers. Every Spring Bank Holiday at Cooper's Hill, in Gloucestershire, England, as many as 15,000 people gather from all over the world for the annual Cheese Rolling.

It's thought to originate in a pagan festival celebrating the arrival of summer, though the current activity probably dates from the early 1800s.

Nowadays a round Double Gloucester cheese weighing 7–9lb (3.2–4kg) is rolled down Cooper's Hill, which is said to have a gradient varying between 1 in 2 and 1 in 1. Foolhardy folk try to run, but mostly tumble and cartwheel, down the green cliff attempting to catch it. As the cheese reaches speeds of 70mph that's practically impossible. But the first person to the bottom wins the prized circular dairy product.

As well as the steepness, the ground is very uneven and grassy and injuries are common. 'Catchers' from a local rugby club try to put the brakes on out-of-control rolls at the hill bottom. It's common for competitors to visit the pub beforehand . . . and the hospital afterwards. Regular winner and local Chris Anderson says one year he took a bang to the head while securing victory. The next day at work he put a kettle in the fridge.

27 May

The Great Wall Marathon
(since 1999)

At most marathons runners dread hitting The Wall, but at this one contact with a huge stone structure is guaranteed – for two miles along the World Heritage-listed Great Wall of China.

The 5,164 stone steps mean you don't see so many elite Kenyan runners at this one. The route starts near the village of Huangyaguan, a couple of hours northeast of Beijing, and *Runner's World* magazine describes it as a 'relentless series of climbs and descents; a mixture of small, shallow steps, and painful, knee-high ones'. The temperature can be well above 30° Celsius and the course record is 3:09:18.

The Great Wall Marathon is not to be confused with The Great Wall of China Marathon, (also called the Conquer the Wall Marathon), a newer event which takes place in the same month but on a different part of the Great Wall. It claims to be on a more remote section, much of it unrestored since 1570, and includes over 20,000 steps.

28 May

Volmari Iso-Hollo sets the record straight
(1933)

Volmari Iso-Hollo was one of the last Flying Finns who dominated distance running between the two World Wars. In May 1933 he set a new 3,000m steeplechase world record, running 9:09.4 in Lahti, Finland.

It made amends for the 1932 Olympics where, despite grabbing gold, he should have been credited with a world record. In the 3,000m steeplechase final the lap-counter had been looking the wrong way, absorbed in the decathlon pole vault, and lost count of the laps. Tragicomically, there was no last-lap bell and the entire field kept on running, covering 3,460m.

When the 1936 Olympics came around he was favourite and justified his status by claiming gold and a fresh world record of 9:03.8 (and a 10,000m bronze to boot).

29 May

The first ascent of Mount Everest
(1953)

Even if Everest is often used down the ages to help describe impossible-seeming athletics goals such as the four-minute-mile (see 23 March), scaling the world's highest peak wasn't technically a moment in athletics history. But it was a moment – probably the greatest since the Poles were reached – of epic human endeavour.

At a whopping 8,848m (29,029ft) above sea level, Mount Everest is split between Nepal and Tibet, where it goes by the name of Chomolungma – in Nepal it's Sagārmātha.

To reach its summit had been a British obsession since the 1920s, especially for George Mallory, who lost his life high on the Himalayan monster on his third attempt to climb it – some believe he may have done so before perishing.

It wasn't until the ninth British expedition in 1953 that success was achieved, from the Nepalese side. Tom Bourdillon and Charles Evans had come within 100m of the summit but were forced to turn back, leaving Nepal's Tenzing Norgay and New Zealand's Edmund Hillary to capitalise on their trail breaking and stashed oxygen to reach the summit, and write their names into history.

30 May

Pre's last drive
(1975)

The very promising career of America's Steve Prefontaine ended in a tragic car crash today in 1975. At just twenty-four 'Pre' held the US record in seven distances from 2,000m to 10,000m and seemed a shoo-in for gold medals at the following year's Olympics.

He had placed fourth in the 1972 Olympic 5,000m final, regarded by many as one of the greatest ever races, and is the subject of two Hollywood films, two documentaries and at least four books. Pre had an eye for a quote to rival Muhammad Ali, with his best two being: 'To give anything less than your best, is to sacrifice the gift,' and: 'I'm going to work so that it's a pure guts race at the end, and if it is, I am the only one who can win it.'

31 May

Comrades' greatest finish
(1967)

The rivalry between Manie Kuhn and Tommy Malone, 'The Flying Scotsman', was already growing. Malone had beaten Kuhn after a long battle in the 1966 Comrades, while a few months later Kuhn was second and Malone third in the London–Brighton race.

It was so tight at the halfway point of the 1967 Comrades that seven runners – including Kuhn and Malone – were all given the time 2:51. On the steep winding hills at Alvestone Malone made a move and opened up a gap. A little later Kuhn found himself three minutes adrift of the surging Scot and a win for Malone looked likely. He was handed the traditional message from the Mayor of Pietermaritzburg to the Mayor of Durban at Tollgate, with a lead of two minutes over Kuhn. But Kuhn had home-town advantage and a partisan Natal crowd egged him on. He began to slowly close the gap.

Inside the stadium, where the race finishes, the 3,000-strong crowd was told the winner was Malone and that he was 180m away. Malone thought Kuhn was still a comfortable two minutes behind him. However, to the dismay of Malone and the delight of the crowd, Kuhn suddenly came into view just 15m behind the leader, with less than 50m to go.

Malone gave it all he had. But as he kicked hard cramps caught him, an agonising – in both senses of the word – 15m from the finish line, and he fell to the ground. The stadium was silenced. Malone tried to get up, but his legs weren't so keen on the idea. The white vest of Kuhn dashed past him, to win by one second. The runners embraced after an epic and famous duel.

JUNE

1 June

The 1,000-mile walk
(1809)

Scotland's Robert Barclay Allardyce began his walk of 1,000 miles (1,610km) in 1,000 hours for 1,000 guineas today in 1809. 'Captain Barclay', or the 'celebrated pedestrian' as he was also known, was the first great pedestrian of the nineteenth century.

Pedestrianism was the eighteenth- and nineteenth-century feat of walking and/or running seemingly impossible distances, usually for a considerable wager. It was the origin of both racewalking and ultramarathon running.

Walking the equivalent of 24 miles per day sounds easy, but Barclay had pledged to walk at least a mile every hour for 42 days. Around 10,000 spectators gathered at a half-mile course in Newmarket, England. Total betting reached £100,000 (£40m in today's money).

Barclay's sage strategy was to walk a mile at the end of each hour, then another one straight after, at the start of the next hour, allowing himself maximum rest before the next one. Predictably the 29-year-old's pace decreased from just under 15-minute miles at the start to around 21-minute miles. His weight dropped from 13st 4lb (84.5kg) to 11st (70kg). A spectator reported that Barclay become so lethargic helpers stuck needles in him and even fired pistols close to his ears to try and keep him awake. But he got there to cement his place as the forefather of the pedestrian movement.

2 June

Alan Robb runs a 40th consecutive Comrades Marathon
(2013)

South African Alan Robb made his first appearance at the 89km (56-mile) Comrades Marathon in 1974, the world's oldest ultramarathon, finishing third. He placed fifth the following year. But 12 months later, Robb won the race. And again the next year. He completed a hat-trick of wins in 1978, breaking the tape in Durban in a record (for the 'up' course) 5:29:14.

Robb won again in 1980. He didn't win in 1981, or indeed ever again. But four times is better than almost anyone else and the seed was sown. He simply loved the race. 'Comrades is my Christmas Day,' he has said. The sexagenarian has an eye on 50 finishes.

3 June

Italy's marathon world-record breaker
(1908)

Umberto Blasi won Italy's first national marathon championship in Rome today, with a time of 3:01:04. This seems almost laughably slow some 100 years later, but Blasi went on to break the world record.

The Italian would be three times national champion at the marathon distance and in capturing his third and final title in Legnano, in 1914, run his all-time PB, a respectable 2:38:00.8. (Although not recognised as a world best by the IAAF, the Association of Road Racing Statisticians lists this mark in their progression of world records, and as the world's fastest for 1914.)

Blasi also competed at the marathon in the 1908 Olympics in London. Though he recorded a DNF at eight miles, he wasn't as unfortunate as compatriot Dorando Pietri who, despite being the first finisher, was disqualified for having been repeatedly helped up from the ground in the finishing straight (see 24 July).

4 June

Thomas Longboat is born
(1887)

This date is Thomas Longboat day in Canada. It marks the birth of one of the world's great distance runners. Longboat was a Canadian Onondaga Indian who grew up working on a ranch, chasing runaway horses.

Longboat won the 1907 Boston Marathon (then a 24½-mile course) in a record time of 2:24:24 and the following year represented his country at the first Olympic marathon, in London, where he was a favourite. He collapsed, however, as did several leading runners on a hot day (though there were also rumours he'd been drugged).

A rematch was organised between Longboat and Italy's Dorando Pietri at Madison Square Garden, New York, in the same year. Interest was huge and thousands were turned away. Pietri went haring off from the start, but was in a state of collapse on 25 miles, when Longboat sauntered casually past him. They raced again at the same venue the following year, with the same outcome, in comically similar circumstances.

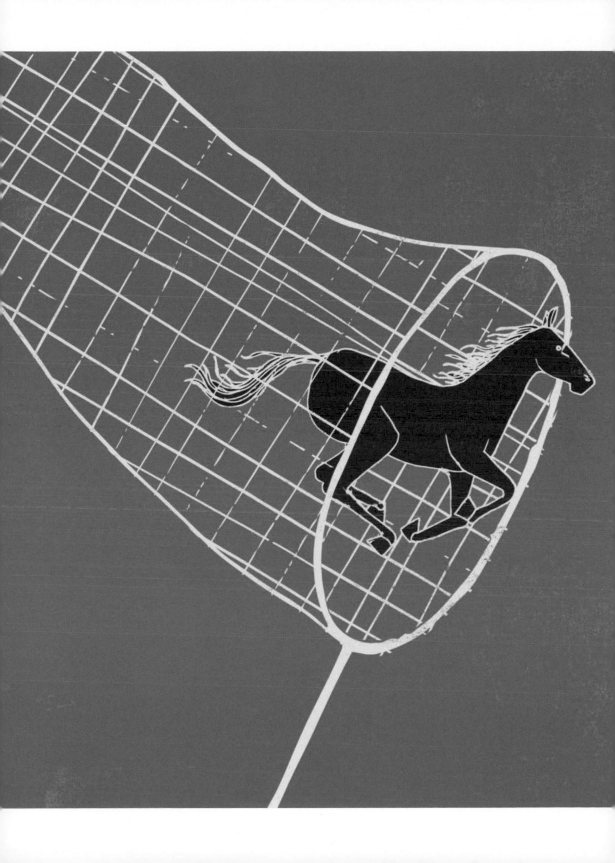

5 June ⫸

5 June

Haile Gebrselassie breaks yet another world record
(1995)

Like Thomas Longboat, Haile Gebrselassie grew up chasing horses and it showed. 1995 saw the great distance runner at his electrifying peak. In May he broke the two-mile world record, with 8:07.46. In August he won the 10,000m World Championships. Just after that he reclaimed his 5,000m world record, chipping nearly 11 seconds off, with 12:44.39. And in between all those achievements that would cap most careers the Ethiopian broke the 10,000m world record on 5 June, rocketing to 26:43.53 at Hengelo, Netherlands.

When he retired from competitive running in May 2015, Gebrselassie had claimed two Olympic golds, eight World Championship wins and set 27 world records. Many see him as the biggest rival to Emil Zátopek as the world's greatest ever distance runner.

6 June

The Norwegian Superman?
(1833)

Pedestrian Mensen Ernst began his second great foot journey today, the small matter of 1,577 miles from Munich, Germany, to Nafplio, Greece.

The first notable achievement of Ernst's 25-year pedestrian career was in 1819 when he ran 72 miles from London to Portsmouth, in nine hours. Ernst's reputation grew further with a 13-day, 1,500-mile journey from Paris to Moscow in 1832 (see 25 June).

The following year the pedestrian tried something marginally bigger, 1,577 miles from Munich, carrying letters from the Bavarian king to his son Otto, King of Greece, in Nafplio. Ernst was thought to have been robbed of his money and maps, arrested as a spy and imprisoned for two days, but he still managed to complete his audacious act in 24 days.

In 1835 his aspirations were even larger. The Norwegian travelled from Constantinople to Calcutta and back, crossing the wilderness region of Asia Minor, Syrian deserts, Persia, Afghanistan and the Himalayas. Again he was reportedly shot at, robbed, and bitten by a snake, as he covered the 5,000-mile round trip in 59 days – averaging 85 miles a day.

He sounds like quite the Superman. But, as you'll see on 25 June, all wasn't quite as it seemed.

7 June

Mr DeMarathon is born
(1888)

American Clarence DeMar finished second in his first Boston Marathon in 1910, but later that year was advised by a doctor that he had a heart murmur and should stop running. The next year DeMar won the Boston Marathon with a new course record of 2:21:39.

After finishing 12th in the marathon at the 1912 Olympics DeMar did heed doctors' warnings and took a break from serious distance running. He ran Boston again, however, in 1917, finishing third, apparently on little training, but was then drafted into the army.

In 1922, he returned to marathon running and again won Boston, with a course record 2:18:10, following up with two further wins in 1923 and 1924 (the latter being the first time the full 26 miles, 385 yards was run at Boston). He won bronze at the 1924 Olympics, then had a brilliant sequence of five consecutive marathon victories: the Baltimore, the Sesqui-Centennial and Port Chester (all 1926); and the Baltimore and Boston in 1927. He won Boston again in 1928 and clocked up a seventh and final Boston win, aged forty-one, in 1930, cementing his well-earned nickname, 'Mr DeMarathon'. Not bad for a dodgy ticker.

8 June

The Astonishing Pedestrian
(1788)

Foster Powell, the most famous pedestrian of the eighteenth century, sometimes called the 'Astonishing Pedestrian', set out today from Hicks' Hall, London, on a journey to York. He then returned to London, completing a 396-mile trip in 5 days, 19 hours, and 15 minutes.

The Yorkshireman was a legal clerk who discovered his aptitude for long distances on his rounds delivering law papers. His pedestrian career had started with a 50-mile run on the Bath Road in seven hours.

Next he clocked up 112 miles in 24 hours. But he really gained fame for his epic walks from London to York.

His last one was in fact his PB, recording a time of 5 days, 15 hours and 45 minutes. Straight afterwards he wagered he could walk another mile, then run another, in 15 minutes. He walked a mile in 9:20 and ran the second in an astonishing 5:23, to win the bet by 17 seconds. This was at the age of fifty-seven.

9 June

The fourth Astley Belt contest
(1879)

The Astley Belt series was the Champions League of nineteenth-century pedestrian racing. Six-day events saw top pedestrians compete on an indoor circuit, captivating huge crowds on both sides of the Atlantic between 1878 and 1889.

American Edward Weston first hit on the idea of trying to walk for six days when he attempted to cover 500 miles. He achieved it at the third attempt in December 1874. After matching Weston's accomplishment, American-Irishman Daniel O'Leary challenged him to an inaugural six-day race in November 1875, to decide the 'World Championship of long-distance walking', in Chicago. O'Leary won with 501 miles to Weston's 450.

In England, parliamentarian and gambler Sir John Astley (see 18 March) arranged a rematch in 1877, with O'Leary again victorious (519 miles to 510), with an estimated 70,000 watching the race live over the six days.

Astley lost £20,000 betting on Weston, but was smitten with the sport and created the Astley Belt series. He made the rules 'go as you please', meaning walking, running or any combination in between was allowed.

There would be seven Astley Belt six-day races (see 29 June). But Weston made a dramatic comeback for the fourth Belt on 9 June 1879, taking an overdue win, clocking 550 miles. The final Astley Belt saw a win for Charles Rowell after overcoming an apparent mid-race poisoning (see 27 September).

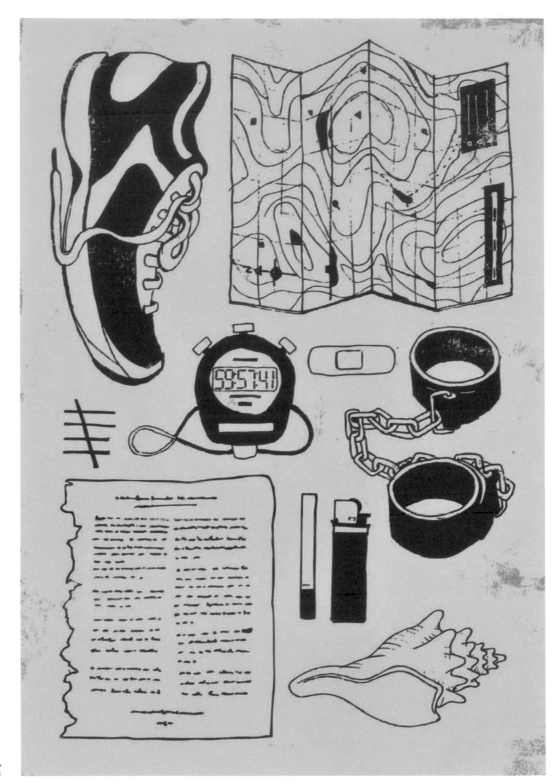

10 June

The Barkley Marathons
(1977)

When Martin Luther King Jr's murderer James Earl Ray escaped from Brushy Mountain State Penitentiary in Tennessee on 10 June, it didn't become a great foot journey – quite the opposite – but it gave birth to one, namely the world's toughest, and quirkiest, 100-mile race.

After running for 55 hours, Earl Ray had only travelled eight miles through the densely wooded terrain when he was captured. On hearing this, ultrarunner Gary Cantrell thought he could do better and the Barkley Marathons was born.

Some insight into why the escaped convict found it so hard to get far can be seen in Barkley's completion statistics. Since its inception in 1986, only 14 runners out of around 800 have completed it (two more people than have walked on the moon, as of 2016).

The race, a series of 20-mile loops, has 54,200 feet of accumulated vertical climb, the equivalent of ascending Mount Everest twice from sea level.

Competitors must find around 10 (it changes each year) books and remove the page corresponding to their race number. Failure to produce these at the finish means disqualification. The books often have titles such as *A Time to Die* and that sardonic humour permeates the idiosyncratic event.

'There is no website,' said Cantrell, 'and I don't publish the race date or explain how to enter.' Potential entrants must write an essay on 'Why I Should be Allowed to Run in the Barkley', though it's not clear where to send it to. Or when. The start time also remains a mystery until one hour beforehand and is signalled by Cantrell lighting a cigarette.

The only thing Barkley isn't tough on is your wallet. It costs $1.60 to enter.

11 June

Henry Rono breaks the 10,000m world record
(1978)

An incredible 81-day sequence saw Henry Rono break four world records in 1978: the 10,000m on 11 June in 27:22.5; the 5,000m in 13:08.4; the 3,000m steeplechase in 8:05.4; and the 3,000m in 7:32.1.

He also won the 5,000m and the 3,000m steeplechase gold medals at the Commonwealth Games in the same year. It's a hot streak unparalleled in the history of distance running.

Rono would also set a new world record for 5,000m in 1981.

Sadly, the Kenyan would never get to compete at the Olympics: his country boycotted both the 1976 and the 1980 Games and by 1984 he was no longer competing.

His 3,000m steeplechase world record stood for 11 years.

12 June

Morio Shigematsu breaks marathon world record
(1965)

Lining up at England's Polytechnic Marathon in 1965m Morio Shigematsu of Japan was blessed with excellent conditions at London's erstwhile Windsor to Chiswick route. 'The flat course, the following wind, the refreshing rain were all there as aids to covering the 26 miles 385 yards of macadam,' reported *The Times*.

Shigematsu, wearing a pair of white gloves, which he said was for wiping sweat from his brow, recorded 2:12:00. He'd knocked 11.2 seconds off Abebe Bikila's world best, a record that would stand for two and a half years, until Australia's Derek Clayton (see 17 November) recorded 2:09:36.4 at Japan's Fukuoka Marathon.

Less than two months earlier, Shigematsu had also set a course record at the 1965 Boston Marathon (2:16:33).

13 June

Bob Graham goes for a fell run
(1932)

Bob Graham was a hotelier and 'fell' walker and runner in England's Lake District. He wasn't a natural athlete. He was short and stocky, teetotal and vegetarian, but he had excellent knowledge of the Lakeland fells. For Graham's 42nd birthday he decided to celebrate by summiting a 'round' (circuit) of 42 Lakeland fells within 24 hours.

In preparation, he walked each fell in bare feet, to both toughen up his skin and save his gym shoes. When the big day arrived (12 June, finishing the next day), he fuelled himself on bread and butter, strong tea, milk, boiled eggs, fruit and sweets. He walked the uphills and ran the downhills – with extraordinary speed – wearing tennis shoes, shorts and a 'pyjama jacket'. Graham got round his Round in 23 hours 39 minutes, thus creating the 66-mile Bob Graham Round.

It has become the biggest challenge of Britain's fell running scene; many have tried to do it since, with approximately one third succeeding.

The record for the Bob Graham Round is Billy Bland's astonishing 13 hours and 53 minutes from 1982.

14 June

The longest race in the shortest time
(2015)

Finland's Ashprihanal Aalto, forty-four, won the world's longest certified footrace – the Self-Transcendence 3,100 Mile Race (see 16 June) – in the shortest ever time.

Aalto completed the race, set around a block in Queens, New York, in 40 days, 9 hours 6 minutes and 21 seconds, an average of more than 76 miles per day. The Finn broke Madhupran Wolfgang Schwerk's nine-year-old record by more than 23 hours.

Four hours and 45 minutes of sleep was the most he ever got, usually less. As the race progressed, Aalto took 10-minute naps during his three scheduled 12- to 15-minute breaks each day, and found that he could fall into a deep sleep.

'This year I used everything I knew from the previous races,' Aalto, who has run the race 13 times and won eight times, told *Runner's World*.

Aalto says that his training included a few 25-mile runs now and then. His work, delivering a daily newspaper back home in Finland, helps him stay fit.

15 June

Buddy Edelen breaks the marathon world record
(1963)

When American Leonard 'Buddy' Edelen broke the marathon world record with 2:14:28 at London's Polytechnic Marathon it was the first one ever run below 2:15.

After graduating the American had moved to Europe to try and improve his distance running in a country 'where you're not just regarded as a track bum if you wish to continue running after college'.

In 1962, he finished fourth at the Fukuoka Marathon in a US record time of 2:18:57, making him the first American to run under 2:20 for the marathon.

'I owe so much to the wonderful club life and tradition of distance running over here in the UK,' he told *The Times* after his win. He also recalled, 'a feeling of tremendous mechanical efficiency'.

16 June

The world's longest race
(1997)

In 1964, Indian guru Sri Chinmoy moved to New York and started teaching meditation, including running to attain enlightenment. In 1996 he created a 2,700-mile (4,345km) race around a block in New York, but he clearly felt that wasn't testing enough because at the award ceremony he declared the 1997 edition would be extended to 3,100 mile. The Self-Transcendence 3,100 Mile Race is the world's longest certified footrace.

Henceforth, runners have undergone 5,649 laps of one extended city block in Queens – they must average 59.62 miles per day to finish within the 52-day limit.

Participation is limited to invited athletes who have a résumé of multi-day running experience and elite endurance abilities. In the 18 years to 2015, just 37 people completed the distance.

Though it's not a prerequisite for participation, most of the event's competitors are followers of the late Chinmoy. The leader lived about a mile from the race's course until he died in 2007.

According to his website, Sri Chinmoy 'felt that peace could be manifested through silent meditation, music, poetry, art and sports. He especially had a fondness for running and felt it provided an excellent opportunity for people to challenge themselves and overcome their pre-conceived limitations – what he referred to as self-transcendence.'

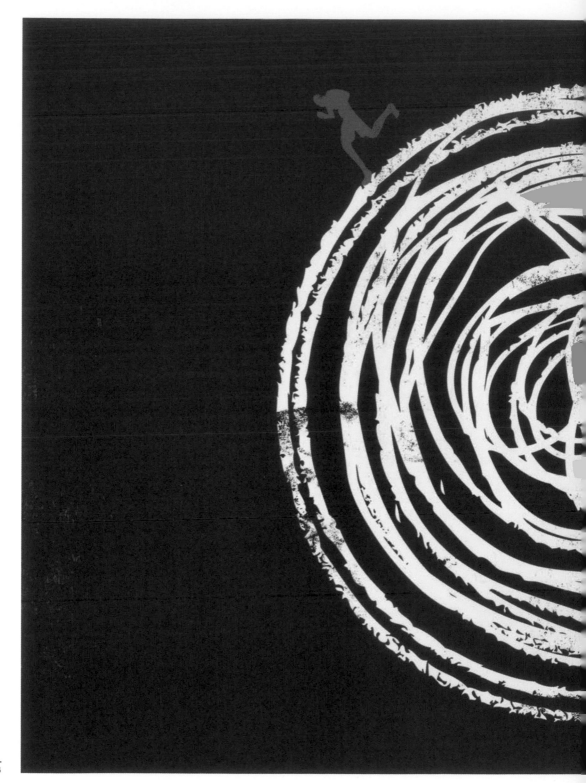

17 June

Derek Ibbotson is born
(1932)

Britain had a wealth of middle-distance running talent in the 1950s and among them was Derek Ibbotson. He achieved more than his contemporaries Sir Roger Bannister and Sir Chris Chataway and yet isn't as well known.

Ibbotson was British junior champion in 1951, but a spell in the army interrupted his athletics career. In 1955 he won the Intercounties Three Miles title and a year later he beat Chataway to become the AAA champion.

In the 5,000m final at the 1956 Olympics in Melbourne Ibbotson faced the Soviet Union great Vladimir Kuts, who'd won gold at 10,000m, as well as Chataway and Gordon Pirie. He came away with a hard-fought bronze behind Kuts and Pirie.

Bannister had broken the four-minute mile in May 1954 and Australia's John Landy had brought it down to 3:58.02 only a month later. But three years later no one had surpassed it.

Ibbotson was at his peak in 1957 and he raced 70 times, setting a European record for the mile with 3:58.4. Then in a meet on 19 July at White City he beat a top line-up to win in 3:57.2, a new world record.

It never got so good again for Ibbotson. Interestingly, in 1958, he finished fourth in a mile race won by Australia's Herb Elliott (see 25 February), in 3:55.4. Ibbotson's time was 4:00.00, making him officially the first man to run a four-minute mile dead-on.

18 June

William Edwards attempts to walk 100 miles
(1875)

Pedestrianism spread from the US and UK to the Antipodes in the nineteenth century and Australian William Edwards was one of the stars of the scene down under.

Edwards had competed in several 50-mile races and on 18 June 1875 in the Drill Shed, Dunedin, New Zealand, he started his first attempt to walk 100 miles under 24 hours. 'After finishing the 50 miles he showed signs of fainting,' reports P.S. Marshall's excellent *King of the Peds*, 'but afterwards revived and continued the walk,

though his feet were bleeding very much through the effects of new shoes he wore.' He reached the crucial century . . . with five minutes to spare.

For his next trick he pledged to walk 3,150 times around Christchurch's Oddfellows Hall, a distance of 105 miles, within 24 hours. This time he wore canvas shoes. He was also plied with brandy and 'some of Gee's calves' foot jelly'. Edwards was again victorious with just seven minutes and three seconds to spare.

19 June

Calcaterra doesn't win the 100K World Championships
(2009)

The 2009 100K World Championships was one of only two times in five years the race wasn't won by former Italian cabbie Giorgio Calcaterra. In 2009 he finished third in Torhout, Netherlands, with Japan's Yasukazu Miyasato winning. In 2010 Miyasato's compatriot Shinji Nakadai triumphed, though Calcaterra wasn't there to try and reclaim his 2008 title. He would be back though, winning in 2011 and 2012 (in a PB of 6:23:20).

In 2000 the 'flying taxi driver' ran 26 marathons in under two hours and 20 minutes, creating a new world record. He also clocked a PB of 2:13:15.

In 2005 Calcaterra won the Utrecht Marathon and in 2006 switched to the ultramarathon distance, where he found his true calling.

20 June

The Trans-America Footrace returns
(1992)

The first multi-day race was probably The Trans-America Footrace, nicknamed 'the Bunion Derby' (see 4 March), which took place in 1928, from Los Angeles to New York. It was repeated the following year, this time from New York to Los Angeles (see 31 March).

Estimated to be over 3,000 miles (5,000km), with an average of 44.5 miles a day for 70 days, and no rest days, it's obvious why it might have had limited appeal. So it didn't happen again until 1992.

For the third incarnation, runners left Los Angeles aiming for New York with 64 days to cover 2,935.8 miles, averaging 45.9 miles a day.

There were 28 starters and 13 finishers in 1992, the fastest being American David Warady in 521 hours 35 minutes and 57 seconds.

'The daily grind was machine-like,' he told Raceacrossusa.org, 'Same boring thing, day after day, but getting used to that boredom, and embracing it was one of the keys to success.'

A pan-American race has struggled to become a regular fixture, with seven in various formats since 1992, the last one being in 2012. Out of all the races, the completion rate is 34.3 per cent.

21 June

Steve Birkinshaw runs up 214 mountains in a week
(2014)

British fell runner Steve Birkinshaw set a new record today for bagging the 214 'Wainwright' peaks in the Lake District and raising £12,000 for multiple sclerosis. Birkinshaw broke the record set by 'Iron' Joss Naylor (see 10 February) in 1987, who completed the challenge in 7 days, 1 hour and 25 minutes. Birkinshaw, aged forty-five, ran 320 miles (515km) and ascended 118,000ft (36,000m) in 6 days and 13 hours.

He ran the equivalent of two marathons each day, with a GPS tracker recording his movements to prove his feat beyond doubt.

Birkinshaw worked out a more efficient route than Naylor, and slept for just four hours a day to Joss's eight, finishing with severely blistered feet and tendonitis, among various ailments.

'There were some really tough times out there,' said Birkinshaw. 'But I was spurred on every time I reached a Wainwright top and met someone else who had made the effort to come out and support me.'

The 214 fells are described in Alfred Wainwright's seven-volume *A Pictorial Guide to the Lakeland Fells* (1955–66).

22 June

Paavo Nurmi breaks his first world record
(1921)

Paavo Nurmi, arguably in the top three distance runners of all time with Emil Zátopek and Haile Gebrselassie, was the eldest of five Finnish children.

Nurmi left school at twelve, and worked as an errand boy for a bakery, dragging carts and sacks around, then military service ensued. His unit had to march 12.5 miles, lugging backpacks full of sand. Nurmi ran the entire route. Within a year he was representing Finland in the 1920 Olympics.

The 'Flying Finn' set 22 world records at distances between 1,500 metres and 20,000m – the first being the 10,000m on 22 June 1921 in Stockholm. He won nine Olympic gold medals (five at the 1924 Olympics) and three silvers. He's the only runner to have held world records for the mile, 5,000m and 10,000m events at the same time.

What made him so good? 'He paid no attention to his opponents before, during or after the race,' said the *Guardian*. 'He never spoke and he never smiled. The sheer inhumanity of the man broke the hearts of those who had to run against him.'

23 June

Timothy Olson wins Western States

(2012)

As well as being the oldest (see 3 August), along with UTMB (see 25 August), the Western States Endurance Run is the world's most competitive 100-mile race. Starting in Squaw Valley, California, it ends 100.2 miles later in Auburn. Runners climb more than 18,000ft and descend nearly 23,000ft but it is seen as a comparatively fast and runable course.

The legendary Scott Jurek may have won Western States seven consecutive times (see 26 June), Tim Twietmeyer five times and Ann Trason (see 24 June) 14 times, but it's Timothy Olson, with his trademark long hair and beard, who has the course record.

He was the first runner to break 15 hours, clocking 14:46:44 in 2012. Olson won again the following year, but in a slower time.

Olson initially took to running cross country to get in shape for basketball, but he found the sport, and runners, to be more to his liking. He went off the rails at college, turning to drink and drugs, but thankfully he rediscovered running and says it may well have saved his life.

24 June

Ann Trason wins Western States
(1989)

Not only did Ann Trason win California's Western States Endurance Run 100-mile race in 1989, but she became the first female to finish in the top 10. Her first two attempts had ended in DNFs, but she went on to win Western States 14 times and held the women's course record for 18 years.

Trason was a good runner at school, but her ultra running started with 1985's American River 50 Miler. Aged just twenty-four she both won and set a course record (she returned eight years later and ran it an hour faster, in 6:09, a course record that still stood in 2015).

As well as Western States, Trason broke 20 world records in distances ranging from 40 to 100 miles, qualified three times in the marathon for the US Olympic trials, and set a course record at the Leadville 100 that has stood for more than 20 years.

In 1998, Trason won all four Grand Slam 100-mile events (Western States, Leadville 100, Vermont 100 and Wasatch 100).

25 June

Ernst arrives in Moscow
(1832)

Norway's Mensen Ernst, famous pedestrian and godfather of ultramarathon running, arrived in Moscow today in 1832, two days ahead of schedule, having travelled on foot from Paris in just 14 days, the first of his three epic trips.

But hold on a minute. The distance from Paris to Moscow, as the crow flies, is 1,500 miles, so that's 107 miles (172km) per day. An averagely fit ultramarathon runner nowadays could maybe cover 107 miles in 20 hours, but they'd need a good old sleep – certainly more than four hours – before doing it all the next day. Norwegian author Bredo Berntsen has found numerous flaws in claims made about Ernest in his biography *Des Stauermannes Mensen Ernst*.

However, some newspaper reports from the time do support aspects of Ernst's second big journey, from Germany to Greece. 'We can't dismiss Ernst outright,' writes Edward S. Sears in the excellent *Running Through the Ages*. 'He was at the very least a popular and colourful long-distance pedestrian.'

26 June

Rookie Scott Jurek wins Western States
(1999)

Scott Jurek is America's greatest ultra runner, but he hated running at first. He began purely as cross-training for the ski season. Everything changed for him in 1994, when Jurek ran his first Minnesota Voyageur 50-miler ultramarathon. He placed second and discovered a hidden taste for ultra-distance races.

In 1999 he was on the start line for Western States, the most prestigious 100-miler in the US, if not the world. He led from start to finish. It would be the first of an unprecedented seven consecutive wins.

The American has also won the 153-mile Spartathlon three consecutive times, the 135-mile Badwater Ultramarathon twice, the Hardrock 100 and many other races, with numerous course records along the way.

Jurek is known for his veganism, his primal howls on the start line and staying at the finish line to clap home the rest of the field.

27 June

Alain Mimoun dies
(2013)

In the decade after World War Two French-Algerian Alain Mimoun would have been the greatest distance runner in the world if it wasn't for the incredible Emil Zátopek.

Mimoun was a medallist at three successive Olympics, and perhaps the most inspirational French athlete of the twentieth century. He showed promise as a teenager and was lucky a shrapnel wound to the leg during the war didn't end his career before it had begun.

Successes in cross country earned him selection for France's Olympic team for London in 1948, where he finished second behind Zátopek in the 10,000m final. At the 1950 European Championship he also finished second to the Czech in the 5,000m and 10,000m finals. The same happened in the 1952 Olympic 10,000m final. And – you've guessed it – in the 5,000m final, too. But Mimoun's moment would come.

At the 1956 Olympic marathon – the French-Algerian's first – Mimoun paced it perfectly as early leaders faded away and an ageing Zátopek laboured behind. He entered the Melbourne Cricket Ground first and alone, crossing the line without another runner in sight. He waited at the finish to embrace his friend the sixth-placed Zátopek.

28 June

Gunhild Swanson makes it with six seconds to spare
(2015)

Not many 71-year-olds become internet sensations. But then not many 71-year-olds run ultramarathons. After 2015's Western States 100-mile ultramarathon a video soon went viral of Gunhild Swanson finishing the gruelling race with just six seconds to spare before the 30-hour cutoff.

The German-born ultra runner wasn't sure she would make the cut after she went off-course at mile 88 when she followed a couple of runners, instead of looking for markers. The mistake added three extra miles to her already brutal race.

The finish was Hollywood scripted with Swanson battling against the clock down the finishing straight and a huge crowd wildly encouraging her. 'I finished the sucker,' she said afterwards.

Swanson became the first person over seventy to ever finish the 45-year-old race. The mother of four and grandmother of nine has been running ultramarathons since 1987.

29 June

The 'Plucky Pedestrian' is born
(1841)

Daniel O'Leary was born in Ireland, but immigrated to the US. Edward Weston was the undisputed king of the pedestrians (or 'peds') at the time and had recently been the first to walk 500 miles in six days. The unheralded Irishman, the 'Plucky Pedestrian' as he would soon be called, challenged him to a race. The rivalry would define O'Leary's early career.

Weston eventually accepted O'Leary's challenge to an inaugural six-day race, in November 1875, to decide the 'World Championship of long-distance walking', in Chicago. Surprisingly, O'Leary won with 501 miles to Weston's 450.

Weston and O'Leary met in another famous race at the Agricultural Hall in Islington, London, in April 1877. O'Leary won again, breaking his own six-day record by covering 519 miles. The *London Standard* reported 35,000 spectators present.

The Plucky Pedestrian also began a custom of walking 100 miles in 24 hours every year when he was thirty-five, a habit he maintained up to and including his seventy-fifth year.

30 June

Eldon wins International Cross Country Championships
(1958)

Stan Eldon grew up cycling, as a grocer's delivery boy and on 100-mile trips to visit an aunt. But he was inspired by the 1948 London Olympics when, as a 12-year-old, he watched the marathon at the cinema in Windsor. He showed great promise in cross country races as a teen and in 1958 he earned his first international vest.

Distance-running in Britain was at an all-time high in the 1950s, with stars such as

Pirie, Chataway, Ibbotson and Sando. So when Stan Eldon suddenly appeared on the scene, it was surprising to see him challenging star runners with aggressive front-running – and often beating them.

By now a policeman, Eldon won the 1958 International Cross Country Championships, beating Alain Mimoun and Frank Sando into second and third respectively, then breaking the British six-mile and 10,000m records. In 1959 he recorded several more international wins. At just twenty-two he was a celebrity.

But then he began to have problems, specifically in his stomach, affecting both his training and racing, and he was never to reach those dizzy heights again. Still, while his flame burned, it burned very brightly.

1 July

Running around the world
(2008)

Danish political scientist Jesper Olsen and Australian ultramarathon runner Sarah Barnett set off from Norway today to run around the world.

Olsen, who held various national records for ultra running, had already done it once. In 2004–05 he went west–east from London, taking 22 months and making him the second verified person to have run around the globe, covering some 16,000 miles.

This time he went via the north–south route – the first known attempt to do so. GPS-tracked all the way, the pair passed through Finland, Denmark, Hungary and Turkey. But on 1 December, in Turkey, after 4,557 miles (7,334km), Barnett had to give up.

Olsen continued alone through Africa, but then had to spend more than six months recovering in Denmark due to dysentery, malaria and two operations to eliminate infections in his right arm.

He continued his run on 1 January 2011 from Punta Arenas, through South America and North America to Newfoundland, finishing at Cape Spear on 28 July 2012 and clocking up 23,000 miles.

2 July

Jules Ladoumègue sets 2,000m world record
(1931)

During the Great Depression the French needed a star and they found one in middle-distance runner Jules Ladoumègue. The sport enjoyed a huge resurgence, fuelled by newsreel coverage.

In 1928, Ladoumègue started to work with famed coach and Olympic silver medallist Charles Poulenard. He won the 1,500m at the French Championships, qualifying for the 1928 Olympics. Racing hard in the final against two Finns, Eino Purje and Harri Larva, Ladoumègue claimed a laudable second place.

In 1930, after Ladoumègue defeated 1,500m world-record holder Otto Peltzer (see 8 March and 3 July), he eyed the record of 3:51.0 himself.

With pacers on a Paris track, Ladoumègue not only bagged the record, he became the first sub-3:50 1,500m runner. He went on to set world records for the 1,000m (2:23.6) and 2,000m (5:21.8).Then he broke the mile record, with 4:09.2.

Ladoumègue was a national hero and a big favourite to win gold at the 1932 Los Angeles Olympics. But the French Federation banned him for life because he had allegedly received payments when he was meant to be an amateur. His career was over.

3 July

A German runs in the British Championships
(1926)

It was controversial when German 800m runner Otto Peltzer was announced as a runner in the 1926 British Championships. Germany had been barred from taking part in the 1924 Olympics and World War One was still fresh in collective minds. Peltzer would be up against Douglas Lowe, the British 1924 Olympic 800m champion.

From the gun, varsity runner Wilfred Tatham took an early lead, with Lowe second and Peltzer on his heels. Lowe was soon in front and passed the bell well under world record speed, but in the back straight, Peltzer made a move; the German repeatedly challenged the Englishman. Over the last 60 yards they ran side by side until Peltzer's strength was too much.

The German hit the tape in a new world record of 1:51.6.

Peltzer got an ovation from the 35,000 spectators, animosity from the Great War temporarily eclipsed by a brilliant athletic performance.

4 July

The Complete Book of Running is released
(1977)

When author Jim Fixx started running in 1967 at the age of thirty-five he weighed 240lb (110kg) and smoked two packs of cigarettes per day. Ten years later, when his book *The Complete Book of Running* was published by Random House, he was 60lb lighter and smoke-free.

The book spent 11 weeks on the top of the best-seller list and is credited with kick-starting America's fitness revolution, popularising running and demonstrating the health benefits of regular jogging.

As well as the physical benefits of running, *The Complete Book of Running* discusses its psychological benefits: increasing self-esteem, acquiring a 'high' from running, and being able to cope better with pressure and tension.

Ironically and tragically, Fixx died of a heart attack, aged fifty-two, while jogging, giving plenty of ammunition for anti-running barflys the world over. In fact he died from a congenital heart disease. His father had his first heart attack at thirty-five and died of another at forty-three.

5 July

Richard Chelimo breaks 10K world record
(1993)

In 1993, aged just nineteen, Richard Chelimo broke the world record – both junior and senior – for 10,000m, recording 27:07.91 in Stockholm. However, compatriot Yobes Ondieki broke it five days later, and Chelimo's contribution to athletics is best remembered as an unlucky or even unjust one.

At the 1992 Barcelona Olympics, with three laps of the 10,000m final to go, Chelimo was racing Morocco's Khalid Skah for gold. As they lapped Moroccan runner Hammou Boutayeb, extraordinarily, Boutayeb stuck with the front two, in order, one can only imagine, to offer support to his compatriot. Rules state a lapped runner cannot 'assist' another athlete and there was no clear advantage gained. But the crowd's spontaneous booing made it clear they perceived it as unsporting behaviour.

Skah won the race, was disqualified, but then reinstated. During the medal ceremony he was roundly booed by the crowd. Chelimo received a standing ovation.

Chelimo retired from running in his mid-twenties, despondent about not reaching the highest echelons, and died of a brain tumour at twenty-nine.

6 July

Lydiard practises what he preaches
(1950)

Placing thirteenth out of fourteen in a race, as New Zealand's Arthur Lydiard did when running the British Empire Games marathon today in 1950, doesn't suggest someone about to make a dramatic impression on the running world. But Lydiard certainly did.

He was a coach who believed effective distance running starts with 'base' training, which for serious athletes had to be 100 miles (160km) a week. The next phase was periodisation, which emphasises different aspects of training, in successive phases, building towards a target race. That was usually four to six weeks of strength work, including hill running and 'springing', to improve running economy. A maximum of four weeks of anaerobic training followed. It's pretty much the way most athletes, from marathon virgins to Kenyan record breakers, still train today.

The pioneering Kiwi coach presided over New Zealand's golden era in athletics, with Murray Halberg, Peter Snell and Barry Magee all winning medals at the 1960 Olympics. *Runner's World* magazine hailed Lydiard as the 'all-time best running coach'.

7 July

Hannes Kolehmainen wins three Olympic golds
(1912)

Finnish distance runner Hannes Kolehmainen, nicknamed 'Smiling Hannes' because of his perpetually happy face, was vegetarian, and a bricklayer by trade, but more notably the first great distance runner of the Olympic Games. He was one of the 'Flying Finns' who dominated the track in the early twentieth century.

Kolehmainen's success predated the peerless Paavo Nurmi and his biggest success was the 1912 Olympics in Stockholm. From his first heat, on 7 July, in the 10,000m, he went on to win three gold medals: for 5,000m, 10,000m and in Cross Country. The 5,000m final was the most memorable (see 10 July).

World War One almost certainly came between Kolehmainen and further success and after it he switched to the roads. He finished fourth in the 1917 Boston Marathon, and won another Olympic gold in the 1920 marathon final at Antwerp. Later he set world records at both 25km and 30km.

8 July

Moses Mosop runs a 5,000m PB
(2006)

Today Kenya's Moses Mosop ran a 5,000m PB of 12:54.46 in Paris Saint-Denis, France, though he's still 17 seconds off the world record (as of 2016). Moses is clearly an incredible runner but there's a hint of misfortune about him.

Take the 2011 Boston Marathon. Mosop and countryman Geoffrey Mutai ran what at the time were the fastest times ever recorded for a marathon – 2:03:06 and 2:03:02, respectively – shattering the world record by nearly one minute. Impressive – except that Boston doesn't meet the criteria for world record attempts.

It wasn't all bad luck for Mosop though. At the 2011 Prefontaine Classic in Oregon, he smashed Toshihiko Seko's 30-year-old 30,000m track record by over two and a half minutes, with a time of 1:26:47 and broke Seko's 25,000m record by a minute and a half. In 2011 Mosop also won the Chicago Marathon with a time of 2:05:37, creating a new course record.

9 July

Lazaro Chepkwony is full of surprises
(1954)

Kenya's Lazaro Chepkwony's appearance in the AAA Six Miles in London had spectators agog. He was the first Kenyan ever to run in Britain, but it wasn't just that. He ran barefoot on the White City cinder track, but it wasn't just that either. It was also the way he raced.

At the gun, he went off like a bullet, quickly opening up a large lead. Then, curiously, he slowed down to let the bemused runners catch him up again. Then off he shot again. Chepkwony repeated his cheeky tactic several times before, after 15 laps, the young Kenyan dropped out of the race.

The press were unimpressed, with the *Guardian* claiming he had 'bedevilled' the contest. But Chepkwony used the same tactics in the Six Miles race at the Empire Games in Vancouver that year, finishing in seventh and setting a Kenyan record.

Chepkwony made the Kenyan team for the 1956 Melbourne Olympics, but injury forced him to drop out. He was never seen again in the world of elite distance running.

10 July

A 5,000m Olympic classic
(1912)

Stockholm was lucky to witness one of the sport's classic races at the 1912 Olympic 5,000m final. France's Jean Bouin and Finland's Hannes Kolehmainen (see 7 July) were the two best 5,000m runners at the time.

Bouin, at twenty-three, wasn't considered a natural talent and relied on potent enthusiasm, yet in 1911 he'd set a 10,000m world record of 30:58.8, which wouldn't be beaten for another 10 years.

Kolehmainen, who was twenty-two, was less experienced than Bouin, though the previous year had won the English long-distance championship over four miles.

The press predicted Kolehmainen would try to run the Frenchman off his feet, but the race started slowly. This should have suited Bouin, but he surprisingly burst into the lead. Soon only Kolehmainen could stay with him

With 50 metres to go they were dead level. Their elbows knocked, there was nothing between them. Finally, it was Kolehmainen who broke the tape first, just one metre ahead of his rival in a new world record of 14:36.6 – an improvement of 24.6 seconds.

Bouin would die in World War One but later deservedly reappeared on a series of French stamps.

11 July

Louis Zamperini shocks at the US Olympic trials
(1936)

It was so hot at the 1936 US Olympic trials for Berlin, held in Randalls Island, New York, that favourite Norm Bright and several others collapsed during the race.

With a sprint finish, the unheard-of Louis Zamperini crossed the line in a dead heat (no pun intended) with American record-holder Don Lash, qualifying for the 1936 Olympics in Nazi Germany.

At nineteen years and 178 days, Zamperini is still the youngest American qualifier ever in the 5,000m. At the Olympics he placed an admirable 8th (Lash was only 13th). But running isn't the most remarkable thing about Zamperini.

During World War Two his plane crashed into the Pacific, with only three of the eleven crew surviving. Zamperini and two men lived on a raft for 47 days; one of them died, the other two were captured, imprisoned and tortured by the Japanese for two years, during which time Zamperini was officially pronounced dead by the US military.

After the war Zamperini became an inspirational speaker, the subject of two biographies and the 2014 Angelina Jolie-directed film *Unbroken*.

12 July

Scott Jurek sets an FKT on the AT
(2015)

The Appalachian Trail (AT) is a 2,200-mile (3,500km) route between Georgia and Maine in the eastern US. It crosses 14 states, with 515,000ft of elevation change. The Appalachian Trail Conservancy estimates that of 2,500 people who started the trail in 2014, only 729 finished.

In May 2015, ultramarathon runner extraordinaire Scott Jurek, who's won almost every ultra race worth running, announced at very short notice that he was going to attempt an AT FKT (Fastest Known Time). The current record, set by thru-hiker Jennifer Pharr Davis, was 46 days, 11 hours and 20 minutes. Supported by his wife Jenny in a campervan, Scott aimed for 42 days.

But in the first week he sustained two injuries and slipped off the pace. He gained some time back in Pennsylvania, but was slowed in Vermont during the state's wettest month in history.

On 12 July though, he completed the trail, breaking the old record by three hours. 'It was the hardest thing I've ever done in my life,' he admitted.

13 July

Ville Ritola wins four Olympic golds
(1924)

Known as one of the 'Flying Finns', Ville Ritola won five Olympic golds and three silvers in the 1920s. Six of those came at Paris in 1924 – still a record for an athlete winning the most athletics medals in one Games. His four golds in one Games is bettered only by his more famous compatriot Paavo Nurmi.

The stringy, versatile runner, who didn't take up the sport until he was twenty-three, declined an offer to attend the 1920 Games as he didn't feel ready. After training in the United States for several years he was certainly ready in 1924.

Ritola had already earned a gold in the 10,000m final, winning by half a lap and knocking 12 seconds off the world record. Next came the 3,000m steeplechase, where on this date, Ritola obliterated the field and bagged a new Olympic record of 9:33.6.

The next day he finished second in the 5,000m, 0.2 seconds behind Nurmi, and later earned another silver, behind Nurmi again, in the individual cross country race. Naturally Finland won team cross country gold too, and team 3,000m.

14 July

Alexis Ahlgren is born
(1887)

On 12 May 1913 Britain's Harry Green broke the world marathon record with 2:38:16. But a mere 19 days later Sweden's Alexis Ahlgren set a world best of 2:36:06 at London's Polytechnic Marathon.

The record would stand until 29 November 1914, when Italy's Umberto Blasi (see 3 June) recorded 2:38:00 at Legnano, Italy. Blasi's run, however, while recognised by the Association of Road Racing Statisticians, isn't ratified by the IAAF. According to the AARS, Ahlgren's record stood for over 17 years – until Finland's Hannes Kolehmainen (see 7 July) ran 2:32:35.

Ahlgren won a spate of marathons between 1912 and 1914, including Stockholm (four times), Malmö and Oslo. His other significant running achievement was competing in the 1912 Olympics, though he failed to finish the marathon. Curiously, before the games he was accused of being 'unpatriotic' by a Swedish sports official. Ahlgren had immigrated to the US and though he represented his country he was a member of an American sports association, when there were apparently Swedish options available. You can't please everyone.

15 July

Harry Green is born
(1886)

Harold 'Harry' Green of Sutton Harriers (London) finished third at London's inaugural Polytechnic Marathon in 1909, with 2:49:00.

The death of King Edward VII put paid to the following year's event, but Green was on the start line for 1911. He trailed the American Michael Ryan until Putney, 23 miles in, where he took the lead and finished four minutes in front of Ryan in 2:46:29.

He ran again in 1912 and finished third. The event doubled as British Olympic trials and Green ran the marathon in the 1912 Stockholm Olympics, finishing top-placed Brit in 14th.

In May 1913 Green stamped his name into the record books when he broke the world marathon record in Shepherd's Bush, London, with 2:38:16. True to his modest place in the grand scheme of things, Green's record lasted a mere 19 days.

But Green's legacy is about more than his running. During World War One he won the DCM, the Medaille Militaire and received a battlefield commission during the landing at Suvla Bay in the Dardanelles.

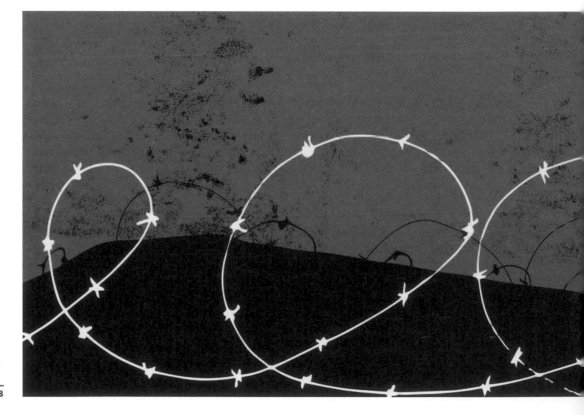

16 July

Commonwealth Games begin in Edinburgh
(1970)

The 1970 British Commonwealth Games, hosted by Edinburgh, Scotland, was a Games of firsts.

It was the first Games not to have 'Empire' in its name, and the first to use metric rather than imperial units. It was also a first Commonwealth Games for Scotland, the first to have a unique logo and the first to use synthetic all-weather tracks instead of cinders.

The marathon was a Games highlight (see 23 July), as was the 10,000m final. Neutral interest focused on Australian great Ron Clarke (see 21 February). This was his fifth major games, and he had yet to win the gold medal he coveted. Clarke was nearing retirement and running out of chances.

In the 18th lap of 25 Clarke made a break and the lead group was soon down to three, with local interest Lachie Stewart and England's Dick Taylor joining the Aussie. With two laps left, a relaxed Clarke moved out and let a weary-looking Taylor run inside him.

With 230m to go, Clarke finally took the lead. But Stewart, who'd been just behind the two all along, matched him with apparent ease. As they entered the home straight Stewart made his move and Clarke had nothing left in the tank.

17 July

The International Amateur Athletics Federation is formed
(1912)

At the end of Stockholm's 1912 Olympic Games 17 national athletics associations met and agreed there was a need for an international umbrella federation to oversee the sport. They arranged to get together again in Germany in 1913 to make it official. One of the IAAF's first tasks was to standardise and publish a list of world records.

The fledgling president was Sweden's Sigfrid Edström, later also president of the International Committee. Edström was at the centre of the controversial decision to ban 'Flying Finn' Paavo Nurmi from competing in the 1932 Olympics at his peak after he was classified as a professional athlete. Nurmi got some kind of revenge during the 1952 Olympics opening ceremony when he carried the Olympic torch in the stadium to a standing ovation, in front of Edström.

In 1982 the IAAF finally changed its rules to allow athletes to receive payment for participation in international competition. In 2001 the word 'Amateur' was dropped belatedly from the organisation's name as it became the International Association of Athletics Federations.

18 July

Arne Andersson and Gunder Hägg race again
(1944)

Arne Andersson and Gunder Hägg represent one of the classic sporting rivalries. The two Swedes had been competing for years at the mile and 1,500m. In 1943 Andersson broke Hägg's world records for 1,500 and the mile, and he beat Hägg in their first 1944 encounter over 1,500m, though Hägg won their second meeting that year. The third meeting, for an 'English Mile' race, was impossible to predict.

The duel, on this date, caught the public's imagination and Malmö stadium was full to its 14,000 capacity, with an estimated 4,000 locked outside. After three laps of close racing, on the bell the two protagonists were neck and neck. In the final straight, Andersson moved alongside and they ran in unison, even glancing at one another. From somewhere Andersson found something extra and outreached his rival to the line, winning by 0.4 of a second.

The only predictable thing about the race was a new world record, of 4:01.6 – Hägg too had run under the previous record.

19 July

Len Hurst wins the inaugural Paris Marathon
(2009)

The first Olympic marathon in Greece had been a popular success and the French wanted in on the action.

English brick-maker Len Hurst won the first event, a 40km race, in 2:31:30, some 17 minutes faster than Greece's Spiridon Louis (see 10 April) less than three months earlier. Hurst repeated the trick in 1900 and 1901, with the former being a PB of 2:26:48.

Hurst had been automatically classed as a professional runner on winning his first race and the £10 prize in 1887 as a 15-year-old. He also ran ultramarathons and indulged in pedestrianism. In 1903 he won the inaugural, 52-mile (84km) London to Brighton run (open to professionals – the first, in 1901, had been amateur only).

Hurst trained for his races by working five to six hours a day, then running six miles or more. He could apparently make 8,000 bricks and run 10 miles, all within 12 hours.

20 July

Emil Zátopek wins 10,000m Olympic gold
(1952)

After winning gold and silver medals at 10,000m and 5,000m at the 1948 Olympics, the legend of Emil Zátopek was already in the making. But everything seemed to be against him leading up to 1952.

In training the 'Czech Locomotive' collided with a tree while skiing and badly hurt his leg. Days before the Olympics he went down with flu and doctors advised him not to race. The night before his 10,000m final, an Australian journalist barged into his room at midnight, attempting to interview him. The gracious Zátopek answered his questions for 20 minutes, then realised the reporter had no room and let him stay the night. Naturally the unstoppable Zátopek still won the race the next morning, with a new world record.

His 1952 5,000m win was perhaps the most dramatic of his four Olympic golds, with an incredible last-bend manoeuvre to tear past three runners to win, setting a new Olympic record.

Then he turned up for the marathon, too, a last-minute decision and not a distance he'd run before or trained for. Zátopek crossed the line in first place with a new Olympic record (2:23:03). He'd secured an unprecedented and as yet unrepeated hat-trick of long-distance golds.

21 July

Catherine Ndereba is born
(1972)

Catherine Ndereba's Kenyan family knew they had an athlete on their hands from an early age. As a child, Ndereba would collect water for the family, often returning in double-quick time compared to her brothers and sisters.

But reaching the very top has required sacrifices greater than most athletes. In 1998, for example, aged just twenty-six, she left her husband and baby daughter for three months so she could run in competitions in the States. It paid off.

In 1999 she ran world-fastest times for the 5,000m, 12,000m, 15,000m and 10 miles – the latter two of which she bettered in 2001 and 2002 respectively.

In 2000 Ndereba won both the Boston and Chicago Marathons, setting a world record at the latter with 2:18:47. In 2003 she claimed gold at the World Championships and in 2004 bagged an Olympic silver medal. In 2007 she won a World Championships gold and in 2008 another Olympic silver.

Surely even her family daren't have predicted just how good Ndereba would become.

22 July

Saïd Aouita breaks the 5,000m world record
(1985)

Growing up in Morocco, Saïd Aouita always wanted to be a footballer. But coaches could see he had more potential as a runner and they weren't wrong. Bagging six world records in all, Aouita was so prolific at middle-distance record-breaking he may as well have been named 'Saïd Aouita breaks world record'.

After success at the Worlds and Olympics, world records came. In 1985 he ran 5,000m in 13:00.40 in Oslo, Norway, on 22 July, then 3:29.46 for the 1,500m on 23 August.

Two years later he broke the 2,000m world record with a time of 4:50.81, then six days later he broke his own 5,000m record, with 12:58.39 in Rome, the first person to go under 13 minutes.

In 1987 he set a two-mile world record with 8:14.08, then in 1989 he broke the world record for 3,000m, in Cologne, Germany, with 7:29.45.

The world's most famous Arabian sportsperson has the fastest train in Morocco named after him and he also features on an Azerbaijan postage stamp.

23 July

Ron Hill runs world's fastest marathon
(1970)

A 32-strong line-up for the 1970 Commonwealth Games marathon included reigning Commonwealth champion, Scotland's Jim Alder; the world's fastest-ever marathoner, Australia's Derek Clayton; current Fukuoka Marathon champion, Canada's Jerome Drayton; and reigning European champion, England's Ron Hill.

Clayton led for the first five miles, but Hill soon pushed ahead, then bizarrely seemed to wait for Ndoo of Kenya and Clayton. A couple of miles later he pushed ahead again.

At the halfway turnaround his lead over Drayton, Alder and Trevor Wright wasn't big. Hill passed 15 miles in 72:18 – a slower pace. Behind him, Alder passed Drayton close to the 20-mile mark, as did England's Don Faircloth.

Alder was tiring, and Hill extended his lead over the last six miles, winning with the second-fastest ever marathon time of 2:09:28.

Hill's time was just short of Clayton's record at Antwerp, but there had been suspicions about the course length in Belgium. Hill's time isn't recognised as a record by the IAAF, but is by the Association of Road Running Statisticians.

Hill would set world records at four other distances. But, rightly or wrongly, he'll never have the satisfaction of the official marathon world record.

24 July

The first 'standard' marathon
(1908)

The marathon had been wildly popular at the 1896 Olympics in Greece, with Boston's marathon starting the following year. Both events, however, were around 25 miles (40km). The 1908 Olympics in London was the first time the marathon was run over the distance of 26 miles and 385 yards it still is today.

London's marathon, too, was originally intended to be 25 miles. However, so that the grandchildren of King Edward VII and Queen Alexandra could view the start, race officials selected for its location the grounds of Windsor Castle. Those extra 385 yards would prove dramatic in 1908.

With only 27 of the 75 starters still in the race, thanks in part to a hot day and a suicidal early pace from some, Italian Dorando Pietri entered the stadium first. But he was by now delirious, he wobbled about and toppled over. Medics and officials rushed to aid Pietri, dragging him up continuously and shepherding him in the right direction. When he collapsed for a fifth time, two metres from the line, he was carried across it – to a waiting stretcher.

American John Hayes crossed the line 30 seconds afterwards, in 2:55:28, in much better shape and without any assistance.

An Italian flag was raised in victory but the Americans rightly protested. An hour later the Italian was disqualified for 'assistance' and the win awarded to Hayes.

25 July

Rob Young falls into deep sleep
(2015)

Less than two hours earlier, at 10.11 p.m. on 24 July, Rob Young had run 373 miles in 84 hours and 41 minutes, breaking the world record of continuous running without sleep set by *Ultramarathon Man* author Dean Karnazes. The Londoner had felt inspired by watching the 2014 London Marathon – and by his partner's belief that he'd never run one – and set out the very next day to ran the marathon distance. And he never really stopped.

Exactly 365 days after his first one, he completed his 370th marathon, raising lots of money for children's charities as he went. He has also completed a number of ultramarathons and the 3,080-mile Race Across USA, which he won by 30 hours.

Next he aimed at the world record for running without sleep, owned by the legendary Karnazes. Rob set off from Eastbourne at 9.30 a.m. on Tuesday, 21 July. By 10 a.m. on Wednesday morning, he had covered 136 miles, but the lack of sleep was taking effect.

'During the second 24 hours, I went through moments of darkness where everything hurt and I didn't want to go on,' Young told the *Independent*. 'I found that if you close one eye and concentrate on it, you can convince yourself that you are sleeping on that side. Even doing that for a minute makes you feel refreshed!'

After 280 miles his body started to 'feel different', he said. 'It felt like I was running barefoot – the pain shot up my legs with every stride, like my heels were being hit with a baseball bat.'

At 1.45 p.m. on Friday, he equalled Dean Karnazes' record of 350 miles non-stop running. Another mile and a new record was his. When Young finally came to a stop later that night he had himself a new world record.

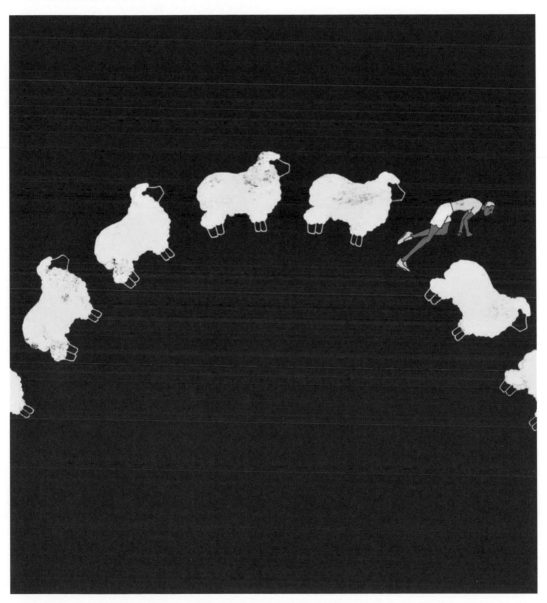

26 July

Yoko Shibui wins the San Francisco Marathon
(2009)

Japan's Yoko Shibui first caught attention by winning the 2001 Osaka Marathon in 2:23:11. In the following three years she ran in the World Championships, the Chicago Marathon and most notably scored a win and a time of 2:19:41 at the Berlin Marathon. Her PB puts her in an exclusive club of only a handful of women who've run sub-2:20 and ranks her within the top ten fastest ever.

She raced in the 2008 Beijing Olympics 10,000m, but surprisingly only placed 17th.

But Shibui was back on song the following year, running 2:46:34 to win the San Francisco Marathon.

In both 2011 and 2012 she would have been disappointed with performances at key marathons (fourth at both the Tokyo Marathon and 2012 Nagoya Women's Marathon). But with her record of bouncing back from disappointment, it will be interesting to see what's next for the Japanese marathon-running great.

27 July

Geoff Smith's Olympic 10,000m final
(1980)

Placing seventh at the 10,000m final at the 1980 Olympic Games in Moscow, while hugely impressive to us mere mortals, probably isn't what Englishman Geoff Smith would most like to be remembered for. And neither is the thing he is actually best remembered for.

His personal best time in the marathon was 2:09:08, enough to win most races back in 1983 when he set it, and still is today. But Smith's best time over 26.2 miles was when he finished second to Rod Dixon in the New York City Marathon in 1983, with one of the all-time great race finishes. Smith only lost by nine seconds, having been agonisingly caught by Dixon on mile 26.

Smith also won the Boston Marathon twice, both times with big margins (over four minutes in 1984). In another cruel twist of fate, he was the last person to win the race before prize money was introduced.

28 July

The first women's Olympic marathon
(1984)

It's staggering to think now that there wasn't a women's Olympic marathon until the 1984 Games in Los Angeles.

Joan Benoit, the first-ever women's Olympic marathon champion, initially only took to distance running to help recover from a broken leg suffered while slaloming, but took to it quickly. She entered the 1979 Boston Marathon as a relative unknown, and won, knocking eight minutes off the course record.

In 1983 she won it again, in 2:22:43, taking two minutes off the world's best time, set by Grete Waitz in the London Marathon the day before.

Training hard for the US Olympic women's marathon trials in 1984, however, Benoit seriously injured her knee on a 20-mile run. She underwent arthroscopic knee surgery just 17 days before the trials.

Benoit somehow won the trials and, three months later, won the first Olympic women's marathon in 2:24:52, finishing several hundred metres ahead of Grete Waitz, Rosa Mota and Ingrid Kristiansen.

29 July

London's 'Austerity Games'
(1948)

The post-war 'Austerity Games' in London cost just £730,000 to put on. No new venues or an Olympic village were built, and Olympians were encouraged to buy or make their own uniforms, though they were allowed extra food rations.

The Netherlands' Fanny Blankers-Koen was one of the big stories. Known as the 'Flying Housewife', the 30-year-old mother of three took home four gold medals (for the 100m, 200m, 80m hurdles and 4x100m relay).

The world also saw the emergence of Emil Zátopek. In the 10,000m final the Czech lapped all but two runners, winning by more than 300m. In the 5,000m final he was trailing by 50m at the start of the final lap but closed the gap with a sensational sprint, though he still had to settle for silver, finishing just behind Belgium's Gaston Etienne Reiff.

30 July

Delany–Ibbotson rematch
(1957)

Irishman Ron Delany's 1,500m win at the 1956 Melbourne Olympics was a sensation. He had only been running seriously for four years, had beaten local favourite John Landy (see 7 August) in an Olympic record time, and was the first Irishman to win an Olympic medal for over 20 years.

Over four seasons (1956–59) he was unbeaten in 40 indoor races in the US – one of the greatest winning streaks of all time. He set several Irish records and also beat the world indoor mile record three times, reducing it to 4:01.4.

But in July 1957, Delany raced in the Amateur Athletic Association 880 yards in London and won. In the mile race he finished second to Derek Ibbotson, who broke the world record.

Ten days later, on 30 July, Ibbotson faced Delany in a rematch in Ireland and a chance for revenge. According to Delany, the 25,000-strong home crowd were 'deranged, distracted and almost dancing with hysterical delight' over his victory against the new world record holder.

31 July

The first Badwater ultramarathon
(1987)

America's Badwater ultramarathon is hardly alone in claiming to be the hardest or most extreme event around. But it has a worthy claim.

The initial concept was a race between the lowest and highest points in the contiguous US: from the Badwater Basin in California's Death Valley to Mount Whitney's summit, at 14,505ft (4,421m).

The two points are only 80 miles apart on the map. But because of detours, around lake beds and over mountain ranges, the distance on land is some 146 miles (235km).

Due to the two mountain ranges that must be crossed, the course's cumulative elevation gain exceeds 19,000ft. But neither of these two challenges are what the event is most notorious for. The race takes place annually in mid-July, when temperatures over 49°C (120°F), even in the shade, aren't uncommon.

1 August

Steve Ovett versus Seb Coe
(1980)

Britons Steve Ovett and Seb Coe were the world's best two middle-distance runners of the early 1980s and one of the sport's greatest rivalries.

They were chalk and cheese: Coe favoured the 800m, while Ovett was stronger at 1,500m; Coe was from the north of England, Ovett from the South Coast; Coe was the more driven, Ovett the more relaxed; Coe was seen as an establishment figure, Ovett more of a rebel. In the British media Coe was the good guy, Ovett less so. He was reluctant to play the press game, while future politician and IAAF president Coe was far more accessible. Coming into the 1980 Olympics, Coe was on fire. He had broken three world records in 41 days – the 800m, mile and 1,500m.

However, in the Olympic 800m he got his tactics horribly wrong. He got boxed in and left it too late to make a move. Ovett finished three yards in front, with gold. Despite silver, Coe called the race, 'the very worst 800 metres of my 20-year career'.

Six days later they met again in the 1,500m final. The first two laps were slow, which suited Coe. With 800m to go East German Jürgen Straub picked up the pace, stretching the field. Coe wasn't going to get boxed in this time. Around the final bend, he kicked past Straub to come home four yards clear. Ovett took bronze. Each had won the event they were thought to be weaker at. For such a big rivalry, the pair rarely raced directly. They only met six times in their entire careers, with four of those meetings coming in Olympic finals.

A film, provisionally starring Harry Potter's Daniel Radcliffe as Coe, is in the pipeline.

2 August

Emil Zátopek's failed comeback
(1948)

Czech newcomer Emil Zátopek, who'd hung back in the early laps of his surprise 10,000m win, surprised again when he went immediately into the lead of the 1948 Olympic 5,000m final. Behind him Belgium's Gaston Reiff, the Netherlands' Willem Slijkhuis and Sweden's Erik Ahldén stayed in touch, biding their time. The pace was suicidal.

In the third kilometre, Zátopek's foolhardy speed began to tell and first Reiff then Slijkhuis passed him, with the Czech slipping back to 60m behind Reiff and 30m behind Slijkhuis.

Round the last bend, Reiff looked to have the race sewn up. As Slijkhuis slowed, however, he was passed by a resurgent Zátopek. Reiff, assuming victory, was also slowing. The Czech realised it and found a spare afterburner. He had 20m to make up and 100m in which to do so.

Hearing the excited crowd, Reiff looked round to see the crazed Zátopek in hot pursuit. He was spent, but terror drove him on. At the tape, Reiff had held on by just two tenths of a second – 14:17.6 to Zátopek's 14:17.8.

3 August

Gordy Ainsleigh leaves his horse at home
(1974)

This story has reached mythological proportions among ultra runners, but is often mistold. The Western States Trail Ride was a 100-mile horse race across the high mountains and deep canyons of California's Sierra Nevada.

Gordy Ainsleigh completed the ride in 1971 on bareback and without stirrups. 'From that excruciating experience,' he said, 'I learned that I could tolerate the pain of doing 70 miles on foot without previous training, when the alternative was an even more painful brutalising of my raw thighs on horseback.'

The following year's race was less painful for him, but approaching the 1973 event he realised his steed wasn't up to covering 100 miles. A friend challenged him to run it instead. And so a year later, in 1974, he did. After 23 hours and 42 minutes Gordy arrived in Auburn, proving a runner could indeed traverse the rugged 100 miles in one day.

'I suffered beyond my wildest imaginations,' he has said, 'but that was the day I ran into history by founding the Western States Endurance Run and the sport of trail ultrarunning.'

4 August

Mo's magic moment
(2012)

The Olympic 10,000m final had been won by an African at every Games since 1984. A British runner had never won a 10,000m or 5,000m gold. Though Somalia-born, Farah moved to London aged eight and at the 2008 Beijing Olympics he had failed to qualify for the 5,000m final. He moved to Oregon, US, and started working with maverick Cuba-born coach Alberto Salazar (see 19 April), running 120 miles a week and training at the same high-altitude camps as his Kenyan opponents. He became world champion, so expectation was huge for his home London Games.

Ethiopian Kenenisa Bekele (see 6 April), reigning Olympic 5,000m and 10,000m champion, led initially, with Farah waiting patiently. With five laps left Farah slipped into third behind Kenyan Moses Masai and Tariku Bekele, Kenenisa's brother.

Crowd noise grew, urging Farah to take the lead, but he showed studied discipline. The leading pack jostled for position. As tension rose, with 500m to go, he finally hit the front. No one could match his kick, and he crossed the line in 27:30:42. 'This is the best moment of my life,' said an emotional Farah.

5 August

Siegfried Herrmann's 3,000m world record
(1965)

Those who believe a flawed, underachieving or less than peerless athlete to be more interesting than the mercilessly dominant might enjoy the career of Germany's Siegfried Herrmann.

The middle- and long-distance runner was a member of the East Germany team for the 1956 and 1964 Olympics – but not for 1960. An Achilles tendon tear put paid to his 1,500m aspirations in the 1956 heats. In 1964 he placed a modest 11th in the 10,000m final. His best European Championships result was sixth at the 1,500m in 1958.

Domestically though, between 1952 and 1966 he won 26 East German titles. Before the 1956 Olympics his 1,500m PB was only 1.2 seconds off the world record, and he set a world record of 7:46.0 for the 3,000m in 1965 – even if, cruelly, it stood for less than a month.

6 August

Jack Lovelock takes Olympic gold in a classic
(1936)

Highly–strung Jack Lovelock needed a masseur to help him relax enough to sleep every night for the week leading up to the 1936 Olympics 1,500m heats and final. And no wonder. The New Zealander had set a world record for the mile in 1933, but hadn't been in such good form of late. In a race that would define a golden era of middle-distance running, his two main rivals were American WR-holder over a mile Glenn Cunningham (see 10 March) and reigning Olympic champion Italy's Luigi Beccali (see 19 November). All three had set world records, had reputations for strong finishes and had raced each other several times, with Beccali usually coming out best.

The final started late, delayed by Adolf Hitler's tardiness as he joined the 112,000 crowd. After 500m, Cunningham, who wanted to keep the race fast, went into the lead. Lovelock retaliated and they were soon one and two, with Beccali still in touch. At the bell there was some jostling and Cunningham was briefly forced off the track, with Sweden's Eric Ny taking the front. Cunningham and Lovelock were right on his shoulder.

With 300m to go – too soon to start a final kick according to standard tactics – Lovelock unexpectedly took off, with Cunningham momentarily stuck behind Ny. Cunningham and Beccali reacted, but the Kiwi's burst had caught them napping and put him three to four metres ahead.

Down the back straight, Cunningham and Beccali couldn't catch him. On the final bend they made up a small distance, but only as Lovelock relaxed for a final surge down the finish straight, which made victory his.

His revolutionary tactic had helped him set a world record of 3:47.8, the highlight of his career.

7 August

The Miracle Mile
(1954)

Roger Bannister's sub-four-minute mile in May had stirred up interest across the world. Australia's John Landy had surpassed the Briton's time in June, with 3:58.0 to Bannister's 3:58.8, making them both international celebrities. Now they were to race over a mile at Vancouver's Empire Games and it felt like the whole world was watching.

The two dealt with the pressure differently. Bannister trained in private and tried to avoid scrutiny, while Landy trained in public and seemed happy to talk to everyone. They were opposites in many ways. Bannister was pale and frail-looking, Landy tanned and muscular. Landy ran with a brisk, high-tempo gait, Bannister with a long-striding form.

Bannister was the faster finisher, so Landy knew he had to make the race quick and he had a five-metre gap over Bannister by 440m. For the next 200m or so the gap remained the same, but then Landy pushed on again, stretching to 12 metres ahead.

At halfway Bannister decided to abandon his race plan and try to catch the tearaway Aussie. Usually the third lap of a mile or 1,500m race is the slowest, but Bannister ran 59.3, to be just five metres behind Landy. At the bell they were close, but Landy pushed on again, opening up a small lead.

Round the last bend, Bannister closed on the straining Aussie. Coming into the straight, Landy thought he had broken Bannister and turned to the left to check . . . at the very moment Bannister surged by on his right.

'This tiny act of his held great significance and gave me confidence,' said Bannister. There's a statue of the moment in Vancouver.

The Englishman was finally in the lead – it was Landy who'd been broken. Bannister hit the tape in 3:58.8 – matching Landy's world record – and collapsed into the arms of an official, with Landy just 0.8 seconds behind. Officials and press swarmed on to the track in excitement, hindering other runners.

For Bannister, it was all about racing. For Landy, the time was everything. He later said, 'I'd rather lose a 3:58 mile than win one in 4:10.'

8 August

A German surprises the Africans
(1992)

Dieter Baumann was one of very few non-Africans to challenge their dominance of the 5,000m in the late 1980s and 1990s. Using his 1,500m speed down the home straight, the German was a surprise 5,000m silver medallist at the 1988 Olympics. He finished fourth at the 1991 World Championships, but unexpectedly beat 5,000m world champion Yobes Ondieki over 3,000m in Cologne. In early 1992 he narrowly missed the 3,000m world indoor record.

In the 1992 Olympic final Baumann got boxed in by four African runners in the final lap's back straight, and was only able to break clear coming into the home straight. But he launched a devastating sprint, passing each of the four runners in turn, to win an extraordinary gold.

9 August

Korean wins gold for Japan
(1936)

Korean Sohn Kee-chung became the first ever medal-winning Korean Olympian when he won gold in the marathon at the 1936 Berlin Olympics. But he competed as part of the Japanese team and was even given a Japanese name, Son Kitei. Between 1910 and 1948 Korea was part of the Japanese empire.

Sohn Kee-chung won his first marathon aged seventeen and between 1931 and 1936 won nine more. In 1935 he ran the Tokyo Marathon in 2:26:42 (see 21 March), a world best and five minutes faster than Argentina's Juan Carlos Zabala's winning time at the 1932 Olympics.

In 1936 Zabala tore off from the front, but Sohn Kee-chung sat in second, some 90 seconds behind, with England's Ernie Harper. On 19 miles an exhausted Zabala tripped, fell and soon dropped from the race. Sohn Kee-chung went on to win, with Harper second and fellow Korean Nam Sung-yong third. On the podium, the two secret Koreans had their heads bowed in what they called 'silent shame and outrage'.

Sohn Kee-chung would later coach Korean Suh Yun-bok to Boston Marathon success and in 1992 watched his protégée Hwang Young-cho win South Korea's second Olympic gold in the marathon. His autobiography is part of South Korea's school syllabus.

10 August

Juha Väätäinen wins the greatest race
(1971)

In front of an excitable home crowd, Finland's Juha Väätäinen was in a group of six runners at the final bell of the European Championships 10,000m final. They followed European record holder Britain's David Bedford, who had led from the start.

Väätäinen and East German Jürgen Haase both kicked past Bedford in a thrilling Hollywood-style last lap, going neck and neck to the line and bringing the crowd to its feet. Väätäinen just edged out Haase, having run the last 400 metres in a stunning 53.8 seconds.

Väätäinen also won the 5,000m final four days later, again with a startling last lap of 53.0 seconds.

11 August

A controversial race that got even more controversial
(1984)

Few races had been as talked about beforehand as the 1984 Olympic 3,000m final. Zola Budd had deserted South Africa, where she was born but they were banned from Olympic competition due to their apartheid regime, for Britain. Her citizenship, available due to British grandparents, was controversially fast-tracked. Anti-apartheid activists were unhappy and her first race meet as a Briton was cancelled at short notice.

Budd, who ran barefoot, had broken the women's 5,000m world record aged just seventeen and most expected gold to go to her or American world champion Mary Decker.

Decker set off at a fast pace, but Budd took over on halfway. At 1,700m, running in a pack, Decker came into contact with one of Budd's legs, knocking her slightly off balance. Not long after Budd's foot brushed Decker's thigh, causing Budd to lose balance and tumble into Decker's path. Decker's spikes came down into Budd's ankle, drawing blood. Budd kept her stride, but an off-balance Decker fell onto the infield, tearing off Budd's number. She was out of the race with a hip injury.

Budd continued to lead, but faded, finishing seventh, well outside her best time, as the crowd booed. Later she said she slowed as she couldn't face collecting a medal in front of the disapproving crowd. An IAAF jury found her not responsible for the collision.

12 August

Carlos Lopes wins marathon gold
(1984)

A week before the 1984 Olympics Portuguese marathon runner Carlos Lopes was run over by a car in Lisbon. Mind you, he had form for this kind of thing. Lopes had failed to finish his first marathon, at New York in 1982, after colliding with a spectator.

Though the Lisbon car collision should have been more serious, this time he was far more fortunate – he escaped unscathed. And at the Los Angeles Games the 37-year-old went on to win the marathon on a hot day as all the favourites gradually fell away. It was an Olympic record (2:09:21) that stood until 2008, and his country's first ever gold medal.

13 August

Fermín Cacho sets 1,500m Euro record
(1997)

Spain's Fermín Cacho burst on to the scene in 1992, but hadn't been considered a potential medallist before he won that year's Olympic 1,500m with a perfectly timed race. Things didn't go nearly so well for him at the 1996 Games in Atlanta when in the final Hicham El Guerrouj stumbled and Cacho lost ground in having to leap over the stricken Moroccan. Cacho finished second by just five metres.

He won silver again at the 1997 World Championships, but in August that year ran a European record and the third fastest ever time of 3:28.95.

It was 16 years before Mo Farah broke his European best.

14 August

Racing footmen
(1660)

It was fashionable for sixteenth-century Turkish nobleman to have couriers, or runner messengers. The Grand Turk was said to have between 80 and 100 *peirles* (lackeys or footmen), usually from Persia and often in jester-esque uniforms, including jangling bells. In *Wonders of Bodily Strength and Skill*, Guillaume Depping tells of one running 120 miles in 24 hours – they were the forefathers of the pedestrian movement.

The trend spread across western Europe in the seventeenth and eighteenth centuries, where they were often used to run ahead of carriages to look for hazards on the rudimentary (i.e. potholed) roads. Sixty miles in a day wasn't uncommon.

Noblemen took pride in the running ability of their footmen, arranging races and betting heavily. We don't know when the first footmen race was, but as of 1660, three times around London's Hyde Park was certainly a fixture each August.

A spate of footmen dying from 'consumption' (tuberculosis) after three to four years breathing in germ-laden air on the dusty roads may have led to the commonly held idea at the time, even by doctors, that running was bad for you.

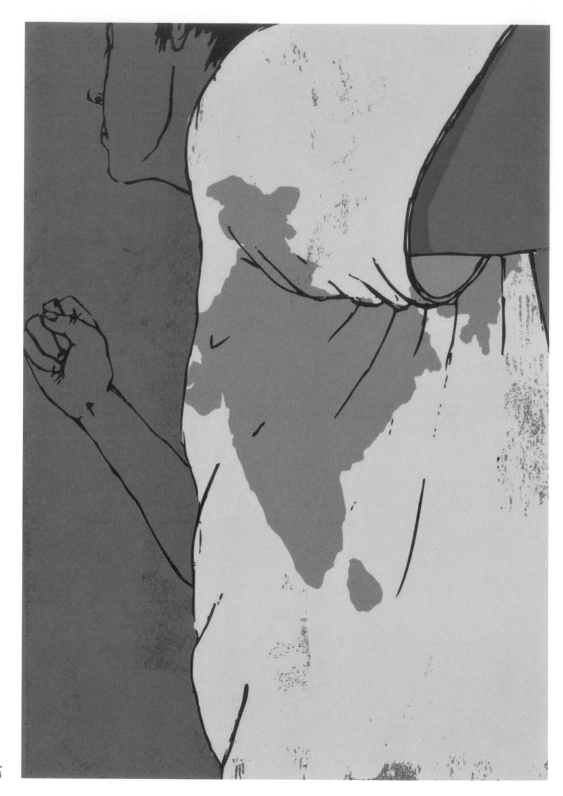

15 August

Raj Vadgama runs around India
(2014)

Raj Vadgama set off today on his 'Bharathon', a 10,000km (6,214 miles) run through 70 Indian cities. The interior designer, who also claims he holds the national record for running 1,500km from Delhi to Mumbai in 30 days, expected it to take four months to run around his country's interior. In the event it took five and a half.

He claims he ran for eight to nine hours per day, starting and finishing (on 26 January 2015) in Mumbai. However, other Indian ultra runners have voiced scepticism at his schedule that jumped from an average of 46km a day to a remarkable 111.5km ... and the fact he looked more rather than less plump by the end.

16 August

The Fastest Man Alive
(1920)

America's Charley Paddock won one of his two Olympic 100m golds on this date. Nicknamed 'The Fastest Human' and 'The Fastest Man Alive', he also placed second in the 200m final – and gained a gold from the 4×100m relay. In 1921 he ran the 110yd (slightly more than 100m) in a world record 10.2 seconds. It wasn't until 1956 that the 100m world record dropped below Paddock's time.

The former marine became famous for his jump finishes – literally jumping at the line. He was said to be largely fuelled by raw eggs and sherry and starred in five B-movies. He was portrayed by Dennis Christopher in the 1981 Oscar-winning film *Chariots of Fire* about the 1924 Olympics, where he didn't match his 1920 standards, though he still collected a 200m silver medal. Paddock died in a plane crash in World War Two.

17 August

Joseph Guillemot shocks Paavo Nurmi
(1920)

The 1920 Olympic 5,000m final is remarkable in that Finland's Paavo Nurmi didn't win it. The Flying Finn won three other golds at these Games, but he only finished second here as Joseph Guillemot beat him. The Frenchman's victory was all the more impressive as his lungs had been severely damaged by mustard gas in World War One, his heart was located on the right side of his chest and he was a pack-a-day smoker.

Nurmi had tried to exhaust his two main rivals, the Swedes Eric Backman and Rudolf Falk, and after three laps only Guillemot was still with the Finn. On the final curve the Frenchman overtook the tiring Nurmi, finishing over four seconds ahead of the runner who would win five golds at the next Olympics, including for 5,000m.

Guillemot had his sights on a double gold, but the 10,000m final was moved forward at the request of Belgium's King Albert – something Joseph only found out at short notice after a large lunch. He battled his bloated belly and shoes two sizes too big to finish second, behind Nurmi. Then he vomited at the awards ceremony.

18 August

Ian Sharman attempts the Grand Slam of Ultrarunning
(2013)

Britain's Ian Sharman winning America's Leadville Trail 100 in the Colorado Rockies, on this date, is impressive but not extraordinary in the grand scheme of things. However, US-based Sharman was attempting the Grand Slam of Ultrarunning, namely racing four prestigious 100-mile races (Leadville, Western States, Vermont 100 Mile Endurance Run and Utah's Wasatch Front 100 Mile Endurance Run), not only in the same year, but within ten weeks. Only about a dozen runners manage to complete the Grand Slam each year. Sharman went on to set a new overall record time of 69:49:38.

The Brit also holds the record for the fastest 100 miles on a trail, with 12:44 recorded at Rocky Raccoon in 2011. Almost as impressively, he's broken 10 world records for running marathons in the fastest time while dressed in various costumes.

19 August

Anton Krupicka wins Leadville 100
(2006)

American Anton Krupicka ran his first marathon aged twelve. In college he was clocking up 200-mile weeks and he dropped out of university to become a professional mountain and ultramarathon runner (though he does now have two BA degrees).

Known for his trademark beard, long hair, big glasses, cap and apparent allergy to wearing a top, Kupricka's biggest achievements have been twice winning the gruelling Leadville 100 (2006 and 2007), despite nearly missing the start of the 2006 race 'because I was taking too much time in the bathroom'. He also beat the existing course record when placing second to Geoff Roes at Western States in 2010, plus the Rocky Raccoon 100 Miler and many other (mostly US) race wins.

20 August

Usain Bolt does the triple
(2008)

On this date, Usain Bolt won the 2008 Olympic 200m in Beijing's Bird's Nest, with a world record time of 19.30 seconds, breaking Michael Johnson's 1996 record – and just hours before his twenty-second birthday too.

The nominative determinist had already won 100m gold, breaking his own world record in the process, with 9.69, despite seeming to ease up at the line (and having a shoelace undone).

Then he and his Jamaican team-mates took three-tenths of a second off the best 4x100m time, to make Bolt the first man to win all three events in world record times.

At the 2012 Olympics he won all three events again.

21 August

Irishman Thomas Conneff takes over the US
(1895)

Back in the late nineteenth century many of the top runners enacted a style of running with arms straight down by their sides, something Irish amateur Thomas Conneff did to good effect in the US. On this date he ran a three-quarter mile in 3:02.8, a record which stood until 1931.

He dominated the mile in America – including the fastest amateur mile of the century with 4:15.6 – and won the national 10-mile championship four years in a row from 1888. All despite apparently not liking training, though Conneff did wisely get himself a coach. Neither his mentor nor he believed in trying to pace themselves evenly throughout a race, rather they simply started out hard and when the going got tough tried to hang on. It was the common tactic of the time and it worked for Conneff's mile world record anyway.

22 August

Paul Tergat finally beats Haile Gebrselassie
(1997)

This was the day Kenya's Paul Tergat finally beat his great nemesis Haile Gebrselassie. Not in person, but he would have gained some satisfaction in breaking the Ethiopian's 10,000m world record, clocking 26:27.85.

The intense rivalry between Tergat and his friend Gebrselassie defines his career. The Kenyan lost narrowly to him in both the 1996 and 2000 Olympic 10,000m finals – the latter by nine/hundredths of a second, in one of *the* great races. He also finished second behind Gebrselassie at the 1997 and 1999 World Championships. Gebrselassie also meanly took back the 10,000m record in June 1998.

Tergat turned his focus to the marathon and got a small victory over his rival at the 2002 London Marathon, placing second to Gebrselassie's third. Tergat went on to hold the marathon world record from 2003 to 2007, with 2:04:55, set at Berlin, before – naturally – it was bettered by Gebrselassie.

23 August

Walter George sets a mile record
(1886)

Walter George's unorthodox training techniques included what he called '100-up' – running on the spot with high knee-lifts and 'springing', and taking baths in brine.

The Briton set numerous world records as an amateur and turned professional to challenge the mile record-holder William Cummings. The two would enjoy a long rivalry, with George defeating him in several highly publicised races (see 24 March).

In a race with Cummings that left him collapsed in the grass 60 yards from the finish, George set a 4:12.75 world record for the mile that wasn't broken for nearly 30 years by either amateur or professional.

24 August

Sammy Wanjiru changes the way marathons are run
(2008)

The 2008 Olympic marathon in Beijing was only Sammy Wanjiru's third and he only knew one way to run. The 21-year-old Kenyan shot to the front of the 95-strong field and set a blistering pace. The standard way to run a championship marathon (as opposed to a potentially world-record breaking city one) was usually a slower, more tactical, race, partly because they tended to be hotter events.

As you could almost hear the sound of race plans being torn up, some runners went with him, while others gambled on him blowing up and stayed put.

Wanjiru passed 10km in 29:25, halfway in 1:02:34. He kept pressing as his chasers took it in turns to drop off. Even when it was clear gold was his, his pace was unrelenting. He finished with an Olympic record by three minutes, in 2:06:32.

Most major marathons have been run the Wanjiru way ever since.

25 August

Ultra-Trail du Mont-Blanc
(2003)

The Ultra-Trail du Mont-Blanc (UTMB) has become Europe's most competitive and popular 100-mile race. Starting and finishing in Chamonix, it's equally renowned for its gruelling trails through the French, Italian and Swiss Alps, on the popular Trail du Mont-Blanc hiking trail with a height gain of 10,000m, as it is for the Eurotrash razzamatazz and relatively 'gourmet' aid stations, (well there's more than one type of cheese anyway). Crowds line the trails right up into the mountains, cheering runners on.

While elite runners complete it in around 22 hours, many will take up to 47 hours to return to Chamonix – a heroic feat of stubbornness and endurance. The 2,500-plus places are so popular it could sell out twice over and a ballot system decides places.

Hundred-mile trail ultramarathons have a longer history in the US, but every August the best male runners from across the Atlantic come to France to try and win – and so far, they haven't. American Rory Bosio, however, has won the women's race twice.

26 August

Munich Olympics opens
(1972)

Sadly, these Games were overshadowed by an act of terrorism that left 11 of the Israeli Olympic team dead. After a pause of 34 hours, the Games resumed in an effort to show defiance of terrorism.

In the marathon, Frank Shorter, who fittingly was born in Munich, became the first American in 64 years to win – amid some confusion. As Shorter neared the stadium, German student Norbert Sudhaus covertly joined the race wearing a track uniform. As he ran the last kilometre, the crowd cheered him, thinking he was a competitor, before officials realised the hoax and Sudhaus was escorted away.

Arriving seconds later, Shorter was perplexed to see someone ahead of him and to hear the boos and catcalls – meant for the prankster. It was the third time an American had won the Olympic marathon and in each instance the winner didn't enter the stadium first.

Elsewhere on the track Finland's Lasse Virén won the 5,000m and 10,000m (the latter after a fall – see 3 September), a feat he repeated in the 1976 Olympics.

27 August

Ashprihanal Pekka Aalto is born
(1970)

For three years in a row, Finland's Ashprihanal Pekka Aalto ran all three of Sri Chinmoy Self-Transcendence Races. That's the Six-Day Race, which he has won three times, the 700 Mile Race and the 3,100 Mile Race.

Aalto has won the 3,100 Mile Race, the world's longest-known ultramarathon event, eight times, including with a new record of 40 days 9 hours and 6 minutes in 2015 (see 14 June).

Aalto averaged 76.776 miles (123.6km) per day, the equivalent to running nearly three marathons, consecutively for over 40 days. The course is simply 5,649 laps of the same tiny block in Queens, New York.

The Finn has occasionally finished second or third in Self-Transcendence, but usually wins, and is never off the podium.

28 August

Super Swede Anders Gärderud is born
(1946)

Sweden's Anders Gärderud was eliminated in both the 800m and 1,500m heats at his first Olympics in 1968. So he chose to focus on the 3,000m steeplechase. He was hotly tipped for 1972, but was again eliminated in the heats – as he was for the 5,000m too. But only seven days later, he set a 3,000m steeplechase world record of 8:20.8. He broke the record twice more in 1974.

Finally, in 1976, Gärderud got his moment, with an Olympic gold medal and another world record at the 3,000m steeplechase.

He still holds Sweden's 5,000m record.

29 August

Bernard Lagat wins 1,500m gold
(2007)

Middle- and long-distance runner Bernard Lagat won the 1,500m final at the World Championships in Osaka today in 2007. By the end of the championships, the Kenyan-born American citizen had become the first athlete to be world champion in both the 1,500m and 5,000m at the same championships. Though both Hicham El Guerrouj and Paavo Nurmi have done so at the Olympic Games. Lagat is a 13-time medallist in World Championships and Olympics, including five gold medals – two 1,500m Olympic medals were for his native Kenya before changing his national affiliation to the US. He's the first American to win a World Championship medal of any kind in the 5,000m.

Lagat donated all his bonus earnings during the 2010 indoor season to the Haiti Relief Fund.

30 August

Egg white and brandy lead to a wobbly athlete
(1904)

Thomas Hicks won the gold medal in the marathon at the 1904 Olympics in St Louis, despite some dubious nutritional choices. On 18 miles the British-born American asked for water but received a wet sponge to suck on and, thoughtfully, an egg white. A few miles later, he received two eggs, a sip of brandy and a small dose of strychnine sulphate (considered to be a stimulant at the time but later used as a rat poison).

Over the final two miles of the hilly route he was given two more eggs and two more shots of brandy. He finished the race in first place, though had to be helped across the finish line and wasn't stable and coherent enough to receive his trophy.

Fred Lorz had crossed the line ahead of him, but had received a lift in a car from mile 9 to mile 20. When he was disqualified he claimed it was all a joke. Lorz would win the Boston Marathon the following year, apparently fairly.

31 August

The original Olympic Games
(776 BC)

Ancient Greece's original Olympic games took place between 6 August and 19 September during a religious festival honouring Zeus, the king of the gods. They were staged every four years for several centuries at Olympia, a valley near the city of Elis. Several other Greek cities had festivals including athletic events, but Olympia's become the biggest.

Koroibos, a cook, won the 200-yard foot race, the only running event initially. A longer foot race was added in 724 BC, and sometime later there were four distances, with the *hoplitodromos* – which roughly translates as 'race of soldiers' – event requiring runners to wear armour and carry a shield.

Race winners had statues made of them, poems composed in their honour and often received cash and free meals for life from their native cities. False-starting runners could be whipped with a forked stick.

SEPTEMBER

1 September

Daniel Komen sets 3,000m world record
(1996)

Kenya's Daniel Komen was another world-class distance runner regularly eclipsed by Ethiopia's Haile Gebrselassie – except for an unprecedented purple patch between 1996 and 1997.

The two-year spell – where he ran as if under a spell – saw Komen win several highly competitive races, including a World Championship 5,000m gold in 1997, and break numerous world records. Still no one has matched his feat of running two consecutive sub-four-minute miles (see 17 May), or broken the record that started it all off.

On this date in Rieti, Italy, the Kenyan ran a 3,000m world record time of 7:20.67, breaking Algerian Noureddine Morceli's two-year-old record of 7:25.11.

In February 1998 he also set the indoor record for the same distance, clocking 7:24.90 in Budapest – the penultimate record of his remarkable peak.

2 September

Surprising tactics in the Olympic 5,000m final
(1960)

The 12 runners stayed together for the first seven laps of the 1960 Olympic 5,000m final in Rome's fittingly re-named Olympic Stadium. Australian Dave Power surged ahead on the eighth lap, but soon eased up and was caught by a pack of seven. Just as the pace eased a little, New Zealander Murray Halberg took off, hitting the front with three laps to go. He was coached by legendary compatriot Arthur Lydiard (see 6 July) and they had an audacious plan.

'I improved my place to second in the field,' Halberg recalls in his autobiography. 'I settled there momentarily, gathered my strength. Then with all I had, I sprinted.'

With two and a half laps to go, Halberg recorded a 61-second lap and was 20m ahead of the field. His pace looked premature or even suicidal to spectators and runners alike, most of whom didn't respond to his breakaway. Convention had it that it was way too soon to put the burners on. Halberg and Lydiard thought otherwise.

The New Zealander's pace inevitably dropped slightly. But at the bell he still had a 15-metre lead. That final lap was a desperate fight to hold his advantage and he was constantly looking over his shoulder to East Germany's Hans Grodotzki. But Halberg held on to win by eight metres, in 13:43.4.

Four of the first six runners had run PBs. It was Halberg's finest moment as a runner.

3 September

Lasse Virén falls in the 10,000m Olympic final
(1972)

The Flying Finns may have dominated the track between the two world wars, but in 1972 Finland had not won a single gold since 1936. Finn Lasse Virén had made the Olympic 10,000m final, but wasn't a favourite. At the previous year's European Championships on home soil in Helsinki the policeman had placed 17th. He had, however, set a world record for the rarely–run two miles a few weeks before the Olympics.

Britain's Dave Bedford led the race, keeping it ahead of world record time. But just before halfway several runners collided, including Virén and one of the favourites, America's Frank Shorter. Tunisia's Mohamed Gammoudi was sent cartwheeling into the infield and lay motionless. But the Finn got up and rejoined the race.

A lap later the relative novice was back with the lead pack. On 6,000m he moved to the front. Then race favourite Miruts Yifter of Ethiopa took the lead, but Virén took it back. With 600m left, the Finn went for it and at the bell he led by three metres. No one could match his final lap and he won with a new world record of 27:38.4 – knocking one second off Ron Clarke's seven-year-old effort.

He would win the 5,000m too, and win them both again in 1976, for an unprecedented distance running double-double.

4 September

Abel Kirui wins marathon World Championships again
(2011)

Kenya's Abel Kirui entered the 2006 Berlin Marathon as a pacemaker but somehow managed to finish ninth overall. He did better the following year when he finished second to legendary Haile Gebrselassie as the Ethiopian set a new world record. Kirui's 2:06:51 in that race remains his PB.

In 2009 he finished first in the marathon at the World Championships, beating compatriot and Olympic silver medallist Emmanuel Mutai (see 12 October). Though at major city marathons he has failed to live up to the promise he showed in Berlin in 2007, he defended his world title at the 2011 World Championships, only the third man to do so, and won silver at the 2012 Olympics, proving championship marathon racing is his forte.

5 September

Men versus horses
(1880)

At the height of six-day pedestrian racing's popularity in the late 1800s, stars of the scene Edward Weston (see 22 February) and Daniel O'Leary (9 June) had a disagreement about whether horses might have superior endurance qualities to men. Weston backed men, O'Leary their equine companions. There was only one way to decide the debate.

A six-day race between seven men and 11 horses took place in San Francisco in October 1879. A horse won, but Weston argued that the men weren't elite-level runners. So an O'Leary-sponsored six-day rematch was arranged in September the following year, this time with five horses and 15 runners, attracted by the $3,000 prize money.

The four-legged racers led initially, but on the fifth day Michael J. Byrne hit the front. However, on the final day the leading horse died while resting in his stable, leaving Byrne with something of an empty victory, despite his 578 miles. A horse finished second with 563 miles.

Every June since 1980, Llanwrtyd Wells in Wales has hosted a 22-mile race between man and horse, where man has been twice victorious.

6 September

Michel Jazy's Olympic 1,500m silver
(1960)

After he failed to progress from the 1,500m heats at the 1956 Olympics, Frenchman Michel Jazy eschewed interval training on a track for running in natural surroundings. Australian Herb Elliott was clear favourite for 1960 gold.

But France's other Michel – Bernard – led for the first 800m, at world record pace. Then Elliott took over, running the third lap in a blistering 56 seconds. There was no matching the Australian, who had a 15m lead into the last 100m and set a new world record of 3:35.6. Behind him though, Jazy, who wasn't expected to get close to the podium, was having the race of his life. He outpaced the Hungarian István Rózsavölgyi and smashed his PB, with 3:38.4, to claim silver. 'I was wonderfully lucid,' he said in his autobiography of his finest Olympic moment.

The runner, a major celebrity in France, was one of the greatest and most elegant runners of the 1960s, setting nine world records.

7 September

First female sub-three-hour marathoner born
(1942)

In the early 1970s, there was still plenty of hostility towards the idea of women running marathons – 1,500m was the longest female race at most official meets.

On 31 August 1971, however, Australian Adrienne Beames (born on this date) is thought to have become the first woman to run a sub-three-hour marathon, with 2:46:30 in Werribee, Victoria, Australia. Cold and rainy weather seemingly didn't hinder her as she finished fifth overall with a time significantly faster than the 3:01:42 set three months earlier by American Beth Bonner (see 19 September).

Beames' attempts to enter marathons had been rebuffed and her coach arranged an event especially. Even the Victorian Women's Amateur Athletic Association refused to verify the time and her result isn't recorded by the IAAF as an official record.

However, her performance inspired other women and a month later Bonner and fellow American Nina Kuscsik would both run the New York City Marathon in under three hours.

Beames later also held women's world bests for 5,000m and 10,000m.

8 September

Pyotr Bolotnikov wins Olympic 10,000m gold
(1960)

Though he made little impact at the 1956 Olympics, in 1957 Pyotr Bolotnikov caused a shock by beating his legendary compatriot Vladimir Kuts over 10,000m and becoming national champion. He was building up perfectly for the 1960 Olympics in Rome, where the 10,000m final was textbook racing from the Russian. He controlled the race, starting a breakaway just before the bell and finishing five seconds ahead of East Germany's Hans Grodotzki and Australia's Dave Power, in 28:32.2 – only two seconds from Kuts' world record. British newspaper *The Times* said Bolotnikov 'ran a race of courage, confidence and intelligence'.

9 September

Mike Morton runs for 24 hours
(2012)

In 2012, two months after winning the notorious 135-mile Badwater Ultramarathon, US Army Master Sergeant Mike Morton won the 24-Hour World Championship in Katowice, Poland, setting a new US record.

On a one-mile loop through a park, Morton led the entire race, running 172.457 miles (277.54km) – the former US record was Scot Jurek's 165.705 miles, set in 2010.

His goal for two years had been to break the US record. His plan was to hit 50 miles between 6:05 and 6:15, 100 miles in 13:11 to 13:30, then hit 150 miles by the 21-hour mark. The first 50 miles were the worst, said Morton. 'About two hours into it the ball of my foot started going numb.' He changed his shoes, but it took him another three hours to feel like he was running well again. He made his 50-mile time target by two seconds. The second 50 miles were relatively uneventful, and he sped up to reach his 100-mile goal early, at 13:10. At the 20-hour mark, Morton was on target to break Jurek's US record by six miles. When he hit it, the soldier's crew urged him to try and set a record that would be out of reach for a while.

He finally broke the US record by nearly seven miles, but was over 16 miles off the world record of 188.590 miles (303.5km) set by the legendary Yiannis Kouros in 1997.

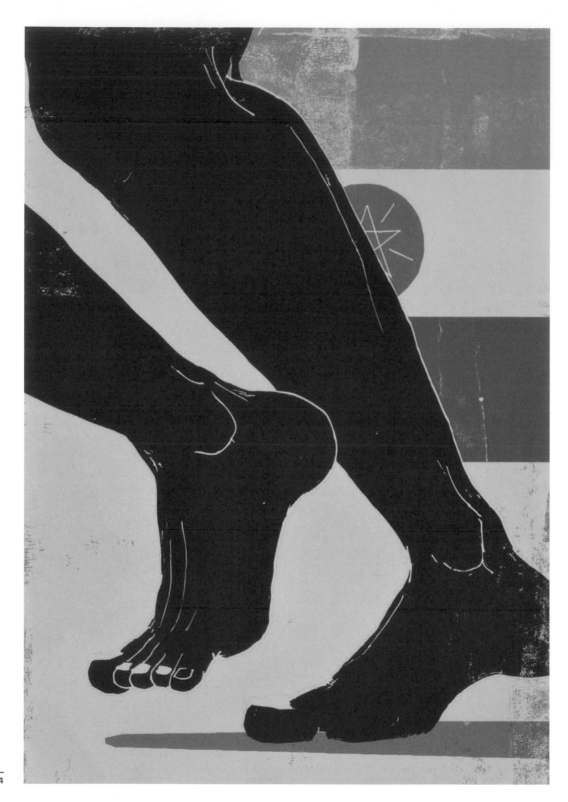

10 September

The first black African to win Olympic gold
(1960)

Ethiopia's Abebe Bikila, a member of Emperor Haile Selassie's bodyguard, was a last-minute replacement in the marathon for injured Wami Biratu, boarding the plane to Rome as it was about to leave. In Italy he quickly wore through his one pair of running shoes and a pair donated by Adidas didn't fit well, causing blisters. So he went barefoot, which only added to the widespread view of Bikila as a no-hoper – he was described by one commentator during the race as 'that unknown Ethiopian'.

By 20km only Moroccan Rhadi Ben Abdesselam remained with Bikila. The Ethiopian had been warned Rhadi, supposed to be wearing number 26, was the one to watch and Bikila spent much of the race searching for his number. But Rhadi was in fact wearing 185 – and could be found right next to him.

As would become his trademark, Bikila increased the pace on 20km. Yet it wasn't until the final 500m that he finally pulled away conclusively. Finishing in 2:15:16, Bikila shattered Emil Zátopek's Olympic record by nearly eight minutes.

His victory came less than 25 years after Italian dictator Benito Mussolini had invaded Ethiopia after a brutal colonial war, but also marked the rise of East African middle- and long-distance runners and was the defining moment of the 1960 Olympics.

11 September

Thomas Wessinghage wins Euro 5,000m final
(1982)

Even though he'd been an international middle- and long-distance runner for a decade, West Germany's Thomas Wessinghage had to wait until the age of thirty for his finest sporting moment.

In 1980 he set a German record of 3:31.58 at 1,500m, even if in the same race Ovett set a world record of 3:31.36. Wessinghage missed a great chance of a potential Olympic medal that year as West Germany joined the US-led boycott of the Moscow Olympics.

At the 1982 European Championships in Athens he decided to run the 5,000m because he'd grown weary of losing to British athletes Steve Ovett and Seb Coe (see 1 August) at his favoured 1,500m. The conservative pace of the final favoured Wessinghage. He was in good form, having recently set a European 2,000m record. With around 250m to go, Wessinghage started his final kick, moving into a decisive lead. He'd stretched it to five metres by 4,800m and almost doubled it by 4,900m. In crossing the line first he beat British world-record holder David Moorcroft, who finished third.

12 September

Jesse Owens is born

(1913)

Austria-born leader of Nazi Germany Adolf Hitler hoped to use the 1936 Berlin Olympics to showcase the ideology of Aryan racial supremacy. But as the Games have since been nicknamed 'the Jesse Owens Olympics', you could say it didn't quite go to plan.

African-American Owens, the grandson of Alabaman slaves, arrived in Berlin already a star, and throngs of fans, many of them young girls, crowded around him, some with scissors trying to get snippets of his clothing.

In one of the greatest performances in Olympic history, Owens won gold for 100m, 200m, 4×100m relay and the long jump – a feat only once matched, by compatriot Carl Lewis at the 1984 Olympics.

Hitler was said to be annoyed, but a myth spread that he snubbed Owens. In fact Owens felt he was treated better in Germany than in the US, and shown more respect by Hitler than by his own president Franklin D. Roosevelt. 'I tell you, Hitler did not snub me . . . Remember that [Roosevelt] did not send me a message of congratulations because people said he was too busy.'

In Germany black and white athletes shared the same transport and hotels, while the US was still segregated, and Owens faced discrimination and limited job opportunities despite his stardom. He was reduced to participating in stunt races against dogs, motorcycles and horses during breaks at football and baseball matches.

Outside Berlin's Olympic Stadium there's now a Jesse Owens Way.

13 September

The inaugural New York City Marathon

(1970)

Now the largest marathon in the world, with 50,304 finishers in 2013 and usually around two million spectators, the New York City Marathon has come a long way. In 1970 just 127 competitors ran several loops around Central Park as about a hundred spectators watched Gary Muhrcke win in 2:31:38.

'I only signed up 15 minutes before the race,' said the 30-year-old New York fireman. 'I hadn't trained for three weeks because of a leg injury, but I felt OK, so I decided to run.' The entry fee of $1 was reflected in the prizes of cheap watches and recycled baseball and bowling trophies.

Nowadays the race takes place in November, is one of the prestigious six World Marathon Majors and the course travels through the five boroughs of New York City.

14 September
A marathon drinking session
(1660)

Held every September in France's Médoc region, near Bordeaux, the Marathon du Médoc may be 26.2 miles long, but that's where the similarity with most other marathons ends.

The route winds through scenic vineyards where, instead of water stations, participants are offered and expected to taste up to 23 glasses of wine – while also stuffing themselves with local specialities such as oysters, foie gras and cheese. Fancy dress is compulsory. The cut-off is a generous six and a half hours and every finisher gets a bottle of wine.

Though it was meant to take place in 1984, the first official race didn't happen until 1985. 'There were some problems with administration – they're very strict about health and safety over here,' said marathon president Vincent Fabre.

15 September
A 5,000m classic
(1962)

The 5,000m final of the 1962 European Championships looked very competitive. Russian Pyotr Bolotnikov (see 8 September) would have been a favourite had his heat not been just 24 hours after his 10,000m final. Expectations lay on Poland's Kazimierz Zimny, France's Michel Bernard and Britain's barefoot Bruce Tulloh. On paper Tulloh had the best speed in the field (having run an 8:33.4 two miles that year), but had recently been beaten by Zimny.

Surprisingly, Bolotnikov forced the early pace. He still led after 3,000m, but slowed noticeably as Czechoslovakia's Miroslav Jurek took over. With 800m to go, Bernard led, followed by Tulloh, Zimny and compatriot Boguszewicz, and France's wonderfully named Robert Bogey. 'Nobody seemed to have much idea of what to do,' wrote Tulloh in his autobiography. When Tulloh took off with 700m to go, only Bernard and Zimny had enough energy to go with him.

At the bell Tulloh had a five-metre lead. Could Zimny catch the Briton? Not when the barefoot runner covered the last lap in 57.4. Tulloh broke the tape with 10 metres to spare, while remarkably Bolotnikov clawed his way back to third.

16 September

Jürgen Haase defends European 10,000m title
(1969)

Trained by pioneering New Zealand coach Arthur Lydiard (see 6 July), East German 10,000m specialist Jürgen Haase is known equally for things that occurred off the track.

He won gold at both the 1969 and 1966 European championships, and silver in 1971, but a scandal erupted in 1966. Haase's teammate Jürgen May persuaded him – with the help of US$500 – to wear Puma running shoes rather than his usual Adidas ones (the two sportswear companies were formed by feuding German brothers).

The episode became a minor political scandal and both athletes were initially banned from the national team. Haase was pardoned, but May was forced to defect to West Germany to compete internationally. When May was selected for the 1969 European championships, East German officials successfully protested, which in turn led to West Germany boycotting the meet where Haase won his second gold medal.

17 September

Dean Karnazes runs 50 marathons in 50 days
(2006)

American former marketing executive Dean Karnazes began his self-created and much-publicised challenge to run 50 marathons in 50 consecutive days in 50 US states.

Before he set off, Karnazes performed a lactate threshold test in Colorado. 'They said the test would take 15 minutes, tops,' he told the *Guardian*. 'Finally, after an hour, they stopped the test. They said they'd never seen anything like this before.'

The *Ultramarathon Man* author started with the Lewis and Clark Marathon in St Louis and finished with the New York City Marathon on 5 November – clocking 3:00:30. Eight of the runs were conventional marathons, but as most events are on weekends Karnazes ran marathon courses in each state on weekdays.

Karnazes is nearly as famous for arranging for pizzas to be delivered to him mid-run as he is for covering vast distances. He once said, 'There's magic in misery,' and treats blisters by popping them and slathering them with glue.

18 September

Was Harry Hutchens 'hog fat'?
(1887)

The day before the hotly anticipated sprint race between Britons Harry Hutchens – generally considered the fastest sprinter in the second half of the nineteenth century – and newcomer Harry Gent, a rumour circulated that Hutchens was 'hog fat'. Hutchens had something of a mixed reputation (see 29 October) already.

When the Londoner returned to Britain from a tour of Australia, his new rival, Gent from Darlington, awaited. A 120-yard race was arranged for the 'Championship of the World', with £200 prize money and over 15,000 paying spectators at Lillie Bridge. But a rumour that Hutchens was uninterested got out and Gent's supporters bet heavily on the outcome.

When Hutchens appeared, looking as fit as ever, Gent's entourage panicked at the idea of losing their money. They kidnapped their man and fled. Sensing an angry crowd, both Hutchens and the promoter followed suit.

The furious crowd demanded their money back and their frustration led to a burned-down arena.

19 September

The other 'first' women's sub-three-hour marathon
(1971)

As far as those who distrust Australian Adrienne Beames' marathon time, apparently recorded a month earlier (see 7 September), are concerned, American Elizabeth 'Beth' Bonner was the first woman to run a sub-three-hour marathon. She recorded a world record of 2:55:22 at the 1971 New York City Marathon, aged just nineteen.

In May the same year Bonner had run a marathon in Philadelphia in 3:01:42, a world best.

She died at the age of forty-six after being hit by an 18-wheel truck while cycling. An annual 5K run in Arthurdale, West Virginia, is named in her honour.

20 September

Ronaldo da Costa breaks ten-year record
(1998)

When Brazil's Ronaldo da Costa ran 2:06:05 to win the 1998 Berlin Marathon he also broke a world record that had stood for 10 years.

Running the second half in an unprecedented 1:01:23, in only his second marathon, his feat was labelled 'one of the most surprising performances in marathon history' by *The New York Times*. The Brazilian smashed Ethiopian Belayneh Dinsamo's record of 2:06:50, which had gone unchallenged for the third longest time span since the first marathon at the 1896 Olympics. The world best made da Costa an instant celebrity in Brazil, to rival another Ronaldo, the footballer.

The youngest of 11 children, the running Ronaldo had dropped out of school early to work: he carried bricks at a factory, farmed rice, beans and corn, among other manual jobs.

Da Costa was the world record holder for just over a year, when Moroccan-American Khalid Khannouchi (see 2 May) ran 2:05:42 at Chicago. Da Costa never showed world-class form again, admitting he'd lost motivation.

21 September

The Loneliness of the Long Distance Runner
(1962)

Based on his 1959 short story of the same name, the screenplay for *The Loneliness of the Long Distance Runner*, released on this date, was written by British writer Alan Sillitoe.

For protagonist Smith, 'Running had always been made much of in our family, especially running away from the police.' Smith spends much of the story in a young offenders' institution, but realises he still has a level of freedom when picked to run races for the prison.

Of running, he says: 'It's the only risk I take and the only excitement I ever get, flying flat out [. . .], crazy like a cut-balled cockerel'. A theme is the joy of running without purpose instead of running to race. It's also an unmistakably political story, with comments on British society.

22 September

First women's marathon World Championships
(1974)

Forty-five women from seven nations travelled to Waldniel, West Germany, to compete in the first International Women's Marathon Championship, a decade before the race was included at the Olympics.

Germany's Christa Vahlensieck and France's Chantal Langlacé gave Liane Winter some competition on the four-lap course, but the German crossed the finish line first in a European record time of 2:50:31.

A year later she set a world best at the Boston Marathon with 2:42:24 (even if she was aided by a 25mph tailwind) and became the first woman from outside the US to win it. At the finish line, via her translator, her first words were to ask for a beer.

Winter, who was an accountant at the Volkswagen factory in Wolfsburg, also won the Budapest, Maryland and Schwarzwald Marathons – the latter three times.

23 September

The Chicago Marathon is born
(1905)

While most major city marathons seem to have started with the apocryphal seven runners and even fewer spectators, the first Chicago Marathon attracted a reported 100,000 spectators. The huge crowd watched a big upset with Rhud Metzner coming from behind to steal a late victory over hotly tipped Louis Marks.

It wasn't until American Frank Shorter's 1972 Olympic marathon win and the subsequent popularity of the New York City Marathon that Chicago really came of age with participant levels close to its rivals.

Prize money in the 1980s attracted elite runners and Britain's Steve Jones won here in 1984 with a world record of 2:08:05 –

he ran without a watch and didn't know he was on course to break it until two miles from the end. Jones won again the following year, finishing just two seconds short of his world best time. Duels between Joan Benoit Samuelson and Ingrid Kristiansen were another highlight.

The world record has been set at Chicago four times: by Jones (1984), Khalid Khannouchi (1999), Catherine Ndereba (2001) and Paula Radcliffe (2002).

Now one of the six World Marathon Majors, Dennis Kimetto (2:03:45 in 2003) and Radcliffe (2:17:18 in 2002) currently hold the course records.

24 September

Naoko Takahashi smiles in Sydney

(2000)

No wonder she famously smiled as she crossed the finish line. In winning the 2000 Olympic marathon, Naoko Takahashi became the first Japanese woman to win an Olympic gold medal.

The race and prize-giving was watched by 84 per cent of TV viewers in Japan and she became an overnight superstar. Her face was soon splashed across newspapers and magazines, and she appeared on talk shows. She even received The People's Honour (only the third woman to do so).

The following year she became the first woman to run a marathon in under 2:20, with a world record of 2:19:46 at Berlin, while her time of 2:23:14 would remain an Olympic record for 12 years.

The secret to her success was said to be hornet juice.

25 September

Patrick Makau breaks marathon world record

(2011)

Kenya's Patrick Makau broke the marathon world record at Berlin running a stunning 2:03:38 (an average pace of 4:42.9 per mile). He also left the legendary Haile Gebrselassie, whose record he trumped by 21 seconds, in his wake at halfway.

'In the morning my body was not good,' he said, 'but after I started the race, it started reacting very well. I started thinking about the record.'

Makau's first marathon, at Rotterdam in 2009, was just 24 seconds short of the fastest ever debut – running 2:06:14. He's a dab hand at half marathons, too, running the second fastest ever in 2009, of 58:52. He held the marathon world record for two years, creating a bridge from Haile Gebrselassie (2:03:59) to Wilson Kipsang (2:03:23).

The last six marathon world records have been set at Berlin. Not since Khalid Khannouchi's 2:05:38 in London in 2002 has one been run elsewhere.

26 September

Wally Hayward breaks London to Brighton record
(1953)

Wally Hayward's running career spanned 60 years. The South African won his first Comrades Marathon in 1930 at the age of twenty-one. In 1950 he returned, but wasn't considered a serious contender. He went on to win, in a time 40 minutes quicker than his previous effort. He returned again the next year and won again, being triumphant at Comrades five times in all. Aged seventy-nine he was back again, completing the 56-mile ultramarathon in a remarkable 9:44.

Hayward achieved similar levels of performance elsewhere. On this date, at the age of forty-five, he shattered the 80km London-to-Brighton record by over 22 minutes, winning in 5:29:40 – recording the first 50-mile world record (5:14:12) along the way.

Just weeks later, Wally broke fellow Comrades hero Hardy Ballington's 100-mile world record on the Bath Road, England, by more than an hour, in 12:20:28 (which was unmatched for 15 years).

Hayward also fought in World War Two, earning the British Empire Medal for bravery for his actions near El Alamein, Egypt.

27 September

The fifth Astley Belt six-day race
(1879)

Public interest in the fifth Astley Belt Series six-day race was great. On 22 September at Madison Square Garden, New York, several pedestrian legends started the event, including Americans Edward Weston (see 22 February) and Frank Hart, and Britons Charles Rowell (see 3 March) and George Hazael (see 22 December).

On the penultimate day it all looked to be going Rowell's way, with him having clocked 419 miles to second-placed Hazael's 385, with American Sam Merritt in third. But after a late-morning rest stop, Rowell failed to emerge from his tent for six hours. And when he did, he looked awful. Clearly unwell, he shuffled on. But Merritt was catching him.

Word spread and crowds grew, to watch the enfeebled Rowell struggle to cling to his ever-dwindling lead. Merritt was only 8.5 miles behind Rowell and he broke into a run. Somehow Rowell followed suit.

Even at 1 a.m. on Saturday morning a crowd of 6,000 watched. *The New York Times* devoted their entire front page to the race the next morning.

By the 9.49 p.m. finish, miraculously, Rowell had hung on, beating Merritt by 15 miles, with a total of 530 (853km). It would later transpire Rowell had been poisoned, but he had the last laugh, pocketing US$30,000 in prize money.

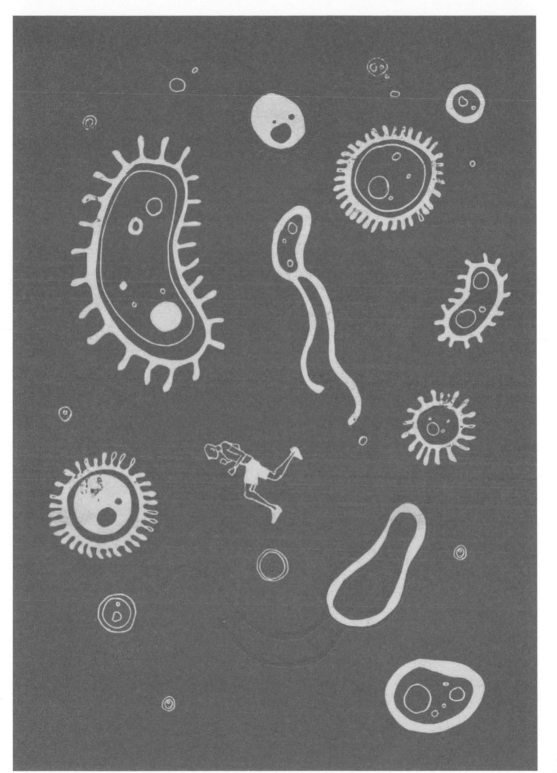

28 September

Haile Gebrselassie breaks his own world record
(2008)

Ethiopia's most famous export, Haile Gebrselassie, broke his own marathon world record at Berlin, running the 26.2 miles in 2:03:59. It was the third of four consecutive Berlin victories between 2006 and 2009 and the 35-year-old had beaten his previous world record by nearly half a minute.

Kenyan James Kwambai went with the Ethiopian as he broke away just after the 33km mark, but Gebrselassie stepped up the pace 6km from the finish and his opponent waned.

'I am so, so happy,' said Gebrselassie, 'everything was perfect. The weather was perfect, the spectators were perfect, everything. I am so happy . . . Berlin is my lucky city.'

A fortnight before the marathon, the Ethiopian was forced to rest for a week because of a sore calf. 'But I knew before I came here I could do something special,' he said.

In a 25-year career, Gebrselassie claimed two Olympic golds, eight World Championship victories and 27 world records.

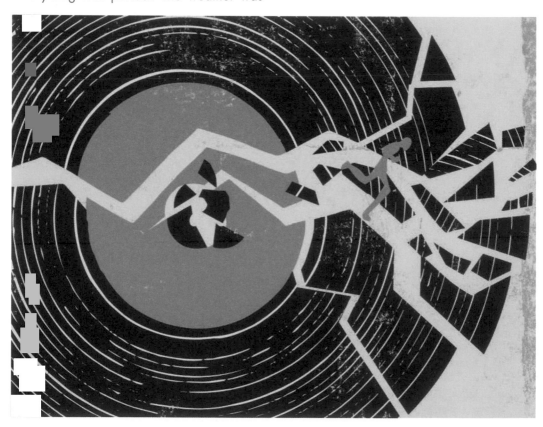

29 September

The first female marathon runner?
(1918)

Rightly or wrongly, neither the IAAF nor the Association of Road Running Statisticians (ARRS) recognise Stamata Revithi (see 11 April) as the first woman to run a marathon.

Instead, French runner Marie-Louise Ledru is often credited as the first female to cover the distance, doing so on this date. Ledru reportedly completed the Tour de Paris Marathon in a time of 5:40, finishing in 38th place. So, a huge moment for both feminism and distance running. But unfortunately things may not be so straightforward.

While the ARRS support Ledru's mark, as usual the IAAF disagrees, instead recognising Britain's Violet Piercy as being the ground-breaking runner (see 24 December), though it has some question marks against it too.

In previous generations the word 'marathon' didn't necessarily mean 26.2 miles, rather a 'long road run'. Which is helpful in a way, but unhelpful in that it probably applies to both Ledru's and Piercy's 'marathons'. Either way though, a woman running for well over five hours when it was commonly thought that would be the last thing they'd ever do, deserves our hearty applause.

30 September

The fastest ever marathon debut
(2012)

Kenya's Dennis Kimetto ran the fastest marathon debut on a record-eligible course today, at Berlin – alongside training partner Geoffrey Mutai for much of it. Two years later, again at Berlin, he would break the world record for the distance, with 2:02:57 – taking 26 seconds off Wilson Kipsang's year-old mark, set at the same race in 2013. Kimetto's wife, Caroline Chepkorir, passed out after watching her husband break the world record on television.

In Kenya the former farmer is part of a large training group which includes Geoffrey Mutai (who ran 2:03:02 at Boston in 2011) and Kipsang. Their collective average PB is a jaw-dropping 2:03:07.

Kimetto has used some of his winnings to fund the building of churches and schools and help provide opportunities for younger athletes in Kenya.

OCTOBER

1 October

Frank Giannino Jr has a rethink

(1980)

American Frank Giannino Jr was one month into his run across the US when he realised he needed to up his game. Initially inspired by Don Shepherd's book, *My Run Across the United States*, this was his second self-powered journey across the continent. The previous year Giannino had travelled from Santa Monica, California, to New York in 60 days and six hours – some way short of Tom McGrath's 1977 record of 53 days.

So 16 months after finishing, he started out again, this time from San Francisco to New York – and, crucially, with a four-person support team. In the meantime Stan Cottrell had run from New York City to San Francisco in 48 days, 1 hour, 48 minutes, averaging 60 miles a day.

At around halfway, Giannino realised he needed to up his mileage to 70 miles per day. He would start at 3 a.m. and run 25 miles before breakfast, then 25 more by lunch, then as many as possible by dark.

He did eventually set a world record for the fastest time, completing his 3,100-mile (4,989km) journey in 46 days 8 hours and 36 minutes, on 17 October 1980. His record remains unbeaten.

2 October

Rosie Swale-Pope heads off around the world

(2003)

On her 57th birthday, inspired by her late husband and wanting to raise awareness and funds for cancer, Rosie Swale-Pope left Tenby, Wales, on foot to run around the world.

In Siberia she got frostbite and almost lost her toes. A wolf also popped its head into her tent to say hello. 'He never hurt me and he and his pack followed me for a while,' she said. 'It was like they were running with me.'

Another morning she woke up to find a man coming at her with an axe. She thought he was yelling at her in anger, only to realise he was yelling with joy. He hugged her and invited her to a party with his fellow woodsman.

It took her four years and 10 months, and 32,000km (just under 20,000 miles), to circle the world, the writer and adventurer returning home on 25 August 2008.

3 October

Mizuki Noguchi wins half marathon silvers
(1999)

Japan's Mizuki Noguchi won two silver medals today – individual and team – at the World Half Marathon Championships in Italy.

It proved her gamble of switching from track to road was paying off. So she took things a stage further and switched to the marathon too. Noguchi went on to win the Nagoya and Osaka women's marathons, and took silver in the marathon at the 2003 World Championships.

But she wasn't done yet. The pinnacle of her career was the 2004 Olympics, where she beat world record-holder Paula Radcliffe and 2003 world champion Catherine Ndereba to take gold in the marathon – by just 12 seconds from the latter.

She won Berlin the following year, too, with a PB of 2:19:12 – a new Asian marathon record.

4 October

Parkrun turns ten
(2014)

When Paul Sinton-Hewitt started getting friends together to run around Teddington's Bushy Park, on the edge of London, on Saturday mornings, he had no idea his idea would become a weekly global event.

But the free, timed, 5K run grew into a small collection of events around the country . . . and then the globe, with parkruns now taking place every week in countries as diverse as Australia, Russia, South Africa, the US and many others.

Sinton-Hewitt got a CBE in the Queen's 2014 birthday honours for 'services to grass roots sports participation', and later that year parkrun celebrated its tenth birthday.

5 October

Yiannis Kouros smashes his own 24-hour record
(1997)

Greek-born Australian ultramarathon running god Yiannis Kouros produced what many believe to be the most phenomenal endurance feat in modern times, when he obliterated his own world 24-hour (track) record in Adelaide, running 188 miles (303.5km) – the equivalent of seven successive marathons – in 24 hours. His average speed was over 12.5km/h or 7:39 minutes per mile.

The superhuman sometime poet also holds world records for 24 hours on a road (290km), 48 hours on both road (433km) and track (473km) and 100 miles on road (11:46:37 – dating from 1984), among others. Kouros also has the record for the Spartathlon race in Greece – in fact he has the four fastest times ever recorded there.

He is said to rarely take a training run longer than 12 miles, never runs more than 80 miles a week and follows a vegan diet of no meat, fish, eggs, or dairy products.

6 October

Zersenay Tadese wins World Half Marathon Championships
(2012)

Zersenay Tadese's 2012 win in Bulgaria added to his four consecutive victories from 2006 to 2009 – and the Eritrean's half marathon world record of 58:23 from 2010. Elsewhere, his bronze in the 10,000m at the 2004 Olympics made him the first ever Eritrean Olympic medallist.

Unusually, the former cyclist rarely resorts to sprint finishes in races, instead relying on a strategy of fast pace-setting.

Two and a half thousand guests attended his wedding, which was broadcast live on Eritrean television, while his brother Kidane Tadese is also a professional distance runner.

7 October

Geoffrey Mutai is born
(1981)

Geoffrey Mutai, the eldest of 11 siblings, was selected to represent Kenya at the 2002 World Junior Championships, but couldn't go as he had no birth certificate. It's not the only time the marathoner has suffered at the hands of the rule-makers.

On 18 April 2011 at the Boston Marathon, Mutai ran the fastest 26.2 miles ever (at the time) in 2:03:02 (at 4:41 minute-per-mile pace). It broke the course record by almost three minutes and was a stunning 57 seconds faster than Haile Gebrselassie's world record. Mutai says he had no idea how fast he was running, or what his split times were.

However, the time was not recognised by the IAAF as a world record as the Boston course doesn't meet the strict criteria – due to the point-to-point nature of the overall downhill course. The Kenyan has also won the Berlin and New York Marathons twice.

8 October

Emiel Puttemans is born
(1947)

In the early 1970s Belgian Emiel Puttemans was the world's fastest 5,000m runner. He set world records for 5,000m (13:13 in 1972), 3,000m (7:37.6, 1972) and 2 miles (8:17.8, 1971). 'Miel' was twice indoor European champion at 3,000m, in 1973 and 1974, and at the 1972 Olympics, during his purple patch, he gained a silver medal at 10,000m, only beaten by a world record run by Finland's irrepressible Lasse Virén.

Puttemans ran at three more Olympic Games, but with less success, though he did win the inaugural Rome Marathon in 1982.

9 October

John Foden runs from Athens to Sparta
(1982)

John Foden, a British RAF Wing Commander and student of Ancient Greek history, reached the statue of Leonidas Sparta, in Sparta, Greece today in 1982. His experiment had been successful.

Foden had been reading about the battle of Marathon in 490 BC. In Herodotus' account, Athenian messenger Pheidippides is sent to Sparta for reinforcements to help see off the Persian incursion. According to Herodotus, Pheidippides arrived in Sparta, 250km (155 miles) away, a day after departing Athens. Foden wondered if a modern man could cover 250km within 36 hours. He and four RAF colleagues tried it out. Running a route as close as possible to Herodotus' description, Foden and two of his colleagues made it.

As a result the Spartathlon race, 136 miles from Marathon to Sparta, was born, with the first event taking place the next year.

The race has since grown to be a major event in the international ultramarathon calendar and the scene of some of the greatest endurance performances ever seen, especially by Yiannis Kouros (see 5 October), Scott Jurek (see 26 June and 12 July) and Lizzy Hawker (see 21 April).

10 October

The Blue Streak tries to prove sceptics wrong in Wales
(1912)

Australian 100m runner Jack Donaldson, or the 'Blue Streak', raced in the northern hemisphere – Wales to be precise – for the first time, to try and prove his doubters wrong.

At the time many UK journalists were dubious about timing procedures down under and therefore record claims from Australian athletes. Donaldson, unusually for the time a professional athlete, had claimed six world records in distances from 100 yards to 400 yards. But they were so fast he simply wasn't believed in Britain.

The Australian raced in Pontypridd against South African 1908 Olympic 100m champion Reginald Walker for the 130-yard world championship. He beat him by five yards – enough time to turn and watch Walker finish – and was timed at 123/16 seconds. His previously claimed record for the distance was 12 seconds flat, which stood for 40 years.

In the 1920s Charley Paddock (see 16 August) became obsessed with trying to beat the record, only to finally give up in disgust, grumpily proclaiming the distance 'unorthodox'.

11 October

Levett versus Jackson
(1852)

In 1852 William Jackson, more commonly known as 'The American Deer' (despite being born in Norwich, England – see 6 January), became embroiled in a year-long 10-mile racing duel with Ireland's John Levett for the Champion's Belt and title of Champion Runner of England.

As in boxing, whoever held the belt had to defeat challengers to retain the title and accompanying much-prized trouser-supporting accessory. George Frost, the 'Suffolk Stag', was the first belt holder in January, but two months later Levett defeated him in front of 25,000 spectators.

William Jackson, fresh back from a trip to the US and amid rumours he was past his peak, challenged Levett (they had just raced over 20 miles with Jackson comfortably ahead until injury struck at around 15 miles).

In the Champion's Belt race Jackson won easily, even lapping the Irishman. His time was 51:34, even though he'd walked the last 200 yards – it wasn't the done thing to exert oneself any more than necessary. His eight- and nine-mile times were world bests. But he would never be as good again.

Levett immediately demanded a rematch and on 11 October he got one. This time when Jackson tried to break away the Irishman stayed with him. With 80 yards to go, they were still side-by-side. But Levett had the faster finish and won by two yards.

Naturally Jackson challenged him to a rematch, but Levett managed to evade it. He lost the Belt back to Frost in 1853, then regained it in 1854, before retiring.

12 October

Emmanuel Mutai is born
(1984)

As of 2016, Kenyan Emmanuel Mutai (no relation to fellow countryman Geoffrey, see 7 October) was the second fastest marathoner in history, with a PB of 2:03:13, recorded at Berlin in 2014.

He also won the 2011 London Marathon with a course record of 2:04:40, but has more of a reputation for coming second.

Mutai won silver at the 2009 World Championships, has come second at London twice, New York twice and once each in Chicago and Berlin. Yes, even his second fastest marathon time in history only earned him second place – in any other race in the world ever he would have won. And that's despite his 2:03:13 being faster than the world record was before the race (race winner Dennis Kimetto ran 2:02:57).

Next time you feel unlucky, think of Emmanuel Mutai.

13 October

Chataway breaks 5,000m record
(1954)

The 1954 international meet in London was the first visit by a Russian team since 1878 and the 5,000m race brought world record holder, European Champion and full-time athlete Vladimir Kuts up against Britain's Chris Chataway, who was less accomplished – he also had another full-time job, smoked, and usually only ran 35 miles a week. He had a faster kick, but had lost to Kuts at the recent European Championships.

In front of a crowd of 40,000 and millions of TV viewers across Europe, Kuts soared off with a first mile five seconds ahead of the world record. He would burst away from Chataway, with the Englishman digging deep to catch up again. The race stayed this way for a while, Kuts bursting, Chataway slowly catching up. But in the final lap, the dogged Englishman was still with the Russian.

'My oxygen debt was horrendous,' Chataway said. 'By the time I was entering the final straight, it was really like throwing oneself over the cliffs.' Somehow Chataway, the amateur runner, found something extra. With five yards to go he lunged ahead of the famous Russian.

Their times – 13:51.6 and 13:51.8 – were both inside Kuts's world record.

'I had almost given up in the final two laps,' Chataway admitted. 'It's the most extravagant race I have ever run and the most painful quarter-of-an-hour of my life.'

14 October

Billy Mills' surprise Olympic gold
(1964)

Track & Field News labelled the 1964 Olympic final 'the greatest 10,000m of all time'. World record holder Australian Ron Clarke was up against former holder and current Olympic champion Russia's Pyotr Bolotnikov. Another favourite was 1960 5,000m Olympic champion Murray Halberg, while US hopes lay with Native American Billy Mills, and Tunisia's with Mohammed Gammoudi.

Bolotnikov went to the front initially, though Clarke took over and led for most of the first half of the race. From halfway a pack of four developed including Mills, Clarke and Gammoudi. Clarke's 'improvised plan' was to make the race his by accelerating every other lap. With three laps left, the commanding Clarke looked the likely winner. But Mills and Gammoudi were still close.

In a large field of 38, the front three were now lapping runners and Mills and Clarke collided as they tried to pass one. Mills staggered across three lanes, which allowed Gammoudi to dash between them – though to do so he grabbed Clarke's shoulder. Mills recovered well and followed Clarke to chase down the Tunisian.

On the last bend Gammoudi led by seven metres, but Clarke caught him at the start of the straight. Mills had looked out of it, but got a sudden second wind; in the penultimate 50m he closed the gap – then exploded past them both to take the tape.

'His burst was so totally unexpected that it deflated both Mohammed and me,' Clarke said. The first four runners all beat the Olympic record, and Mills had a PB by 42 seconds.

15 October

Don Ritchie's extraordinary 100 miles
(2014)

Scotland's Don Ritchie (see 3 February) set a world record for the fastest 100 miles (on a track) with 11:30:51 on this date – just one of many for the serial ultramarathon record breaker.

His record stood for a full 25 years – a long time in athletics. But in 2002 it was finally beaten, fittingly in a race organised at the same venue by the British Road Runners Club, to celebrate the anniversary of Ritchie's achievement.

A race between two Russians, Oleg Kharitonov and Denis Jalybin, came down to the wire. Jalybin had the lead for much of the event and was a full four laps ahead of Kharitonov with just seven miles to go. Kharitonov somehow picked up his pace and passed Jalybin at the end of the 402nd lap – just 135 metres from the end.

A crushed Jalybin took two minutes to cover that last 135 metres.

Kharitonov had run 100 miles in 11:28:03, an average of 6:53 per mile pace – roughly the equivalent of four marathons in a row at an average of 3:00:16.

16 October

The 'American Wonder' is born
(1817)

George Seward, the modestly self-titled 'American Wonder', was born on this date. He was another American pedestrian who spent his best years across the Atlantic in the UK. As a youngster he would win wagers by jumping over small horses. When he became a pro runner, he specialised in sprinting and is credited with inventing the crouch start. When Mr Wonder ran out of people to race in the US he sailed to the UK with a reputation as 'America's first great runner'.

Arriving in Liverpool he arranged a match with local sprinter Jack Fowler, pretending to be a novice. He turned up dressed as a sailor and acted the part of the greenhorn, playing up to the crowd's mocking. The odds were 10 to 1 against Seward and his £10 was the only money placed on him. He promptly undressed to reveal racing silks and put on his running shoes as the crowd hushed. He beat Fowler easily and collected his payout. But no one in the area would race him. As he travelled the country he soon ran out of competitors. In 1844 he ran 100 yards in 9¼ seconds, which may well have been the fastest time of the century.

Undaunted, he teamed up with the 'American Deer' and toured the UK in 1846, appearing in specially staged running contests (see 8 February).

17 October

Geronimo Jim
(1964)

Jim Alder set a record on this day for the longest distance covered in a two-hour track race, 37.994km (23.6 miles). But it was bittersweet. He was only there because he hadn't quite made the British marathon team for the 1964 Tokyo Olympics, an event which would be run just four days later.

'I cried in the showers afterwards,' he said. 'You only have these purple-patch days three or four times in your career – running at world-record marathon pace for two hours – while the Olympic marathon was taking place in Tokyo.'

Early life hadn't been kind to him either. His mother died of tuberculosis and his father was killed on the last day of World War Two, so he was raised an orphan.

Britain's 1960s distance-running great worked as a bricklayer and would cry out 'Geronimo!' whenever he crossed the finish line, earning himself a nickname. Alder also set a 30,000m record of 1:34:01 and won Commonwealth gold in 1966 for the marathon, his specialist distance – but that almost went very wrong.

Alder arrived at the stadium in Kingston, Jamaica, in the lead but found no officials to guide him into the arena. When he finally made it on to the track, the Scot found England's Bill Adcocks 50 yards ahead of him, with 300 yards left. Alder put his head down and charged for the line – as he breasted the tape first he of course bellowed his signature 'Geronimo!'.

18 October

Another 5,000m Olympic final classic
(1964)

Australia's Ron Clarke had a chance to erase his 1964 Olympics 10,000m final disappointment (see 14 October) just four days later in the 5,000m final. But Frenchman Michel Jazy, America's Bob Schul (coached by Hungarian Mihály Iglói – see 4 January) and Bill Dellinger, and Germany's Harald Norpoth all looked strong contenders too.

The race started slowly, then after two laps Clarke took over. He again practised the surging technique he'd used (unsuccessfully) in the 10,000m final, pushing a fast lap, then dropping to a more sensible pace, then pushing again. Jazy was on his shoulder, with Norpoth close behind.

Schul and Dellinger joined the lead group as Clarke tried a third surge. But he was burned out and Jazy took over. With 600m left there were nine runners in the lead pack.

Dellinger pushed from the back of the pack to the front. On the curve Jazy took the lead and accelerated off the bend, opening up a small gap. Norpoth and Schul tried to go with him. With 200m to go, Norpoth was within four metres of Jazy, with Schul on his shoulder. On the final bend Schul passed Norpoth and closed on Jazy.

'When I came off the bend,' said Schul, 'I wasn't that far behind him. His shoulders had tightened, and he looked back a few times. I thought, "I'll be able to catch him".'

Schul did pass the Frenchman with about 60m to go and reached the tape first. Behind him Norpoth also passed Jazy with 40m to go. Dellinger, too, caught the floundering Frenchman at the line, for bronze.

It was a stunning run by Schul, who had wisely avoided getting caught up in wasting energy during Clarke's surges.

19 October

The Flying Nun is born
(1929)

American nun Marion Irvine became the oldest person to compete in the US Olympic trials in 1984, aged fifty-four. Afterwards she ran city marathons, gaining media attention and the 'Flying Nun' moniker. But it wasn't just a jape – she broke several age-group records.

Irvine only began running at the age of forty-nine, on the recommendation of her niece, who was concerned about her health. At the Boston Marathon Irvine won her 50–59 age-group and finished another marathon in 3:01. She hired a coach and started setting more national age-group records.

At the California International Marathon, her time of 2:51.01 was a world record for female runners over 50 – the time also qualified her for the 1984 US Olympic trials. But her time there of 2:52.02, while thoroughly respectable, didn't get her close to qualifying and is a reminder that this is real life, not a Hollywood film. But it got her into magazines and on TV shows and gained her sponsorships from a large sportswear company.

She continued to break world age-group records and at the 1989 World Veterans Games won five gold medals.

20 October

The loser is a winner in the 1968 Olympic marathon
(1968)

An hour and five minutes after the first finisher of the 1968 Mexico Olympic marathon, the last runner crossed the line. Normally that runner would be a mere footnote in Olympic history. But John Stephen Akhwari wasn't a normal runner. His heroic performance somehow stood for something bigger than winning races.

Akhwari wasn't a medal prospect, and soon found himself suffering in Mexico City's altitude, which triggered cramps. Then at about 19K, amid a jostle of runners, he fell to the ground, smashing his shoulder on the pavement, gashing his knee and dislocating it.

It looked like his race was over. But after some medical treatment he continued.

His progress was slow, but his determination was huge. The Tanzanian crossed the finish line in 3:25:27, limping, bloodied and bandaged, with most of the crowd having gone home.

When asked why he hadn't quit he said, 'My country did not send me 5,000 miles [it was actually nearer 9,000] away to start the race. They sent me 5,000 miles to finish it.'

Akhwari would finish fifth in the marathon at the Commonwealth Games in 1970, but this is the performance he's remembered for.

21 October

Grete Waitz breaks 2:30 marathon barrier
(1979)

Norway's Grete Waitz became the first woman to run the marathon in under two and a half hours, at the New York City Marathon, in 2:27:32.6 – breaking her own world record of 2:32:29.8.

Rarely has the bond between a runner and a race, or perhaps a city, been as strong as for New York and Waitz. 'She became a celebrity in the city,' said a *New York Times* obituary. 'Cabdrivers and the homeless called her by her first name'. Waitz won nine New York City Marathons between 1978 and 1988, more than any other runner in history, setting three world records there. Her first run in 1978 saw her beat the course record by two minutes. She was the world's first great woman marathoner. (See also 15 May.)

22 October

Emil Zátopek sets world record
(1949)

Emil Zátopek set a new world record on this day for 10,000m, with 29:21.2 in Ostrava, Czech Republic. With a level of brilliance that was almost tedious, the 'Czech Express' broke his own record the following summer. And again in 1953. Oh, and again in 1954.

He was thought to be the hardest trainer of his era – and it showed – with ideas based loosely on what he'd read about the great Finnish runner Paavo Nurmi, including intervals. 'Why should I practise running slowly?' he said. 'I already know how to run slow.'

Zátopek wasn't just remarkable on the track. Off it he took night classes and would eventually speak six languages. He used his fame to stand up to political bullies too. In the lead-up to the 1952 Helsinki Olympics, Czechoslovakia's Communist Party omitted fellow runner Stanislav Jungwirth from the team because his father was a political prisoner. 'If he does not go, neither do I,' Zátopek declared. The Communists stuck to their word. Zátopek didn't board the plane to Helsinki. The government caved in and sent both runners to the Games.

In 1968, as Russian tanks invaded his homeland, Zátopek openly protested the intrusion. After Soviet forces had brought a bloody end to the uprising Zátopek was stripped of his rank of colonel, kicked out of the army and forced to collect rubbish on Prague's streets – then spent seven years working in a uranium mine. He was finally pardoned.

23 October

An extraordinary finish in New York
(1983)

The New York City Marathon sees one of the all-time great finishes – here or anywhere. England's Geoff Smith, who had run 10,000m and the marathon at the Olympics, led through the second half of the race.

He was pursued by 1972 Olympic 1,500m bronze medallist, New Zealander Rod Dixon, though with six miles to go, the race looked already over. Smith had a solid two-and-a-half-minute lead – about half a mile – over Dixon. But the New Zealander hadn't given up yet.

Smith was caught just 400m from the tape, in Central Park, and Dixon passed the exhausted Briton to win by just nine seconds.

Dixon explained afterwards how instead of running down the middle of the road, he ran what's become known as the racing line, trying to minimise the distance travelled – a tactic many have copied since.

Smith would go on to win Boston twice, but is equally well remembered for this dramatic race denouement.

24 October

Jim Peters is born
(1918)

England's Jim Peters broke the marathon world record four times in the 1950s, including the first sub-2:20 in 1953.

But he's equally well remembered for a bizarre – and horrible to watch – end to the marathon at Vancouver's 1954 Empire and Commonwealth Games (now just Commonwealth Games).

On a swelteringly hot day, Peters arrived in the stadium with a 17-minute lead and just 400m to go, but fell on the track. He got up. He fell again.

'I could see that tape in front of my eyes,' he remembered. 'But as I got up and ran, it didn't seem to get any nearer.'

Ten minutes later and he'd moved just 200m. The British team masseur finally rescued him and rushed him to hospital. Peters was lucky not to have died and he never ran again.

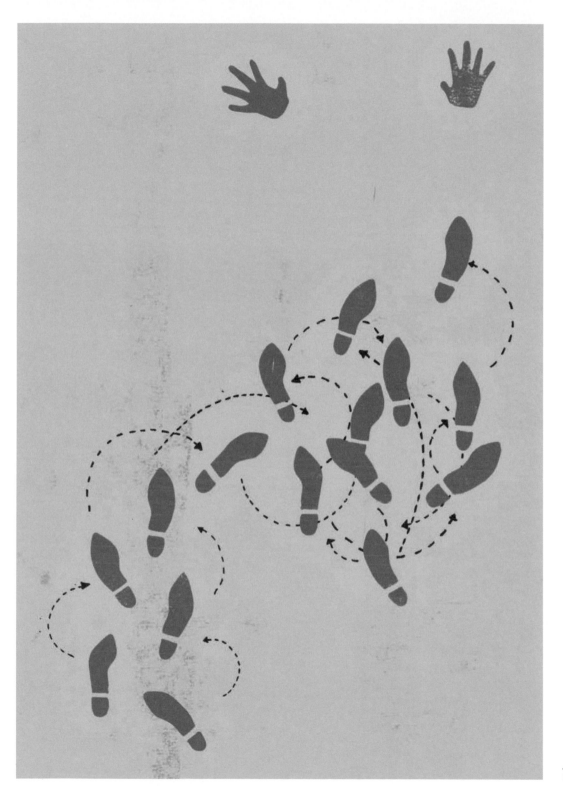

25 October

Alberto Salazar's disputed marathon world record
(1981)

In winning the 1981 New York City Marathon today in 2:08:13, Alberto Salazar thought he'd broken the marathon world record. It was after all the fastest marathon time ever recorded – surpassing the 12-year-old 2:08:33 set by Australian Derek Clayton in Antwerp.

Infuriatingly for him, however, the course was remeasured and found to be around 148 metres (the equivalent of about 27 seconds) short, and the record was officially taken away from the Cuban-American. He wasn't particularly cheered up by the fact the Association of Road Racing Statisticians considers Clayton's performance to have occurred on a short course, too.

Salazar had won New York the previous year and would do so again in 1982. In the same year he would also win the 'Duel in the Sun' with Dick Beardsley at the Boston Marathon (see 19 April), running himself unconscious.

26 October

Joyce Esther Smith is born
(1937)

In 1981 Joyce Esther Smith, in only her second year of competitive running, won the inaugural London marathon in 2:29:57. In doing so she also became the first woman over forty to complete the distance in less than two and a half hours.

A year later, she won the event again, in 2:29:43, setting a new British record, and becoming the oldest woman to win the race at forty-four years, 195 days, a record which still stands. Her time would still have placed her in the top ten in 2013 and 2014.

She also finished ninth in the 1983 World Championships in Helsinki.

27 October

Siah Albison beats The Crowcatcher over a mile
(1860)

The creation in 1860 of the UK's Champions Belt for the mile helped increase interest in the distance. The mile seems to attract epic duals more than any other distance and there have been some legendary efforts at lowering the world record down the years, from Swedes Gunder Hägg and Arne Andersson in the 1940s to Roger Bannister and John Landy in the 1950s.

The first race for the Belt included William Lang, 'The Crowcatcher', Jack White, 'The Gateshead Clipper' and Siah Albison (who was presumably yet to think up a fitting moniker). Mr Crowcatcher wasn't on great form and Albison came from 30 yards behind to catch White. Of course, White instantly demanded a rematch and got one on 27 October.

With 4,000 watching, Lang shot off at a blistering pace, attempting to exhaust Albison and got 10 yards ahead. But his rival slowly reeled him back in and beat him to the tape in a record 4:22¼.

A year later, to win a wager that he could run a 4:15 mile, Lang ran it in 4:02, on a downhill course.

28 October

Christa Vahlensieck
(1973)

Christa Vahlensieck (née Kofferschläger) ran a European best for the marathon, and the first sub-three-hour one, on this date at Waldniel, Germany, recording 2:59:26. But she would do better.

In May 1975, she set a world record time of 2:40:16 at Dülmen, topping Liane Winter's (see 22 September) 2:42:24 from the previous month. In the same year, she won the Schwarzwald Marathon in 2:45:43, which remains the course record.

From 1973 to 1989, Vahlensieck won 21 marathons, including victory at the 1977 Berlin Marathon in 2:34:48, regaining the marathon world record.

She held it for a year before Grete Waitz came along with a 2:32:29.

29 October

Harry versus Harry
(1887)

The burning down of Lillie Bridge by irate fans (see 18 September) was the end of an era for sprint racing in London if not the world. However, Britons Harry Hutchens and Harry Gent did finally meet, in October 1887.

Gent beat Hutchens in Gateshead, but it wasn't the end for the sprinter. At the age of thirty-eight he won his fourth Sheffield Handicap. However, Hutchens had a mixed reputation. He was the master of winning by the smallest margin possible. He knew it wasn't always best to win, or to win easily – that isn't clever business when there's money to be made from bets.

While touring Australia, for example, Hutchens twice lost over 150 yards to Aborigine Charlie Samuels, who according to Edward Sears's *Running Through the Ages* trained on 'a box of cigars, tobacco pipe and plenty of sherry'. For the third race, with a lot more money on the outcome, Hutchens won easily.

30 October

Seven marathons in seven days on seven continents
(2003)

British adventurers Sir Ranulph Fiennes and Dr Michael Stroud ran the fourth of seven marathons in seven days on seven continents. On this date it was the turn of Singapore, amid tropical heat, humidity and pollution. Fiennes, who had recently undergone heart surgery and ran with a defibrillator, collapsed at the end and found himself in an ambulance on a drip. 'I hit the pavement and nearly fainted,' he said.

'I felt completely knackered and not able to do another one.' Dr Stroud walked much of the way after suffering a stomach upset.

But the British adventurers did end their challenge, completing the New York Marathon, which Fiennes finished in 5:25. The pair's 183 miles that week were also run in the Falkland Islands, Santiago, Sydney, London and Cairo.

31 October

Frank Shorter is born
(1947)

Frank Shorter's win at the 1972 Munich Olympic marathon is frequently credited with starting the running boom in the US – which spread to other countries.

It's estimated that as many as 25 million Americans, including President Jimmy Carter, took up some aspect of running in the 1970s and 1980s, partly as a result of watching Shorter win Olympic gold and his resultant celebrity, which is often said to represent the convergence of many middle-class American ideals. Many running events and sportswear companies popular today date to this era.

As well as Munich, fittingly the city of his birth, he gained silver at the next Olympics too, becoming the only American to win two Olympic marathon medals. Shorter was also a four-time winner of the Fukuoka Marathon (1971–74), the premier city marathon at the time.

NOVEMBER

1 November

Meb Keflezighi wins New York

(2009)

One of 10 Eritrean siblings, Mebrahtom 'Meb' Keflezighi (pronounced ka-FLEZ-ghee) didn't see a car until he was ten and when he did, tellingly, he ran away from it. 'That was one race I didn't win,' he has joked. The Keflezighi family arrived in the US as refugees in 1987 and Meb became a naturalised US citizen in 1998.

In winning the New York City Marathon in 2009 he became the first American to do so since Alberto Salazar in 1982. At the line he dropped to the ground, tears streaming down his face, winning with a PB of 2:09:15 – 41 seconds ahead of a four-time Boston winner, Kenya's Robert Cheruiyot. Keflezighi said he followed his wife's advice to be patient in the race. 'She said, "Don't lead",' he said. 'That's why you saw me in the back the whole time, trying to put it together.'

Similarly, when Keflezighi won Boston in 2004 he was the first American winner since 1983. He is the only marathoner in history to win New York, Boston and an Olympic medal.

2 November

Boston's first lady, Bobbi Gibb, is born

(1942)

In 1966 Roberta 'Bobbi' Gibb changed the world by running the Boston Marathon. Before then it was thought women simply weren't capable of doing such a thing.

She grew up as an active child. 'As soon as you became an adolescent, everything changed,' Gibb told *Women in the World*. Gibb watched the 1964 race. 'Something inside of me said, "I'm going to run this race".' She had applied for a place, but was rejected. Allowing a woman to run 26 miles, the letter said, would be a tremendous liability. 'It wasn't until later that I realised I was going to be making a social statement.'

After three nights and four days travelling on a bus from San Diego, Gibb concealed her face with a hoodie and hid in bushes near the start pen wearing her brother's Bermuda shorts, nurse's shoes (women's running shoes didn't exist then) and no number. When the men rushed by, she jumped from the bushes and into the race.

Gibb soon overheated, but didn't want to remove her hoodie and give the game away, however seeing the encouragement from spectators and runners alike, she finally did.

Gibb's feet were covered in blisters and by mile 20 she couldn't do much more than tiptoe along. 'I had this huge weight of responsibility on me. Here I was, making this very public statement. If I had collapsed or hadn't finished, I would have set women back another 50 years.' But she placed in the top third of the field.

The Boston Marathon finally opened to women in 1972. Gibb is recognised by the Boston Athletic Association as the pre-sanctioned-era women's winner in 1966, 1967 and 1968.

3 November

The Everest Marathon
(1985)

The idea of an Everest Marathon was born in 1985 when a British couple organised an impromptu race from Nepal's Namche Bazaar to Tengboche monastery and back.

After the *Daily Telegraph* condemned the concept, warning that people would die, the race took off in November 1987 and has been run every two years since – often in the first week of November.

Starting at 5,184m (17,000ft) above sea level at Gorak Shep, a settlement about two hours from Everest Base Camp, the route descends to Namche (3,446m/11,300ft)

before a punishing three-mile loop up to the village of Thamo and back, to complete the 26.2 miles.

The first mile, notwithstanding the -20°C temperatures at the 6.30 a.m. start, is tough. It includes four uphills over the moraine of the Khumbu glacier, a narrow path strewn with boulders, stones and yak dung.

As well as being the world's highest marathon, it can claim to be the most spectacular. It's ringed by the world's biggest mountains, including Everest. There are usually around 70 runners.

4 November

Paula Radcliffe wins New York
(2007)

Less than 10 months after giving birth, world record-holder Paula Radcliffe won her second of three New York City Marathons (2004, 2007, 2008).

The Briton's 27-hour labour took its toll on her tiny frame and left her with a stress fracture in her sacrum – a bone at the base of her spine. 'I think your body is just a little bit stronger after pregnancy,' she said.

Her fierce rivalry with Ethiopia's Gete Wami (who had won the Berlin Marathon 35 days beforehand) continued, with the two out in front alone from four miles in.

Radcliffe tried several times to shake her opponent off, gaining a slight advantage,

only to see it quickly disappear. In the final half-mile, along Central Park South, Wami drew slightly ahead of Radcliffe.

'Coming into the park I had a lot of support,' said Radcliffe. 'But it was so noisy I didn't know where anyone was. I thought I had a gap, and then she was right there, and then she came alongside me and then went past me at Columbus Circle. And I was thinking . . . this is mine, she's not getting past me.'

Wami didn't have a kick left to match Radcliffe, who won in 2:23:09.

5 November

Alfie Shrubb breaks one-hour record
(1904)

Alfie Shrubb's talent for running was discovered one night when, wearing working boots, he beat a horse-drawn fire tender to the scene of a fire four miles from his home (see 23 April) and a watching captain of the local athletics club invited him to join.

At his peak the wiry Englishman, nicknamed 'The Little Wonder', was virtually unbeatable at distances up to 15 miles. From 1899 to 1912, as both an amateur and professional, Shrubb won over a thousand races, becoming perhaps the first 'superstar' runner. At Ibrox Park, Glasgow, on this date he broke the one-hour record, running 11 miles and 1137 yards (18.7km). His run also broke all amateur records from six to 11 miles, and all professional records from eight to 11. Altogether Shrub set 28 world records, some of which remained unbeaten for almost half a century.

He has two races named in his honour, one in the Sussex village of Slinfold, where he was born.

6 November

Wrong-way Silva
(1936)

In the 1994 New York City Marathon, Mexicans German Silva and Benjamin Paredes were jockeying for position at the front of the race. But just half a mile from the finish, Silva followed a police vehicle turning right into Central Park, and off-course. He'd gifted his rival a 40-yard advantage – huge at that stage of a race.

An easy win seemed inevitable for Paredes, but Silva retraced his steps with surprising calmness. He then accelerated, caught his compatriot, passed him and won the race by a few feet. It was going to be a thrilling finish anyway, but this doubled the drama.

7 November

Canada's marathon man dies
(1988)

'Sy Mah runs in marathons the way some people go to the movies,' wrote *The New York Times*. 'Maybe once a weekend, maybe twice, sometimes even three if there are good ones nearby.'

A professor of exercise science at the University of Toledo, his family's history of high blood pressure piqued an interest in cardiovascular fitness. He began running in 10 marathons a year, then 15, then 20. Then, he recalls, 'I began wondering if I could do a double – two marathons on one weekend.' The Canadian ended up with a Guinness World Record for the most lifetime marathons with 524.

Mah also coached marathon prodigy Maureen Wilton (see 6 May).

8 November

Cor Vriend is born
(1949)

Dutch distance runner Cornelis 'Cor' Vriend, born on this date, was another good distance runner who endured the misfortune of being a similar age to a slightly better one.

The marathon specialist won the Amsterdam Marathon twice (1983–84), the Enschede Marathon (1981) and Japan's Beppu-Ōita Marathon (1984). But during the 1980s he was often overshadowed by compatriot and 1982 European champion Gerard Nijboer.

Vriend is also the Dutch record holder for the rarely-run 25,000m and 30,000m track events and he ran at two Olympics, finishing 41st (1980) and 39th (1984) in the marathon.

9 November

The Athens Classic Marathon
(since 1972)

The Athens Marathon (sometimes also called the Athens Authentic or Classic Marathon) is based on the myth of Pheidippides, a messenger in Ancient Greece, thought to have run from the Battle of Marathon to Athens to announce victory over the Persians (see 1 March).

The first modern marathon, too, has its roots in the Greek capital, as it was during the 1896 Olympics when an official marathon was first run.

This marathon is one of the most difficult around: it's uphill from 10km to 31km. The route begins in Marathon itself and, following that mean long hill, the course then goes downhill to Athens. After passing a statue of a runner the route finishes at the Panathinaiko Stadium, a site for athletics competitions in ancient times and the finishing point of both the 1896 and 2004 Olympic marathons.

10 November

Caballo Blanco is born
(1953)

Born Michael Randall Hickman, but also known as Caballo Blanco (white horse) and Micah True, the US ultra runner was the protagonist of Christopher McDougall's mega-popular running book, *Born to Run*.

In 2003 True, a former professional boxer, organised a 51-mile ultramarathon for the legendary endurance runners the Tarahumara people in Mexico's Copper Canyon that became central to the book's narrative, with Scott Jurek and Ann Trason also showing up.

True died in March 2012, during a run in the Gila Wilderness, but his Copper Canyon Ultra Marathon lives on.

11 November

Ivan Babaryka is born

(1982)

Ukrainian distance runner Ivan Babaryka began his career as a track athlete and was Ukrainian indoor champion over 3,000m in 2006. After switching to marathons he won the 2007 Moscow International Peace Marathon, in severe weather conditions, in a time of 2:20:34. He returned to defend his title in 2008, and did so, finishing 23 seconds faster.

In 2008 he finished second place behind compatriot Andriy Naumov at Germany's Mainz Marathon, and the following year he was runner-up there again.

He made the Ukrainian Olympic team for the 2012 London games, but only placed 59th.

12 November

Daniele Justin becomes a record breaker (for a week)

(1978)

Belgian athlete Daniele Justin set a new women's half marathon record of 1:17:48 today at Nizare, Portland. Her time was ratified by the ARRS, but not the harder-to-please IAAF (almost invariably because of the course distance), which made things a bit awkward.

Perhaps everyone except Justin was relieved then when America's Miki Gorman came along and beat the time just seven days later, running 1:15:58 in Pasadena, a new world record both IAAF and ARRS were happy with.

13 November

Caroline Walker wins at cross country
(1971)

Caroline Walker set a world best in the marathon in February 1970 in Oregon, with 3:02:53, remarkably while she was still in high school.

She won the Junior AAU Cross Country Championship on this date and began running competitively at the University of Oregon, where she was coached by Steve Prefontaine (see 30 May). After his death, she lived in his house with his girlfriend and sister. '[Prefontaine] gave me the compliment of saying that I was the person most like him of anybody he'd ever met,' she has said.

Walker ran in the 1972 International Cross Country Championships and 1973 IAAF World Cross Country Championships, winning team medals. Injuries and her cross country training prevented her from running another marathon and she would later claim mercury in dental fillings negatively affected her health and running performance. A lower-back injury, sustained at a chiropractor's office, ended her running career.

14 November

Andrés Espinosa wins New York
(1993)

Mexican Andrés Espinosa's win at the 1993 New York Marathon, in 21°C (70°F) heat and 65 per cent humidity, was especially sweet as he'd placed second the two previous years. 'I was not going to take second place,' said the erstwhile steelworker, who became sponsored by his former company.

Around three miles from the finish, on Fifth Avenue, Espinosa was still being matched by Bob Kempainen, a 27-year-old American medical student. Espinosa decided to see what this little-known challenger was made of. 'He shifted into another gear I didn't have,' said Kempainen, as the Mexican averaged 4:55-minute miles over the last three miles.

Espinosa had trained for three and a half months in the mountains outside Mexico City and was one of five Mexicans to finish in the top 15 that day. He went home with $40,000. Not bad for a man who'd had to scrape together the bus fare from Mexico City to Dallas to run his first marathon in 1989 (which he won).

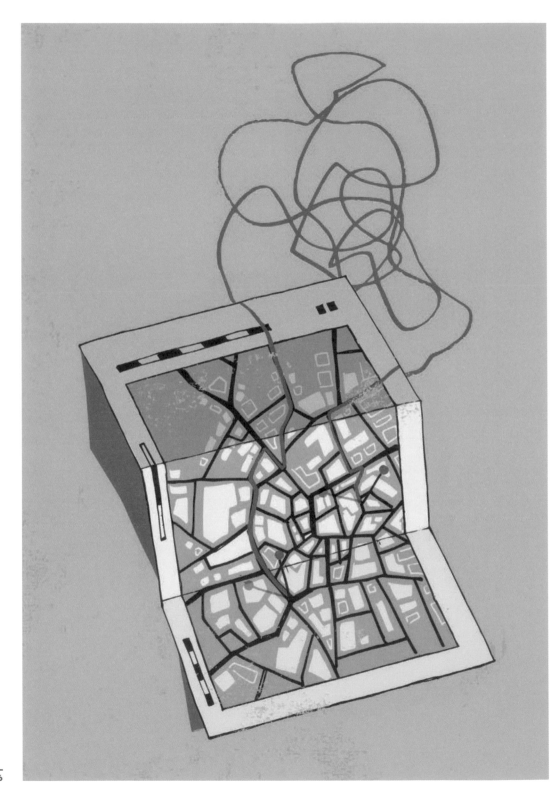

15 November

Bangkok's 17-mile half marathon
(2015)

A mishap on this day turned Bangkok's half marathon into the world's longest. A race official responsible for pointing runners in the right direction inadvertently directed them to U-turn at the wrong place. It added more than 3km to each lap and more than 6km to the whole half (and a bit more) marathon.

Despite the bonus miles, making it good value for money and news all around the world, some runners voiced annoyance on social media, and organisers 'admitted that a technical error happened during the half-marathon event'.

16 November

The Marathon Monks of Mount Hiei
(1885)

The so-called 'marathon monks' are more accurately known as Kaihigyo, from the Tendai Sect of Buddhism, found at Mount Hiei, near Kyoto, Japan. They run (and quite often walk) for spiritual enlightenment. Their ultimate achievement is the completion of the 1,000-day challenge (over the course of seven years), which only 46 men have completed since 1885. Of these, three have completed the circuit twice, most recently Yusai Sakai, who first went from 1973 to 1980, then, after a half-year pause, finished his second round in 1987 at the age of sixty.

Initially monks must cover 40km (25 miles) per day for 100 consecutive days. In the fourth and fifth years their target is 40km each day for 200 consecutive days. In the sixth year they must complete 60km each day for 100 consecutive days, and in the seventh year they have to do 84km each day for 100 consecutive days.

Along the way, monks need to stop at some of the 250 shrines and temples and all runs are conducted in straw sandals, carrying books with mantras to chant. They also carry a knife and a rope, to be used by the monk if he fails, whereby he must take his own life, by hanging or self-disembowelment. Though this now appears to be a custom more honoured in the breach than the observance.

17 November

Derek Clayton is born
(1942)

Born in England and raised in Northern Ireland, Australian long-distance runner Derek Clayton is one of the greatest marathoners to never win an Olympic medal. The six-foot two-inch runner set a world best in the Fukuoka Marathon, Japan, in 1967 of 2:09:36.4 – the first sub-2:10 marathon.

He went on to break this time in Antwerp in 1969, with the first sub 2:09-marathon (2:08:33), which stood as the world best for nearly 12 years. The IAAF back his time. The ARRS, however, consider the course to have been short.

Clayton represented Australia at the 1968 Olympics in Mexico City, finishing in seventh place (2:27:23). Four years later he placed 13th (2:19:49) in the same event. He was said to run 160 miles per week.

18 November

Sandy Barwick starts running
(1990)

In Campbelltown, Australia, Sandra 'Sandy' Barwick today began her attempt to break the women's world record for distance covered in six days.

Eventually covering 549 miles and 110 yards (883.6km) the New Zealander set a record that still stands over 25 years later.

In 1991 she set four ultra-distance road world records, all at the Chinmoy 1,300-mile multiday race in New York: for 1,000km (7 days 1:11), 2,000 km (17 days 3:01), 1,000 miles (12 days 14:38:40) and 1,300 miles (17 days 22:46:07).

'I know it looks crazy to people on the outside, living in a tent and running around in a circle for 18 or 19 days,' said Barwick. 'There was an empty place in me after my mother died, and I think running, which to my surprise I was good at, filled it.'

19 November

Luigi Beccali is born
(1907)

Luigi Beccali was both the first Italian to win an athletics European Championship title and the first to win an Olympic gold on the track. He debuted at the 1928 Amsterdam Games but was only fourth in his 1,500m heat.

Combining athletics with work, he trained twice a day – emulating modern professional training schedules – in the 1930s.

'I trained more than the others,' he said, 'even secretly. Taking advantage of my job situation (I was a council surveyor, responsible for road maintenance, so I was on the road, unsupervised), I would go to the track and allow myself a few kilometres. Then in the afternoon, I would work on speed.'

The 1932 Los Angeles Olympics was the high point of his career, when he came from behind to take gold in the 1,500m. A year later, he equalled the world record in Turin with 3:49.2 and a few days later he bettered it in Milan, with 3:49.0.

20 November

Record breaker and activist Jacki Hansen is born
(1948)

Jacqueline 'Jacki' Hansen won 12 of her first 15 marathons – including Boston in 1973 – and twice broke the women's marathon world record, bringing it down to 2:38:19 in 1975. Yet those weren't the American's most important contributions to the sport. Rather that was her relentless lobbying of the IOC to add women's distance-running events to the Olympics – and this was while she was still running.

In the late 1970s she served as president of the International Runners Committee, garnering support for women's distance events. Success came, but it was gradual. A marathon was added to the Olympics in 1984, 10,000m in 1988 and 5,000m in 1996. *Runner's World* called her: 'One of the most important women in the evolution of women's distance running'.

For her Boston win, only her second marathon, she wore two pairs of hiking socks, one being thick wool, and on a hot day her coach had advised her not to drink any water.

21 November

Eamonn Coghlan is born
(1952)

Eamonn Coghlan was knock-kneed as a child and had to wear orthotic corrective shoes. He dreamed of being a footballer, but he also loved running errands, and learned to move fast to escape gangs of street kids.

The Irishman earned a sports scholarship to the US and went on to break the indoor mile world record on three occasions, and set world records for 1,500m and 2,000m.

He was one place from a medal at both the Montreal 1976 Olympics (1,500m) and the Moscow 1980 Games (5,000m).

After competitive retirement, he continued to race and became the first man over forty years old to run a sub-four-minute mile.

Coghlan went on to become a senator in the Irish legislature.

22 November

The first Cliff Young Australian 6-Day Race
(2004)

Though the pedestrian-era boom of six-day racing has long since passed, there are still a handful of races around the world and from 1984 to 2006 the Cliff Young Australian 6-Day Race was one of them.

Fourteen runners entered the inaugural race, including the great Yiannis Kouros (see 13 February) and British multi-day runner Eleanor Adams-Robinson. Kouros won, covering over 1,022km (635 miles) and setting a new world record. Adams-Robinson broke 11 world records.

In 2005, Kouros was back to set a new six-day world record, covering just over 1,036km, also setting new world record times for 500km and 1,000km in his age group.

Originally named the Colac Ultra Marathon, then the 'Australian Six Day Race – Colac', the event was renamed in 2004 after Cliff Young, the surprise 61-year-old winner of the inaugural Sydney to Melbourne Ultramarathon (see 12 April), after his death in 2003.

23 November

Kuts and Pirie duel for 10,000m gold
(1856)

From the gun there were only really two runners in contention for the 1956 Olympic 10,000m gold. Front-runner Vladimir Kuts had defeated the until-then unbeatable Emil Zátopek over 5,000m at the 1954 European Championships and the Russian was the new star on the scene. Britain's Gordon Pirie meanwhile was renowned for his finishing kick and held world records for 3,000m and 5,000m. Though his 10,000m PB was 47 seconds slower than Kuts' world record of 28:30.4, Pirie had outsprinted the Russian for a 5,000m win earlier that year.

After the nervous Pirie caused a false start, the Russian was soon leading the field with the Briton just behind. On lap five Kuts performed one of his trademark surges, though Pirie gradually caught him again. Kuts began ending his surges so abruptly they would surprise Pirie, then he would offer his rival the chance to take the lead, which would be declined.

Kuts continued to offer Pirie the lead, the offer always declined, and always followed by a burst by Kuts on the back straight. Unsurprisingly this intense duelling led to a drop in the overall pace.

After 20 laps Kuts finally began to look tired. Was the race Pirie's now? But on lap 22 the Russian put in a final burst the Briton couldn't recover from and the gap was 4m with a lap to go.

Pirie was broken and Kuts was first to the tape, with his exhausted rival falling back to eighth.

'He murdered me – that's all there was to it,' said Pirie immediately afterwards. Years later Kuts would say he felt spent and that if Pirie had matched his last burst, he wouldn't have been able to fend him off. Such is the margin between defeat and victory.

24 November

The Galloping Granny is born
(1924)

As a child Mavis Hutchison suffered three nervous breakdowns and spent months in bed, all of which kept her away from sport. But the South African certainly made up for it. She had a spell as a race walker, then ran marathons and ultramarathons, rising to prominence in 1978 when the 53-year-old grandmother became the first woman to run across the US. The 2,871-mile (4,620km) route from Los Angeles to New York took her 69 days, two hours and 40 minutes.

Mavis has also run 1,000 miles from Pretoria to Cape Town in 22 days, twice, and a circuitous 3,200km run around much of South Africa in 1985. She set a new women's record for John o'Groats to Land's End in the UK and has set women's world records for 100-mile and 24-hour running.

She claims to be the third woman to ever finish the Comrades Marathon, in 1966, and has completed the race six more times.

Hutchison has also set South African W80+ masters records for 100m, 200m, 400m and 800m.

25 November

Dorando Pietri versus Johnny Hayes: the rematch
(2003)

After the marathon at the 1908 London Olympics had ended in such drama and controversy (see 24 July), a rematch between protagonists Dorando Pietri and Johnny Hayes was arranged. Italian confectioner Pietri travelled to Hayes's homeland, the United States, to race an indoor marathon on a track measuring one tenth of a mile (requiring 262 laps) at Madison Square Garden, New York.

Despite the seemingly limited appeal of watching two men run in small circles, Hayes versus Pietri II was a sell-out, and the atmosphere 'raucous', said *The New Yorker*.

A journalist called the contest 'the most spectacular foot race that New York has ever witnessed'. Pietri won by 43 seconds, in 2:44:20, and with partisan feeling running high, *The Times* reported that a riot was only 'narrowly averted'.

Marathon mania had taken hold, soon spreading across the US, Canada and Europe. For the next two years, contests between long-distance runners sold out halls in New York, London, Berlin and Montreal. Pietri ran 22 races in the six months afterwards, winning 17 of them.

26 November

Murray Halberg defends his three mile title
(1962)

New Zealander Murray Halberg had been a rugby player until his left arm was left paralysed in a tackle. He was still able to run, holding his limp limb tucked up and, as he himself described it, 'pumping myself along with my right'. He turned to running and became another protégé of legendary coach Arthur Lydiard (see 6 July).

After a nightmare 1,500m race at the 1956 Olympics in Melbourne where he'd led the field only to finish 11th, he did the opposite in the three-mile race at the 1958 Empire and Commonwealth Games. Running conservatively in ninth place, as the blistering pace finally slowed on the eighth lap he started moving to the front, calmly pushing on to secure gold. Similar tactics worked at the 1960 Olympics, Halberg's career highlight, where he secured the 5,000m gold (see 2 September).

At the 1962 E&C Games three mile final, young Canadian Bruce Kidd was considered his main threat, so he stuck close to Kidd for the first 11 laps. Kidd tried to break away a couple of times, but Halberg seemed untroubled in staying with him. On the last lap he performed a decisive break Kidd couldn't match, to gain gold and retain his title.

27 November

Gunder Hägg dies
(2004)

Growing up, Sweden's Gunder Hägg would walk, run or ski the three miles to school. Despite little international racing success, he went on to set over a dozen middle-distance world records in the 1940s, ranging from 1,500m to 5,000m. In the extraordinary summer of 1942, when aged twenty-three, he set 10 world records in the space of just 12 weeks. He seemed untouchable, winning all 32 races he entered in that period.

Hägg played out an intense rivalry with fellow Swede Arne Andersson (see 1 April and 18 July) and the two pushed each other to numerous world records. Feeding off his nemesis, with six records between them in three years, Hägg lowered the mile record by five seconds. His 4:01 wasn't broken for nine years, when Roger Bannister became the first sub four-minute miler.

28 November

Nyandika Maiyoro finishes seventh in 5,000m final
(1956)

Nyandika Maiyoro was a Kenyan running pioneer. In fact, he missed out on becoming the first Kenyan ever to race in Europe by one day. Lazaro Chepkwony beat him to it by 24 hours, competing in the 1954 AAA Six Miles in London. Maiyoro's race, over three miles, was the following day.

As with Chepkwony, it wasn't just seeing an African runner, and a barefoot one at that, that had the crowd spellbound. He had unusual tactics. Rather than employing bursts like Chepkwony (see 9 July), Maiyoro roared into a lead of some 25m. He stayed there for six laps or so, on world record pace.

Gradually the more experienced runners closed on him, and started passing him. The Kenyan was resilient though, holding on for third place and beating some respected runners.

At the 1954 Commonwealth Games Maiyoro placed fourth, running more conservatively, just pipped by Chris Chataway (see 19 January).

At the 1956 Olympics in Melbourne he became the first Kenyan to complete an Olympic final, in the 5,000m, and finished a very credible seventh, behind the likes of Kuts and Pirie (see 23 November). He would place sixth at the 1960 Olympics, eight seconds from bronze.

He also won a 3,000m race at the 1953 Indian Ocean Games in Madagascar, despite only joining it when the other runners had covered more than 100m.

29 November

Brian Kilby wins Commonwealth marathon
(1962)

There's something more heart-warming somehow about athletes who have less than a handful of great results or just a year or two of success, than there is about the supernatural machines who smash endless world records and wolf up gold medals seemingly on autopilot.

Britain's Brian Kilby is one of the former. He won the marathon at both the Commonwealth Games and the European Championships in 1962. The marathoner also recorded an apparent world record of 2:14:43 the following year, but his mark isn't ratified by IAAF.

Kilby would also finish a very commendable fourth in the 1964 Olympics in Tokyo, considerably better than his 29th in 1960.

30 November

Tim Twietmeyer is born
(1958)

This American runner won the prestigious and always competitive Western States 100-mile ultramarathon five times (1992, 1994–96 and 1998). But he can add to that 25 finishes, all of which are sub-24 hours, and his record includes 15 consecutive top-five finishes – both of which are unprecedented achievements. He also has the masters' course record.

His record hints at an element of obsession with Western States and it's perhaps not surprising to learn that he's served on the popular race's board of trustees for 10 years and is currently the president of the Western States Endurance Run Foundation.

He has completed over 200 marathon and ultramarathon races. But none of them 25 times.

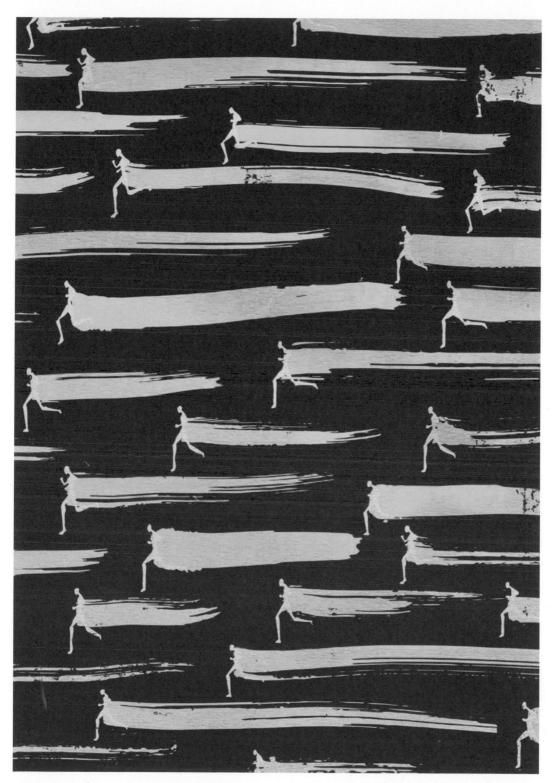

DECEMBER

1 December

Alain Mimoun's last laugh
(1956)

An aging Emil Zátopek was back to defend his title at the 1956 Olympic marathon in Melbourne. This time he was running just one event, but he had recently had a hernia operation. Other than the 'Czech Locomotive', the favourite was French-Algerian Alain Mimoun (see 27 June), who had spent most of his career overshadowed by Zátopek, finishing second to him in three Olympic finals and two European championships. Like Zátopek in 1952, Mimoun was making his marathon début and he dominated the race. By 25km, he had almost a one-minute lead on the field.

He maintained momentum from there, winning in 2:25:00, 1:32 ahead of Yugoslavia's Franco Mihalić.

Zátopek, clearly not at his best, finished sixth. Mimoun waited at the finish line for his Czech nemesis and close friend and said, 'Emil, it was I who won.' Zátopek turned and saluted Mimoun and the pair embraced. 'Oh, for me that was better than the medal,' said Mimoun.

Mimoun confessed to 'gorging' himself on 40km-a-day runs for two years to get fit for the 1956 Olympic marathon.

2 December

George Littlewood sets six-day record despite foul play
(1888)

George Littlewood set the last of the nineteenth century's six-day world records today, with 623¾ miles (1,004km) covered in 144 hours. It remained a world record for 96 years.

At the end of the fifth day though, Britain's 'Sheffield Flyer' nearly fell foul of a saboteur – fairly common in pedestrian racing where big bets were wagered. Taking a break to soothe his aching feet in an alcohol bath, a match was deliberately dropped into his trackside tub. His feet and legs were badly burned but he hobbled on heroically to complete 85 miles on the last day and secure the record.

In the 1960s, physiologist B.B. Lloyd described Littlewood's achievement as 'probably about the maximum sustained output of which the human frame is capable'.

In 1984, Yiannis Kouros finally beat the record, covering 635 miles 1,023 yards in New York. Littlewood's distance is still a British record, though in 1990 James Zarei finished one mile short of it.

3 December

The Comrades King is born
(1955)

In 1977, when Bruce Fordyce first ran South Africa's famous 56-mile Comrades Marathon, he placed 43rd out of 1,678 runners. The next year he placed 14th; in 1979 he placed third; he was second in 1980. The next year he finally won it.

Not content, he won it for an unprecedented eight consecutive years from 1981 to 1988. And again in 1990. His period of dominance coincided with huge growth in the event's popularity, while his record for the 'down' run of 5:24:07 stood for 21 years. He continues to run Comrades now, with over 30 finishes to his name.

An outspoken critic of apartheid, Fordyce and other athletes wore black armbands for the 1981 race after organisers aligned it with the 20th anniversary of the Republic of South Africa. Some of the crowd reacted with hostility to the protest.

Fordyce also won the London to Brighton Marathon three years in a row and held a world record for 50 miles.

4 December

The original globe-trotter passes away
(1979)

In 1908, the Touring Club de France announced a contest for walking around the world, with a prize of 100,000 francs – a fortune then. The concept caught the imagination of four Romanian students studying in Paris. They learned languages, studied cartography, practised Romanian folk songs and dances (to perform in exchange for money en route), did weight training and walked 45km per day in preparation. In 1910 the group set out on their voyage accompanied by a dog, Harap.

In July 1911, in India, one of the quartet died of opium poisoning. Two years into the trip, another died, trying to cross a narrow mountain pass in China's Nanling Mountains. A third Romanian wanderer, suffering leg problems from an old accident, was advised to stop by doctors in Florida. So he (and the dog) did. After having both legs amputated, he died in 1915.

The final one of the gang of four, Dumitru Dan, put his trip on hold during World War One. But he completed it in 1923. Dan had crossed five continents, three oceans, been through 76 countries and worn out 497 pairs of shoes.

Guttingly for Dan, given post-war inflation however, the value of the prize (in current terms) had shrunk from about €500,000 to €40,000.

He had however earned a place in the *Guinness Book of Records* for being the first person to travel around the world on foot. He died on this date in his native Romania.

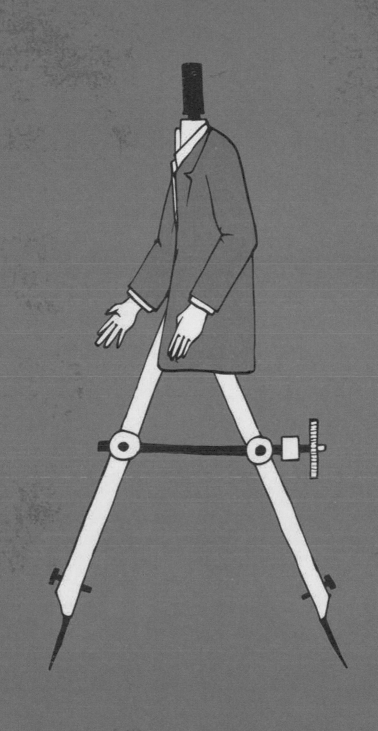

5 December

Fukuoka's deliberately elitist marathon
(since 1947)

Next to sumo wrestling and baseball, marathon running is one of Japan's sporting obsessions. First run in 1947, the Fukuoka Marathon is traditionally staged in the first Sunday in December and is shown live on TV.

In the 1960s, 70s and early 80s it was the de facto marathon world championships – well before the IAAF organised the first World Championships in Helsinki in 1983. 'The goal was to invite the winners of all the major marathons of the year and set up a head-to-head competition,' said Japanese historian Ken Nakamura.

Among former victors are Olympic gold medallists Frank Shorter (a four-time Fukuoka winner), Haile Gebrselassie, the late Sammy Wanjiru of Kenya, Belayneh Dinsamo and Derek Clayton. Perhaps the most memorable race was 1981 when Clayton's fellow Australian Rob de Castella (see 6 December) set a world record.

Fukuoka is unusual in being a city marathon that wholly targets elite runners. To qualify, you either need a sub-2:40 marathon time, a 30km under 1:50 or a half marathon under 1:10. It's also known for its demanding cut-off times.

6 December

Rob de Castella sets world record at Fukuoka
(1981)

With a sustained drive over the final 12km, Australia's magnificently moustached Rob de Castella won today's Fukuoka Marathon in a time of 2:08:18.

It was the fastest time recorded for an out-and-back course, but it wasn't initially known to be a world-best time. De Castella's 2:08:28 was five seconds slower than Alberto Salazar's at the same year's New York City Marathon.

But it later emerged that the New York course was about 148m short so de Castella's time was ratified as the world record.

Nicknamed 'Deek' or 'Deeks' in Australia, and 'Tree' by his competitors due to his thick legs and inner calm, Rob went on to win the Boston Marathon, the Commonwealth Games (twice) and, in 1983, the marathon World Championships.

In 2003 he launched a specialist chain of grain- and gluten-free bakeries and cafés, called Deeks.

7 December

Gordon Pirie dies
(1988)

In 1965 readers of *Athletics Weekly* voted long-distance runner Gordon Pirie the greatest British athlete in history, ahead of runner-up Roger Bannister. Yet, despite being one of the country's biggest crowd-pleasers in the 1950s and early 60s, the Yorkshireman is one of the forgotten heroes of the sport today.

In a golden era of distance running, Pirie defeated legends such as Emil Zátopek in 1955 and Vladimir Kuts in a thrilling race in Bergen in 1956. He was said to train 200 miles a week, won the prestigious English national cross country title three times and was named BBC Sports Personality of the Year in 1955, before a career-defining clash with Kuts at the 1956 Olympic 10,000m final (see 23 November). Pirie also won silver behind Kuts in the 5,000m.

Pirie set five world records, including 5,000m and 3,000m, and the runner had a reputation for always speaking his mind.

8 December

South Pole-bound Amundsen surpasses Shackleton's mark
(1911)

In one of the most efficient and ground-breaking endurance journeys of all time, Norway's Roald Amundsen passed Ernest Shackleton's 'Furthest South' mark on his way to the South Pole.

The primary quest of the Heroic Age of Antarctic Exploration was to reach the hallowed centre of the bottom of the world. Britain's Captain Robert Scott had already tried, as had Shackleton. Scott had another expedition en route to the Pole in 1911 as the Norwegian too raced towards it. Amundsen's expedition had caught Scott off guard – he'd set sail from Norway with most of his crew and expedition backers believing they were aiming for the North Pole.

Five men, four sledges and 52 dogs (of which only 11 would make it back – Antarctic travel is hungry work) made the trip, reaching the South Pole on 14 December 1911.

Amundsen is recognised as the first person, without dispute, to have reached both poles.

9 December

The Reggae Marathon
(since 2000)

Famed, as you might expect, for its atmosphere, Jamaica's Reggae Marathon takes place in Negril, the country's 'capital of casual' on the island's west coast. It promises 'pulsating Reggae music on course [keeping] participants in an "irie" spirit, as they burn the mileage'.

The looped, mostly flat, internationally certified course starts at Long Bay Beach Park by Negril's famed seven-mile white-sand beach. It loops into the town then heads north towards another town, Green Island. Temperatures are usually around 24°C (76°F), kept a little lower by a pre-dawn start, and runners are given a sendoff by a crescendo of drums. Male and female winners are awarded the Bob Marley and Rita Marley trophies.

10 December

The End of the World Marathon
(2012)

This Belize marathon gets its memorable name because it was first held just days before the end of the Mayan Calendar. That date, often referred to as the 'End of the World', was salient in Belize, where Mayans have lived for hundreds, if not thousands, of years.

Although the world didn't end in 2012, the event kept the name, apparently in honour of the writer Aldous Huxley, who wrote in 1934 about Belize (then known as British Honduras), 'If the world had any ends, British Honduras would certainly be one of them.'

Taking place in Placencia, southern Belize, the course promises multiple views of the Caribbean Sea along the way. There's a heat-dodging 5 a.m. start and a huge party afterwards and, though the race was conceived primarily to raise funds for high-school scholarships, US$10,000 in prizes. Water stations are themed, so expect to be handed cups of water by superheroes.

11 December

Freak races
(1763)

In the UK in the seventeenth and eighteenth centuries, plain old running was clearly deemed a tad dull and a craze for 'freak races' gathered momentum. The more bizarre the concept, the more popular the spectacle. Sometimes both runners were equally comical, sometimes the freak was the superior and therefore handicapped runner. For example, in 1763 a race between a runner over 100 yards and a stilt walker over 120 yards was won by the latter. In the same year, a fishmonger tried to run from Hyde Park Corner, London, to Brentford with 25.4kg (56lb) of fish on his head. He bet he could do so in one hour, and did so with 15 minutes to spare. In another recorded instance, an unusually rotund gentleman raced against a young runner with a jockey on his back. Running was never this good again.

12 December

The father of long-distance running runs out of time
(2007)

Ted Corbitt, who passed away on this date, was labelled 'the father of long distance running' by Fred Lebow, the founder of the New York City Marathon. Corbitt was an ultramarathon pioneer who claimed he'd run 199 marathons and ultramarathons, winning 30, and never dropping out of one until he was seventy-five.

At his peak the African-American was US marathon champion and a member of the national team for the 1952 Olympics in Helsinki. He held US records in the marathon, 100 miles, 25km, 40km and 50km. Even at eighty-one, he walked 240 miles in a six-day race. The next year, in the same race, he walked 303 miles.

Corbitt also founded the Road Runners Club of America, was later president, and was among the first five athletes inducted into the National Distance Running Hall of Fame. In his prime he ran 200 miles a week in training and had only one alcoholic drink in his life, a can of beer while in the army.

13 December

Record Year for the Santa Dash
(2015)

The phenomenon of the Santa Dash is becoming nearly as popular as Christmas itself in Britain. Primarily a fundraiser, the idea is simple, but the spectacle wonderfully strange and hilarious. The race is usually 10K or shorter and the only rule that makes a race qualify as a Santa Dash is that runners wear Father Christmas outfits.

The scene is usually a sea of red-faced, red-suited Santas, bobble hats bobbing, white beards flowing as the sound of puffing and panting fills the air. The Santas dash along like they've just slipped off the back of the sledge and are desperately trying to catch the getaway reindeer, clasping want-away bits of ill-fitting costume as they do so.

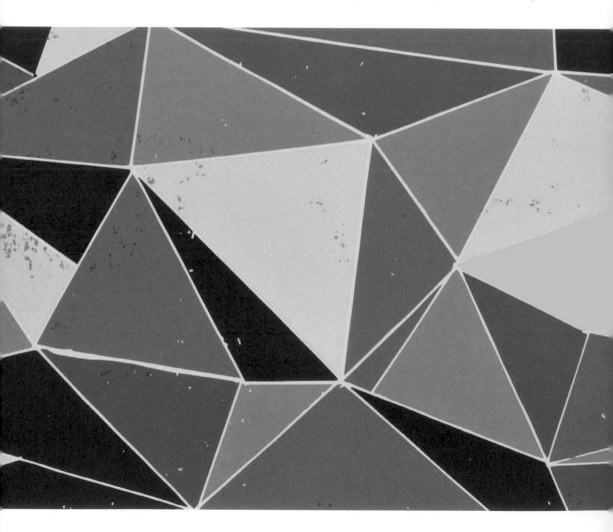

14 December

The Cambridge Wonder's first win
(1874)

Charles Rowell recorded his first race win as a professional pedestrian on this day, earning £5 for running nine and a half miles inside an hour. Rowell was initially a pacemaker for Edward Weston (see 22 February and 17 March) for his various pedestrian record attempts, but it wasn't long before he was gaining attention for his own achievements. Posters advertising the Briton's appearances would later boast that running 150 miles in a day wasn't a problem for the 'Cambridge Wonder'.

Rowell won four of the seven Astley Belt Championships of the World between 1878 and 1881, finally winning it three times in a row and bringing the series to an end. His winnings were sometimes worth as much as US$1,000,000 in today's money.

15 December

America versus England III
(1844)

After the Beacon Race Course was built in Noboken, New Jersey, a series of three international meets between Britain and America took place in 1844. At the first, in October, the 10,000 crowd were shocked at the flesh-baring of the British runners, wearing just shorts, while the Americans wore jockey-style outfits. Plus a confused crowd invaded the track before the 10-mile race was over. But nonetheless, American John Gildersleeve came first. Edward Sears's *Running Through the Ages* reports that one newspaper labelled it 'one of the greatest foot races that ever took place in America or England'.

At November's meet, 30,000 watched England's John Barlow run a world best 10 miles in 54:21.

For the third meet, in a very cold December, the Brits still wore just shorts and, with Barlow having already sailed home with his winnings, it was left for compatriot Tom Greenhalgh to win over 12 miles, after an intensely close duel with Gildersleeve. After a victory speech Greenhalgh was warmly cheered and would later move to America.

16 December

Whitey Michelsen is born
(1893)

Albert 'Whitey' Michelsen was an American long-distance runner who ran the first sub-2:30 marathon, setting the world's best in 1925, with a time of 2:29:01 at the inaugural Port Chester Marathon, New York. Michelsen held this record for 10 years, until Fusashige Suzuki posted 2:27:49 in 1935.

But Michelsen perhaps stays longer in the mind for the remarkable feat of finishing fourth at the Boston Marathon four times. One of those qualified him for the Olympics and he represented the US at the 1928 and 1932 Games, finishing ninth and seventh.

When not pounding the roads, Albert was a plumber.

17 December

Peter Snell is born
(1938)

New Zealander Peter Snell had a short career yet achieved enough to be voted his country's 'Sports Champion of the Century'.

Snell stunned the running world in 1960 when he won the Olympic 800m. It was surprise enough that he'd made the Olympic team for Rome in the first place. Snell had no international experience and *Sports Illustrated* called him 'completely unknown'.

In the race, the Kiwi was well positioned in fourth, but found something extra in the final straight. However, the finish was so close he had to ask his coach, the legendary Arthur Lydiard, who'd won. Snell improved his 800m PB three times in four days at the Games, such was his rise.

After Rome, Snell became the dominant 800m and 1,500m runner of the early 1960s, winning three Olympic and two Commonwealth Games golds and setting world records in the mile, 1,000m, 880yd and 800m. The latter still stands as a record on a grass track.

Just as his arrival had been a shock, so too was his sudden retirement in 1965. He later moved to the US and became an academic. In his sixties, though, he won his age category in the 2003 United States Orienteering Championship.

18 December

The Grand Ladies' International Tournament
(1879)

An overexcitedly titled second six-day race for women took place today at Madison Square Garden, New York. Among the 25 competitors hoping for the US$1,000 prize and championship belt were Madame Exilda La Chappelle from Paris, Madame Ada Anderson of London, Madame Sarah Tobias from Brooklyn and a grey-haired May Marshall, 'The Mother of Female Long-Distance Pedestrianism'.

Unknown 17-year-old American Amy Howard took an early lead, though Madame Tobias took over on day two. Howard's trick when flagging was to pop into her tent for a change of dress and hair makeover, which always seemed to rejuvenate her, albeit temporarily.

On day three Howard retook the lead, and 5,000 spectators packed the venue out for the finale. Howard took the win with a world record 393 miles (632km).

Tobias instantly challenged Howard to a rematch, but New York hurriedly passed a resolution banning women's six-day racing. So instead they all headed for San Francisco (see 10 May).

19 December

Sandra Kiddy wins the Desert Big Macathon
(1981)

Sandra Kiddy won this sponsored Californian race (no prizes for guessing by whom) today in 1981, but it was the least of her pioneering achievements for women in ultramarathon running. Her first ultra in 1979 when aged forty-two was a world best 3:36:56 for 50km. In 1982 Kiddy won the Chicago Lakefront 100km, the premier American road ultra at the time. A year later she won the women's invitational World Cup 100 Mile in Germany. In 1984 she won the Edmund Fitzgerald 100km outright – this distance was her speciality and she racked up several victories in Europe, including London to Brighton.

Of the half-dozen 100km races Kiddy ran in her prime she was undefeated and her average time was under eight hours. When a Hall of Fame for ultramarathon runners opened in the US, she was one of the first two names – and the first female – entered.

20 December

Pyotr Bolotnikov dies
(1948)

Life didn't start well for Russia's Pyotr Bolotnikov. He lost his mother aged four and lived with his stepmother in the Ural Mountains while his father fought in World War Two, where both he and Pyotr's brother were killed.

Bolotnikov initially preferred ice skating and didn't start running until he was twenty, when in the Soviet Army and feeling inspired by Emil Zátopek. He'd found his forte.

After disappointment at the 1956 Olympics, Bolotnikov won 10,000m gold at the 1960 Olympics (see 8 September), beating several more eminent runners. Later that year he set a 10,000m world record of 28:18.8, lowering it by almost 12 seconds. For his achievements he was awarded the Order of Lenin.

In 1962 he lowered the record further, by 0.6 seconds, and at the following European Championships he easily won the 10,000m, but was surprisingly beaten to third in 5,000m.

21 December

Jean Bouin born
(1888)

French middle-distance runner Jean Bouin's 1912 Olympics 5,000m duel with Finland's Hannes Kolehmainen (see 10 July) is considered one of the all-time great races.

Kolehmainen and Bouin quickly created a gap from the rest of the field, with Bouin leading and Kolehmainen constantly trying to get past him. Kolehmainen finally succeeded, winning by just 0.1 seconds. Both of them had broken the old world record.

It was the pinnacle of Bouin's career, though he also competed at 1,500m and 5,000m at both the 1908 and 1912 Olympics. He also set three more world records: for 3,000m, 10,000m and one-hour (19,021m – 11.8 miles).

Bouin was killed in September 1914, serving in World War One. He is featured on stamps, Paris's Stade Jean-Bouin (home of the Stade Français rugby club) is named after him, and a 10K race in Barcelona also bears his name.

22 December

George Hazael versus Achille Bargozzi
(1877)

In December 1877 an 'International Running Match' pitted pedestrian George Hazael against champion runner of France and Italy, Achille Bargozzi, at Lillie Bridge in Hazael's home city of London. It was a mere 30-mile race, a sprint by Hazael's standards. And he won, pocketing the prize of £50.

Hazael would travel all over the UK – and later the US – to race for money and in the remarkable book *King of the Peds* he is described as having a 'bull dog face, short cropped hair and almost deformed stooped shoulders which gave him the most displeasing appearance'.

Nevertheless, he was the first man known to run 600 miles in six days, in 1882 in New York, winning the sum of US$18,380 for his troubles – worth around $400,000 today. He also set a 100-mile world record of 17:04:06.

Hazael later settled in the US, purchased a hotel and constructed a race track outside it to practise on.

23 December

Kilian Jornet runs up Americas' biggest mountain
(2014)

Professional mountain athlete Kilian Jornet set a new speed record on Argentina's 22,841ft (6,962m) Mount Aconcagua, the highest mountain in both the southern and western hemispheres.

Jornet ran up and down the Normal Route, which ascends 13,327 vertical feet in around 50 miles round trip to the summit and back. Starting at 6 a.m., the Catalan sped 15 miles to the Plaza de Mules base camp at 14,108ft, normally a two-day hike, then started the much steeper ascent of the mountain, reaching the summit about nine hours after starting – slower than he'd hoped. He made up time on the descent, covering just under marathon distance in less than four hours. He returned in 12:49. The previous record was thought to be 13:46.

Jornet has set speed records for Denali (previously Mount McKinley, Alaska, US), Mount Kilimanjaro (Tanzania), Mont Blanc and the Matterhorn (both Alps).

24 December

Violet Piercy is born
(1889)

Violet Piercy is one of three (see 11 April and 29 September) women usually recognised as being the first to run a marathon. She was an English long-distance runner who the IAAF credit with a running time of 3:40:22 on 3 October 1926, her mark set approximately on the Polytechnic Marathon course between Windsor and London.

However, research by *Runner's World* magazine suggests this run was more likely to have been 22 miles, and a solo run rather than during an official race. The IAAF list her marathon as 'Chiswick' but the 'Poly' didn't go through Chiswick until years later. Perhaps crucially, the magazine also points out that at the time the word 'marathon' didn't necessarily mean 26.2 miles, instead it often referred more generally to a 'long road run'.

The best compromise is probably to see Piercy as the first woman to be timed over the marathon (with the caveats above), and deserves recognition nonetheless. According to the IAAF, Piercy's mark stood for 37 years, until Merry Lepper ran 3:37:07 to better her, at 1963's Western Hemisphere Marathon (see 31 December).

25 December

Basil Heatley is born
(1933)

On 13 July 1964 Heatley broke the marathon world record at the England's Polytechnic Marathon, running 2:13:56 to surpass Leonard Edelen's world best from the previous year's race by 32 seconds.

Heatley's career highlight arguably came three months later at the 1964 Olympics in Tokyo. There, defending champion Abebe Bikila won another marathon gold with another world record time. But Heatley, who suffered throughout the first half of the race with a stitch in very humid conditions, managed to out-sprint Japan's Kokichi Tsuburaya to the line, to win silver. Not bad for someone who said, 'I can honestly say I didn't like the marathon. It's just a bit too far for me.'

26 December

Serge Girard is born

(1953)

Serge Girard is a French ultramarathon runner who ran across five continents between 1997 and 2006. In 1997 he crossed the US from Los Angeles to New York, recording 4,597km in under 53 days. The following year the determined Frenchman ran across the Australian continent, from Perth to Sydney, running 3,755km in under 47 days (a world record at the time). In 2001 he crossed South America, from Lima to Rio de Janeiro, recording 5,235km in just over 73 days (another world record). In 2003 and 2004 he ran across Africa, from Dakar to Cairo, logging 8,295km in 123 days (bagging another world record). Then in 2005 and 2006 his feet took him across Eurasia, from Paris to Tokyo, recording 19,097km in 262 days.

With something of a void to fill once finished, in 2010 Girard set a Guinness World Record for the longest run in 365 days, covering 27,011km (a massive 16,784 miles) through 25 European countries, beating India's Tirtha Kumar Phani's record of 22,581.09km in 365 days.

Girard claims he went through 50 pairs of shoes, 100 pairs of socks and, a little curiously, 50 pairs of shorts, too.

27 December

The Flying Scotsman at the Grand World Championship

(1881)

Taking part in the snappily titled 'Grand World Championship six-day go-as-you-please Tournament' in New York, George D. Cameron, often called Noremac (his surname backwards, inventively) or 'The Flying Scotsman', finally made a name for himself. Noremac had won prize money in the UK, but his career really took off in the US. In this tournament he caught the eye with 565 miles and 95 yards and second place, earning a mouth-watering $800.

He did well again in the following year's Police Gazette Diamond Championship Belt, in Boston, and was back at Madison Square Garden in October. This time he improved on his previous best, scoring 576 miles (and four laps) – a Scottish indoor record which still stands today.

More impressively still, in April 1884 he walked 5,100 miles over 100 successive days on a track in New York. Sadly, things did ultimately go rather sour for him in the States (see 7 February).

28 December

The origins of cross country

(circa sixteenth century)

The earliest form of cross country racing as we know it today most likely dates all the way back to Middle Ages hunts in Britain, where runners would follow packs of hunting beagles, who in turn sniffed out foxes or rabbits. It was such good fun it was realised the dogs weren't essential to the enjoyment and were dispensed with.

The winter sport of cross country became prevalent in sixteenth-century English private schools; it was originally called 'hare and hounds' or 'paper chases' and also had

origins in the sport of steeplechasing, where horses were raced to church steeples (early running versions were sometimes called 'steeplechases on foot').

There are anecdotes from Rugby School in the nineteenth century of spontaneous, teacher-free races across the countryside to the school, involving plenty of fence-jumping and ditch-falling-into. A 'hare and hounds' version became endorsed by the school, where one group of 'hares' would lay paper trails (i.e. a scent) for the 'hounds' to follow – this included deviously laying false ones.

In 1828 Rugby School held its first 'Crick' run, a 12½-mile cross country race which still exists today – one of the world's oldest races.

Many British running clubs bear the name 'harriers', which comes from 'hare hunters'.

29 December

The Ancient Egyptian ultramarathoners
(1303–1213 BC)

It's impossible to put a date to it, but Rameses II (1303–1213 BC), pharaoh of Ancient Egypt, was a runner. He had to run, alone and in front of crowds, before his coronation to ostensibly prove himself worthy of the throne. Then he had to repeat the feat 30 years later at a festival, to clarify that he was still 'fit' for the job, and run the same one-man race every third or fourth year to prove he was still up to the task – right up until the age of ninety. A physically weak king was seen as undesirable and the ceremony was thought to renew his powers.

The earliest known foot races, known as 'city races', can also be traced to Ancient Egypt, dating to 2035 BC, and (naturally) concluding with animal sacrifices.

In fact, Egyptian soldiers may have also run the first ultramarathons. Records point to a 100km race from Memphis to Fayum and back, run partially at night to avoid heat, in around 690–665 BC.

King Taharqa took part (for a bit anyway), and the winner of the 31-mile return leg took a very respectable four hours.

30 December

JC Santa Teresa runs 21 consecutive ultramarathons
(2014)

According to the *Guinness Book of World Records*, America's JC Santa Teresa set a world best for the most consecutive days running an ultramarathon. Between 10–31 December 2014 he managed 21 days of running 50km each time, throughout California and Texas. Overall he clocked up 1,050km (652.5 miles) in three weeks. He lost 8lb (3.6kg) and mentioned missing family holidays – presumably a fair chunk of Christmas.

In 2012 he ran 30 marathons, raising money for breast cancer after his mother had the illness. He is also a 50-Stater – meaning he's run a marathon in all 50 US states – and aims to run a marathon on all seven continents.

31 December

Merry Lepper is born
(1942)

In 2014, 42 per cent of marathon finishers in the US were female, but in the 1960s, officially 0 per cent were. They weren't allowed. But some rebellious pioneers still ran.

Much like Bobbi Gibb would at Boston three years later (see 2 November), Merry Lepper and her friend Lyn Carman hid at the sidelines of the 1963 Western Hemisphere Marathon (also known as the Culver City Marathon and a prestigious one at the time), California, and joined the men just after the start.

A race official attempted to remove them from the course, but Carman yelled, 'I have the right to use public streets for running!' Carman unfortunately dropped out on 20 miles, but Lepper was given the time of 3:37:07 by a sympathetic official.

Carman would win the Santa Barbara Marathon in 1966, 1969 and 1970, and the World Masters Marathon in 1969. Lepper would never run another marathon, concentrating instead on her studies. But her 1963 time is on the record as a world best (even if the sniffy ARRS think the course may have been short).

GLOSSARY

24 Hour Races
Typically taking place a standard athletics track or 1- or 2-mile looped course, runners simply have 24 hours to see how far they can run.

Association of Road Running Statistics (ARRS)
An association independent of the IAAF who hold elite distance running records for distances of 3,000m and upwards.

Back straight and home or final straight
A standard 400m athletics track has two 100m straights and two 100m bends. The final 100m in a race is known as the home or final straight, while the other straight 100m is the back straight.

Commonwealth Games
Previously known as the British Empire Games, British Empire and Commonwealth Games and British Commonwealth Games, an athletics championship event between athletes from Commonwealth Nations, the 53 former British territories.

European Championships
A biennial (every two years) athletics championship event organised by the European Athletics Association since 1934. It used to be every year, but has been held every two years since 2010.

Fastest Known Time (FKT)
The assumed record for covering a certain route, which could be from a certain start point to the summit of a mountain, an established trail (such as America's Appalachian Trail) or a bespoke route.

Fells
Northern English word for mountains, from the old Norse word 'fjall'.

Final or home straight (see **Back straight**)

International Association of Athletics Federations (IAAF)
The world athletics governing body (see 17 July for more).

Interval Training or Intervals
Popular training method whereby an athlete runs at a fast pace for a short time, has a rest 'interval' (usually slower running), before resuming the set of faster repetitions.

Kick
An increase of speed towards the end of a race.

Lactic acid
Anaerobic (high-intensity) exercise produces lactic acid in muscles which makes them feel heavy and fatigued.

Oxygen deficit
When the lungs demand more oxygen than the runner is able to breathe in. Not a situation that can be sustained for long.

PB
A runner's Personal Best time (known as Personal Record in the US).

Pedestrianism
The popular late-eighteenth and nineteenth-century sport of travelling long distances, either around a track (six-day races attracted big crowds for a several years) or DIY challenges such as Paris to Moscow in a stipulated time, competitively and often for large wagers. Pedestrianism was initially a walking challenge but transformed into a hybrid sport as some pedestrians preferred to run, trot or shuffle. The practice can be seen as the origin for both racewalking and ultramarathon running.

Six-day races Popular in the 1870s, attracting tens of thousands of spectators, this form of pedestrianism saw individuals race around a track usually in an arena for six days, with rest and sleep breaks. Though there are still some six-day races today, the 1870s Astley Belt series was the sport's apex, with Irish-American Daniel O'Leary and Charles Rowell the two biggest stars.

Ultramarathons Any running event longer than the modern marathon distance of 26.2 miles.

World Championships The World Championships in Athletics is organised by the IAAF every two years. From 1983 to 1991 it was held every four years.

World Marathon Majors: The Tokyo, Boston, London, Berlin, Chicago and New York City Marathons. It works as both a championship event for elite runners (also including the World Championships and Olympic Games Marathons) and a challenge for amateur runners.

ACKNOWLEDGEMENTS

Though there were long hours, late nights and very occasional disagreements (always both minor and entirely amicable), working on this book has been hugely enjoyable – which isn't always how it goes.

That's down to both the fascinating subject matter, but also the very professional, personable and deadline-dodging forgiveness of the fine staff at Aurum Press. Especially Daniel Seex for his wonderful illustrations, the heroically diligent Ian Allen, Lucy Warburton, Daniela Rogers, Robin Harvie and everyone else involved.

A huge thanks also to Barbara and Kelvin for teaching me love the outdoors, as well as Jonathan Manning, Graham Coster, John Shepherd, Paul Simpson, Alyssa White, Paul Hansford, Mario Cacciottolo, Amy, Indy and Leif.

BIBLIOGRAPHY

This book required reams of research and some of the excellent books I used more extensively are:

Algeo, Matthew, Pedestrianism: *When Watching People Walk was America's Favourite Sport*, Chicago Review Press, 2014

Askwith, Richard, *Feet in the Clouds: A Tale of Fell-Running and Obsession*, Aurum Press, 2004

Finn, Adharanand, *Running with the Kenyans: Discovering the Secrets of the Fastest People on Earth*, Faber & Faber, 2013

Finn, Adharanand, *The Way of the Runner: A journey into the Fabled World of Japanese Running*, Faber & Faber, 2015

Harvie, Robin, *Why We Run: A Story of Obsession*, John Murray, 2011

Hawker, Lizzy, Runner: *A Short Story About a Long Run*, Aurum Press, 2015

Jean, Shirley & Tucker, Roll, *The Amazing Foot Race of 1921*, Heritage, 2011

Jornet, Kilian, *Run or Die: The Inspirational Memoir of the World's Greatest Ultra-Runner*, Viking, 2014

Jurek, Scott, *Eat and Run: My Unlikely Journey to Ultramarathon Greatness*, Bloomsbury, 2013

Karnazes, Dean, *Ultramarathon Man: Confessions of an All-Night Runner*, Jeremy P. Tarcher, 2006

Marshall, P S, *King of the Peds*, Author House, 2008

McDougall, Christopher *Born to Run: The Hidden Tribe, the Ultra-Runners,* and the *Greatest Race the World Has Never Seen*, Random House, 2010

Noakes, Tim, Pro, *Lore of Running*, Human Kinetics Europe, 2002

Owen, Paul, *The Joy of Running*, Summersdale, 2013

Sears, Edward S, *Running Through the Ages*, McFarland, 2001

Stevens, John, *The Marathon Monks of Mount Hiei*, Echo Point Books & Media, 2008

Sillitoe, Alan, *The Loneliness of the Long Distance Runner*, HarperCollins, 1959

Whitaker, Mark, *Running for Their Lives: The Extraordinary story of Britain;s Greatest Ever Distance Runners*, Yellow Jersey press, 2012

The excellent website www.racingpast.ca was also very useful.

A YEAR
ON THE
RUN

an Hall is an author and outdoor journalist who contributes regularly
tdoor Fitness and most of the running, fitness and outdoor press. The
ife-crisis ultramarathon runner is happiest running long distances in
y places and has completed the Spine Race, the Dragon's Back Race
and UTMB. But his children only seem to remember the time he
got beaten by a 13-year-old at parkrun.
www.damianhall.info

iel Seex has been a professional illustrator for over three years
has worked for a number of high-profile clients including Google,
el 4, Johnnie Walker and Chivas Regal and for cycling publications
Ride Journal and *Boneshaker*. Daniel works primarily in pen and
dding colour and texture digitally and often building a picture from
multiple drawings. He lives in Edinburgh with his partner Julia.
www.thejoyofseex.co.uk